Powerful
Leadership
Development

Bridging
Theory
and
Practice
Using
Peers
and
Technology

Powerful
Leadership
Development

David H. Lepard
Alice G. Foster

CORWIN PRESS, INC.
A Sage Publications Company
Thousand Oaks, California

For information:

 Corwin Press, Inc.
A Sage Publications Company
2455 Teller Road
Thousand Oaks, California 91320
www.corwinpress.com

Sage Publications Ltd.
6 Bonhill Street
London EC2A 4PU
United Kingdom

Sage Publications India Pvt. Ltd.
B-42 Panchsheel Enclave
New Delhi 110 017 India

Printed in the United States of America

Library of Congress Cataloging-in-Publication Data

Lepard, David H.
Powerful leadership development: Bridging theory and practice using peers and technology / David H. Lepard, Alice G. Foster.
p. cm.
Includes bibliographical references and index.
ISBN 0-7619-4587-3 (cloth) — ISBN 0-7619-4588-1 (pbk.)
1. School management and organization. 2. Educational leadership. I. Foster, Alice G. II. Title.
LB2805b .L336 2003
371.2—dc21   2002151361

This book is printed on acid-free paper.

03 04 05 06 07 08 8 7 6 5 4 3 2 1

Acquisitions Editor:	Robb Clouse
Editorial Assistant:	Erin Clow
Associate Editor:	Kylee Liegl
Production Editor:	Diane S. Foster
Typesetter/Designer:	Bramble Books
Proofreader:	Olivia Weber
Indexer:	Molly Hall
Cover Designer:	Michael Dubowe
Production Artist:	Michelle Lee

Contents

Preface

Congratulations! You have found a book containing a refreshingly new and challenging approach to leadership development. The book bridges theory and practice with realistic job-related simulations, guidance for in-depth performance analysis, and with a partner and a video camera. For most of the activities, you will be working with your partner who will also need a personal copy of this book.

Never has there been a more persistent need for more effective educational leadership.

1. The public perceives a need for educational improvement.

2. Politicians perceive that educational reform in the preparation of school leaders is becoming a major issue in a growing number of states.

3. Policymakers demand increased accountability at all levels of the educational system.

4. Reports sound the alarm regarding a growing shortage of individuals willing to serve as school principals.

5. A cost-effective way is needed for individuals to diagnose their readiness for leadership positions.

6. A cost-effective means of strengthening the skills of present and future leaders is urgently needed.

7. Professional standards need to be accompanied by development of performance skills needed for implementation.

8. Universities and school districts need relevant skills-based activities to augment course content.

9. Proven methods of technology and cooperative learning need to be applied in leadership courses, workshops, and preparation programs.

This book addresses these nine needs head on and encourages you every step of the way to become involved by completing all the activities with a partner. It will not be a quick study. It requires practice and specific performance feedback from a peer who will serve as your developmental partner and coach. You, in turn, will also serve as your partner's coach. What a deal!

If you are currently a school leader or think you might like to be one, the activities you complete will probably affirm what you always thought you were expected to be able to do. This book will teach you how to document your colleague's performance and then help you create you personal action plan based on a unique self-rating process.

The processes used in this book are built around a practical set of cooperative-learning concepts. They were developed, tested, and successfully used in a leadership academy program for over 10 years. The material in this book is adapted from *Coach and Director Training Manual* (Associates for Better Classrooms International, 2000), which was used in the program. You will be better prepared for school leadership roles—whether you are a staff development director, teacher, department chair, supervisor, assistant principal, principal, or university student—after completing this book.

The ultimate goal of this book is to begin the process of making a significant contribution to the identification and development of better-prepared and stronger leaders.

In summary, this book focuses on the following:

- Important skills of leadership and their linkages to the Interstate School Leader Licensure Consortium (ISLLC) Standards and the National Policy Board for Educational Administration's (NPBEA) Domains and Dimensions

- Hands-on learning that bridges theory and practice with job simulations, video technology, performance documentation, and peer analysis

- A combination of best practices from teaching, instruction, and staff development

- Directions for developing personal action plans for continuing professional development

Acknowledgments

I would like to thank my friend, colleague, and superb editor, Robb Clouse, for his guidance in the development of this book. In preparing this book—as well as throughout my career—I have been particularly blessed with the love and support of my mothers Ruth Gill and Frances Foster; my children Bill, Michael, Robin, and Elizabeth; and my grandchildren.

And, as always, I am indebted to Robert Lowell Foster.

—*Alice G. Foster*

This book began with the encouragement of colleagues who, along with me, were seeking new and practical cost-effective ways to significantly improve the leadership skills of graduate students hoping to become successful school principals. I was seeking a new amalgamation of learning with practical applications of technology. After directing a diagnostic and prescriptive leadership program for over 2 decades, I had a unique opportunity to combine job simulations, video technology, and software to generate reliable performance reports and recommendations for improvement. The software opened the door for new possibilities for putting instant feedback in the hands of the student. And from that beginning grew the ideas for this book. My coauthor and I were able to write this book on strengthening leadership skills without using the software.

The original project could not have been done without the influence of many, many people. The changes we have made to traditional leadership development courses, workshops, and books, could not be successful without their help. Some, as often happens with many teachers, may not realize the important role they played!

Among them are at least 30 colleagues I want to name. First is Paul Hersey, for beginning and shepherding the first principal assessment center at the National Association of Secondary School Principals (NASSP); Scott Thomson, former executive director of NASSP, for consistent support and encouragement to find a way to use peer partners for strengthening leadership; Ray Cowart, president and CEO of Digital Discoveries, for assisting in creating what may be the first personal computer assessment and report-generating software; Bill Byham, former president and CEO of Development Dimensions International (DDI), for providing real encouragement to our time-saving ideas, as well offering an international venue for sharing and testing out ideas at DDI's annual International Congresses on Assessment Center Methods.

I am grateful to Milton Hakel, eminent professor at Bowling Green University, who recognized early on the value of our approach to leadership development; Edward Pavur for his wise advice and process development validation; Charlie Allen, Maryland State Department Assessment Center Director, who was most encouraging and advised me regarding the early developments of the Professional Enhancement Program (PEP*) materials; and Ronald Jones, outstanding staff developer, who was the first to take the bold step of statewide implementation of the ideas in this book. Thanks also to a true friend and outstanding educator, Mary Ann Wright, who helped and encouraged me every step of the way; Richard Flanary, who assisted me through a career transition; Dwight Allen, former dean of the Graduate School of Education, University of Massachusetts, who provided an unbelievable opportunity to realize my dreams; Jim Sacco, a true friend and colleague; and John Caughlin, my capable doctoral assistant who provided generous support in all phases of the development of PEP*, including research, technical issues, teaching, and encouragement of the concept of peer evaluation and assessment.

Then there is Alice Foster, my coauthor, who, after attending a national staff development association meeting in Dallas, Texas, where I had been on the program, promptly responded to an e-mail inquiry from me asking if she was the same person I knew years ago in the field of staff development. The answer was no, but she followed it with, "Would you like to write a book about the leadership development topic of your presentation in Dallas?" Alice gently initiated me into the field of authorship; Lawrence Mann, formerly on the editorial staff of the Association for Supervision and Curriculum Development, who provided needed suggestions for making this book more accessible to the reader; Bettye Topps, former director of the District of Columbia Office of Staff Development, who provided early ideas for the program; Lilla Wise, former associate director of personnel in the Arlington County Public Schools in Virginia, who aggressively encouraged and field-tested many of the simulations in this book to guarantee relevancy; Marlene Reagin, my Leadership Academy development center director, who worked diligently to make the technology work; Clark Dobson, associate dean, who made it possible to sustain the academy's program for so many years; and Ronald Areglado, formerly of the National Association of Elementary School Principals, who provided encouragement and wise advice over the years.

There is one other category of colleagues and friends I wish to acknowledge—the professionals across the country, many of whom were former assessment center directors, and the many who are now delivering the program outlined in this book. This list would not be complete without including Ray Lemley, formerly of NASSP; Bob Carleson; George Ann Rice; Kate Kinley; Dode Worsham; Jean Brown; Vic Verdi; Michael and Tricia Goode; Joyce Skaff; and Dori Bisbey.

All of these staff developers, teachers, administrators, leaders, and friends have been instrumental in validating the underlying concepts in this book. We couldn't have developed and tested our programs with hundreds of students without the tireless support of administrative assistants like Bonnie Miller, Janice Gentry, Alice Regan, and Ann Ludwik. They put up with my persistent determination to "make it all work." And finally, I wish to thank Robb Clouse, senior acquisitions editor of Corwin Press. Robb has been amazingly patient throughout the entire process of insisting that we translate the ideas in this book so others could understand; and for this, I am eternally grateful.

I am especially grateful to have had consistent encouragement to seek innovative answers to professional challenges from five very special people: my mother, who is in her 9th decade of life; my loving wife, Millie, with whom it all began; my brilliant, kind, and thoughtful son, Brian, who recently published his first international law and ethics book; my bright, thoughtful, and loving daughter, Julie Miller, who puts into practice both leadership and technology for teaching and learning; and my supportive and thoughtful partner, Alan Kousen; a sound science educator, curriculum developer, and techology advisor. Without the patience and encouragement of these special human beings, this book would never have been written. They provide the energy and continuing puffs of support to keep this eagle feather soaring.

—*David H. Lepard*

Corwin Press gratefully acknowledges the contributions of the following reviewers:

Connie F. Ballard
Executive Director
    of Alternative Schools
Houston Independent
    School District
Houston, TX

Stephen D. Shepperd
Principal
Sunnyside Elementary School
Kellogg, ID

Gary E. Martin
Associate Professor
School of Education
Northern Arizona University
Flagstaff, AZ

Jesse Jai McNeil, Jr.
Assistant Professor
School of Education
University of Texas, Arlington
Arlington, TX

Kermit G. Buckner
Professor
Educational Leadership
School of Education
East Carolina University
Greenville, NC

About the Authors

David H. Lepard began his career in education in Pomona, California, completing his master's degree at Claremont Graduate University and his doctorate at the University of Massachusetts, where he directed a microteaching clinic for future teachers. He assisted with early pilots for the National Association of Secondary School Principals' (NASSP) principal assessment center program and later directed the first principal assessment center program in Prince William County, Virginia.

He trained principals throughout the country as a lead trainer for NASSP's development and assessment center programs. Dr. Lepard was invited to join the faculty of George Mason University (GMU) to establish a regional prinicpal assessment center program. He secured funding for four regional principal assessment centers in Virginia, and founded and directed GMU's Leadership Academy for 15 years. While at GMU he tested, applied, and developed many of the principles expressed in this book.

His career in education includes elementary, middle, high school, and university teaching and administration. He presently manages his own consulting company, ABC International (ABCI). ABCI specializes in development processes combining job simulations, technology, and cooperative learning for diagnosing and strengthening leadership skills. He is a frequent presenter at national and international conferences.

Alice G. Foster is Senior Program Specialist, Secondary Education, for Stockton Unified School District. She earned her Ph.D. from the University of Southern California. Her 38 years in the field of education include high school teaching and administration, Stockton Teachers' Association president and negotiator, grant writer, change agent in implementing school reform, and acquisitions editor. She has presented at state national conferences, served for 3 years on the Association for Supervision and Curriculum Development publications committee, and published articles in professional journals.

Background and Fundamentals

OVERVIEW

In this first chapter, you will become acquainted with the ideas that make this program work, and we'll introduce you to some activities, technology, and processes for strengthening your leadership skills. You will find a Self-Inventory for gaining perspective on how others may see your performance. You will also find performance on the job linkages to the Interstate Leadership Licensure Consortium's (ISLLC) standards for school principals. Using paper and pencil, video, and a computer, you will bridge leadership theory and practice. We know you're eager to begin, but be sure to complete this chapter before attempting the activities that follow.

You are an educator with experience. Your feelings about learning and school improvement run deep. And because of your experience, you probably agree that one of the requisites for improving schools is strengthening the leadership skills of teachers and principals. You know that educators with effective leadership skills can help improve instruction and more effectively shape the culture, values, and vision of a school. They are the teachers and principals who are able to address the concerns of their constituents and have a strong influence on the motivation, drive, and commitment of staff, teachers, and students. They seem to get things done better. They have leadership.

LEADERSHIP

What Is Leadership?

Leadership is easy to spot but difficult to define. A plethora of books on leadership enter the marketplace each year. If you've read any of them, you know that each new leadership bestseller offers yet another perspective on what leadership is—complete with definitions, examples, case study formats, and discussions. Professors and practitioners collect more books on leadership each year in hopes of finding the proverbial silver bullet.

Will this book be the silver bullet for you? Yes! But only if you practice, practice, practice. This approach works only if you are willing to learn and practice specific leadership skills. Completion of all the readings and activities in this book will require about 24 hours of your time. If you hope only to be inspired by lofty ideas about leadership, are not willing to dedicate real time to practicing leadership skills, this may not be the book for you.

Recognizing the effects of leadership is one thing, but defining leadership and changing our leadership behavior is quite another. We need first to know what it is about our leadership behavior that needs to be strengthened and then to practice with regular feedback. To craft your personal leadership development, you will need clear definitions and performance indicators. Fortunately, that's exactly what you will find in the activities in this book.

Strengthening leadership behavior is a difficult challenge, and most trainers know it. However, some have concluded that knowledge and expertise are not as important as what they call *native emotional intelligence*. For them, emotional intelligence includes personal qualities and traits such as initiative, trustworthiness, self-confidence, and drive for achievement, along with empathy, political awareness, the ability to leverage diversity, and the ability to work effectively in team settings. Goleman (1998) states that emotional intelligence is the necessary foundation on which other skills and attributes rest. We certainly agree with that. But for us, the challenge for leadership training and development is to clearly specify skills, dimensions, aspects, and dispositions so that they may be understood, learned, and mastered.

In certain settings, leadership occurs naturally, especially where role expectations are defined and understood. You've probably noticed this kind of leadership in senior members of families, elected officials in communities, officiators at sporting events, and in a variety of religious and cultural groupings. Leadership occurs in government, military, business, and schools. In each of these settings, leadership is likely to be performed differently. For example, the leadership role of an elementary school principal is different from the leadership role of a dean of a school of education—yet they both may be recognized as highly effective leaders. If we are to develop skills for meeting particular leadership role expectations, we need to define and clarify the kind of leadership skills we want to strengthen.

As we noted at the beginning of this chapter, we often feel we know what leadership is when we see it but find it almost impossible to define adequately. In this book, we'll explore working definitions of some of the key aspects of leadership. You will clarify your definitions of leadership so that you can understand it, learn it, and master it.

Assessing and Selecting Leaders

In the early 1900s, German psychologists explored the idea that some kind of screening process might help identify individuals suited for leadership roles. By the 1930s, the German military began using a screening process to select unit leaders and others by seeing how well they could assume difficult roles under pressure. British psychologists, after formulating information on the screening and selection process used by German psychologists, began formulating their own process. Screening was based on two principle sources of information on a candidate: written tests and observation of performance in job-related tasks (Caughlin, 1997).

British psychologists finally settled on using multiple assessment techniques with highly trained observers. Later, they applied their methodology to the selection of military officers. They defined performance expectations, and trained teams of assessors to systematically observe candidates. A key innovation involved the use of problem-solving simulations in group settings but without an appointed leader—a situation where some group members took the opportunity to demonstrate their individual leadership skills. This innovation represented a significant contribution to the field of assessment methodology.

Other government organizations soon formed assessment centers for the selection of middle- and high-level civil servants—the first nonmilitary use of the assessment process. Assessment centers are still used for many civil-service appointments and promotions. Eventually, American industry adapted and developed the assessment center concept. AT&T and Michigan Bell were among the first to use it. The process was later used in department store chains, the automotive industry, stockbroker firms, airlines, oil companies, government agencies, and, finally, in public schools.

Improving leadership skills often begins with identifying those elements that leaders need to do well in a given profession. This is not a new challenge. For the past 3 decades or more, education leaders and professional associations have investigated effective ways of identifying and developing individuals for key leadership roles. Business, industry, and government have also sought improved ways of selecting, placing, and developing individuals in leadership roles.

In education, traditional approaches to selecting new administrators often begin by creating or updating existing job descriptions. Advertising the position, developing a pool of applicants, reviewing résumés, seeking recommendations, and, finally, interviewing candidates. Since all parties involved are likely to have different experiences and, therefore, different perspectives on the advertised job, their approaches are often not consistent with one another.

Another approach, considered by some to be a more reliable method for identifying leadership potential and selecting candidates for leadership positions, is found in the assessment center process.

During the 1970s, the National Association of Secondary School Principals (NASSP) developed and implemented an intensive assessment center program for prospective school principals. Their program targeted management competencies and began by observing, analyzing, and interviewing successful incumbents to document what they actually did on the job. Later, the National Association of Elementary School Principals (NAESP) developed a similar program but with a greater emphasis on instructional leadership. Assessment centers use a group of trained professionals who have learned in advance a set of performance criteria for a given position. Applicants demonstrate their readiness for a position by performing simulations under the watchful eye of trained observers. The observers script their behavior in simulations and then reach consensus on the applicant's level of skill. Both organizations found broad acceptance for their assessment programs. Several states even began requiring satisfactory performance in an assessment center as a requirement for licensure of prospective principals.

And some universities integrated assessment programs into their preparation requirements. However, success using the assessment center model was limited because of the extensive demands it made on staff time. Other educational organizations also took steps to develop assessment programs to recommend to their membership, but after some experience with it, many organizations concluded that the assessment center process was too labor-intensive and expensive to continue. Some organizations switched their emphasis from selection to staff development. One clear but unexpected benefit often reported was the strong learning gains experienced by individuals trained and serving as assessors (Byham, 1980). The task of examining and documenting the performance of others resulted in personal growth for assessors who documented performances and drew conclusions about skill levels demonstrated by participants. In contrast, completing job simulations and receiving feedback from others did not result in comparable growth for participants. In spite of the thorough and rigorous process of assessment centers, nagging questions remain: "How can we improve the performance of existing leaders?" and "How can they develop their own performance?" This book gives a new perspective on answers to these questions.

Selecting Leadership Competencies

Two key questions arise: Which leadership competencies should we attempt to develop? How can such competencies be understood and mastered in a practical and cost-effective way? The leadership competencies you will develop with the help of this book are rooted in the NASSP

Assessment Center experience. They also embrace leadership skills in the National Policy Board for Educational Administration's (NPBEA) Leadership Domains and Dimensions (Thomson, Hill, & Conny, 1993) and in the Interstate School Leaders Licensure Consortium's (ISLLC) (1996) Leadership Standards. Also, we have included observable performance indicators that we have distilled from the leadership literature of many state departments of education.

As you use this book, you will notice the importance we place on observable behaviors. We believe that leadership standards that are difficult to observe or measure are not very useful in preservice settings. The first ISLLC Standard, for example, opens with, "A school administrator is an educational leader who promotes the success of all students by facilitating the development, articulation, implementation, and stewardship of a vision of learning that is shared and supported by the school community." At first reading, this is a highly commendable standard, but on further examination, we can see how difficult it is to observe and measure. Fortunately, ISLLC explains the standard by adding, "The administrator has knowledge and understanding of: learning goals in a pluralistic society; the principles of developing and implementing strategic plans; systems theory; information sources, data collection, and data analysis strategies; effective communication; effective consensus-building and negotiation skills; etc." Some of these are more observable than others, and it is with this in mind that we have developed the leadership activities in this book.

Observing Leadership Performance

To help you further develop your leadership competencies, we have identified a limited set of expectations with specific observable performance indicators. We have observed that many preservice and inservice courses in leadership do not use agreed-on performance indicators and that they often fail to strengthen their participants' leadership skills. Too often, they assume that students enrolled in graduate leadership programs already possess the fundamentals of leadership, so they offer only personal experiences and case studies coupled with textbook readings. This book is nothing like that.

The exercise of leadership is sometimes viewed as an art that resists measurement. However, even art can be described in terms of basic elements such as color, form, shape, intensity. Leadership, too, can be described in terms of its basic elements, which can be applied to leadership assessment, training, and development.

In this book, we present a limited number of fundamental leadership competencies. Just as athletes master the fundamentals of their sport; artists master combining, blending, and applying primary colors; and musicians master the 12-note scale—you can master 14 skill areas and apply them to the art and craft of leadership.

Raising Standards

When NASSP created their principal assessment center program in the 1970s, they developed and defined a set of performance indicators that centered on 12 key skills related to management issues. NAESP's program focused more on issues of classroom supervision and instruction. For the most part, the only place to learn the skills identified by the two associations was in their assessment center programs.

Nearly 20 years later, a new organization, the NPBEA (1993) published *Principals for our Changing Schools: The Knowledge and Skill Base*. This handbook was a significant step in bringing together the work of the national associations and others into a concise and useable framework of 21 skill areas. These were classified into four domains: functional, programmatic, interpersonal, and contextual. The work of the NPBEA created a more concise and usable format for use in preparing and evaluating school leaders.

One year later, in 1994, a new consortium was formed to develop a set of standards to help define and guide the practice of school leaders. This consortium included interested chief state school officers as well as national association representatives. By 1996, the group officially adopted the ISLLC Standards. Initial states represented were Arkansas, California, Connecticut, Delaware, Georgia, Illinois, Indiana, Kansas, Kentucky, Maryland, Massachusetts, Michigan, Mississippi, Missouri, New Jersey, North Carolina, Ohio, Pennsylvania, Rhode Island, South Carolina, Texas, Virginia, Washington, and Wisconsin. These participating states now require adherence to the ISLLC Standards (or variations of them) for the development and licensure of both prospective and current administrators.

Candidates must pass a 6-hour written examination, the School Leaders Licensure Assessment, developed and administered by the Educational Testing Service (ETS). Staff members that have been trained in the standards and content specifications score the exams.

SKILL CLUSTERS, PERFORMANCE INDICATORS, AND ASPECTS

Although the practice of leadership is not an exact science, leadership, like all performance fields, has performance aspects that can be analyzed. In this book, we have identified 14 fundamental performance areas that we believe are essential to effective school leadership. These areas include performance in instructional leadership as well as school management.

We have grouped the 14 areas into four leadership skill clusters that include capsule definitions, their relationships to both the ISLLC and NPBEA published leadership standards and domains, and their related performance indicators. The skill clusters include: (a) problem-solving skills, (b) interpersonal skills, (c) communication skills, and (d) personal characteristics. For the most part, the performance indicators are observable. In a few instances, whether positive or negative, the presence or absence of a behavior may be emphasized, such as, "not fabricating information" or "not showing tact." You will find more specific information about ISLLC performance aspects included in the activities that follow in subsequent chapters.

14 SKILLS CLUSTERS

I. Problem-Solving Skills Cluster

1. ANALYZING PROBLEMS

Capsule Definition: Seeking relevant background information to use in solving problems, following directions, analyzing information.

ISLLC Relationships
Standard 1 (Vision), Standard 2 (Instruction), Standard 3 (Management), Standard 4 (Community), Standard 6 (Context)

NPBEA Relationships
Domain 1 (Functional), Domain 2 (Programmatic), Domain 4 (Contextual)

Performance Indicators
- Clarifying directions
- Following directions
- Seeking information
- Seeking additional information
- Clarifying information received
- Using appropriate information sources
- Analyzing information received
- Adhering to activity guidelines
- Seeking policies
- Connecting related issues
- Analyzing performance
- Summarizing processes

2. EXERCISING JUDGMENT

Capsule Definition: Setting priorities, showing appropriate caution, not fabricating information, making quality decisions.

ISLLC Relationships
Standard 2 (Instruction), Standard 3 (Management), Standard 4 (Community), Standard 5 (Ethics), Standard 6 (Context)

NPBEA Relationships
Domain 1 (Functional), Domain 2 (Programmatic), Domain 4 (Contextual)

Performance Indicators
- Identifying and recognizing important issues by giving them priority
- Supporting decisions made by self or by individuals in authority
- Acting with appropriate caution, qualifying recommendations
- Acknowledging own mistakes

14 SKILLS CLUSTERS *continued*

- Following directions given by individuals in authority
- Informing superiors of critical issues and possible solutions
- Taking action on critical issues
- Making commitments to handle important problems
- Recognizing differing cultural backgrounds of individuals groups
- Confirming information before taking action
- Not fabricating information
- Supporting recommendations with information

3. ORGANIZING AND PLANNING

Capsule Definition: Completing tasks, organizing information, planning solutions to problems.

ISLLC Relationships

Standard 1 (Vision), Standard 2 (Instruction), Standard 3 (Management), Standard 4 (Community), Standard 6 (Context)

NPBEA Relationships

Domain 1 (Functional), Domain 2 (Programmatic), Domain 4 (Contextual)

Performance Indicators

- Completing a large volume of work
- Organizing tasks to be completed
- Outlining clearly
- Preparing documents that are easily understood
- Planning tasks, meetings, and events
- Preparing plans for intended actions
- Preparing to-do lists
- Making notes on calendars for scheduling and planning
- Preparing meeting agendas
- Writing notes to self for follow-up actions
- Taking actions to move work ahead
- Preparing materials for meetings and events
- Taking notes on important topics
- Drafting clear, concise questions
- Drafting outlines, visual aids, and so on, for oral presentations
- Showing awareness of time limitations
- Completing a large volume of work

4. MAKING DECISIONS

Capsule Definition: Taking prompt action to resolve problems; showing confidence; making clear, decisive presentations.

ISLLC Relationship

Standard 3 (Management)

NPBEA Relationship

Domain 1 (Functional)

Performance Indicators

- Establishing high-priority issues
- Taking prompt action on assigned tasks
- Taking prompt action on urgent issues

14 SKILLS CLUSTERS *continued*

- Taking prompt action to get assigned tasks underway
- Completing assigned tasks on time
- Establishing clear deadlines
- Asking or drafting brief, clear questions
- Preparing clearly and concisely worded documents and reports
- Showing behaviors of confidence—eye contact, firm gestures, and so on
- Making decisive oral presentations

II. Interpersonal Skills Cluster

5. GROUP LEADERSHIP

   Capsule Definition: Setting direction for groups, keeping groups on task, assisting in accomplishment of group tasks.

   ISLLC Relationships

   Standard 1 (Vision), Standard 3 (Management), Standard 4 (Community), Standard 5 (Ethics)

   NPBEA Relationship

   Domain 1 (Functional)

   Performance Indicators

   - Initiating group discussions
   - Suggesting solutions to problems
   - Suggesting approaches to solving problems
   - Clarifying or restating group tasks
   - Initiating new topics for discussion
   - Redirecting discussions
   - Keeping groups on task
   - Summarizing and restating others' points
   - Calling attention to time constraints
   - Pointing out areas of agreement
   - Supporting others when they are leading discussions
   - Freely participating in group discussions
   - Stopping irrelevant discussions

6. DELEGATING EFFECTIVELY

   Capsule Definition: Clearly assigning responsibilities, clarifying expectations, providing prompt feedback.

   ISLLC Relationship

   Standard 3 (Management)

   NPBEA Relationship

   Domain 1 (Functional)

   Performance Indicators

   - Asking others to assist with tasks appropriate to their skills and job
   - Delegating the gathering of information to individuals based on their knowledge and abilities
   - Delegating authority to individuals based on their knowledge and abilities
   - Delegating with deadlines
   - Delegating with planned follow-up

14 SKILLS CLUSTERS *continued*

- Delegating with clear, specific instructions
- Delegating the gathering of information to individuals based on their knowledge and abilities

7. INTERPERSONAL SENSITIVITY

Capsule Definition: Acknowledging others' viewpoints, taking action promptly and tactfully on concerns of others.

ISLLC Relationships — Standard 1 (Vision), Standard 2 (Instruction), Standard 3 (Management), Standard 4 (Community), Standard 6 (Context)

NPBEA Relationship — Domain 3 (Interpersonal)

Performance Indicators

- Involving others in program or task development
- Promptly getting back to individuals with concerns
- Acknowledging the concerns of others without necessarily agreeing or disagreeing with them
- Sharing information with individuals who need to know
- Using tact when responding to others
- Planning meetings with individuals face to face to address their concerns
- Planning telephone calls to individuals with concerns
- Suggesting compromises
- Using others' names
- Acknowledging positive actions of others
- Not interrupting others or talking over their comments
- Not engaging in side conversations while others are speaking
- Dealing tactfully with aggressive members of a group
- Helping others save face
- Using tension-reducing language and showing willingness to assist others
- Sharing information with others
- Showing evidence of listening attentively to others

8. MANAGING STRESS

Capsule Definition: Remaining outwardly calm under pressure, not expressing criticism strongly, coping successfully with professional challenges.

ISLLC Relationship — None

NPBEA Relationship — Domain 3 (Interpersonal)

Performance Indicators

- Accepting criticism
- Not showing anger
- Not raising voice when challenged
- Not patronizing others
- Not withdrawing from discussions after criticism
- Not showing personal aggressiveness toward others
- Not showing hostility or criticism of simulations or of others

14 SKILLS CLUSTERS *continued*

- Staying on task when under pressure

- Not showing defensiveness

- Maintaining composure when criticized

- Expressing thoughts clearly when under pressure

- Managing available time well

III. Communication Skills Cluster

9. ORAL COMMUNICATION

    Capsule Definition: Orally expressing ideas clearly, effectively; using appropriate eye contact; using correct grammar, diction, pronunciation.

    ISLLC Relationships

    Standard 1 (Vision), Standard 3 (Management), Standard 4 (Community), Standard 6 (Context)

    NPBEA Relationships

    Domain 3 (Interpersonal), Domain 4 (Contextual)

    Performance Indicators

    - Speaking with appropriate volume

    - Articulating words clearly

    - Pronouncing words correctly

    - Making no errors in grammar

    - Making eye contact when listening or speaking

    - Expressing ideas clearly

10. WRITTEN COMMUNICATION

    Capsule Definition: Expressing ideas clearly, effectively in writing; using correct grammar, spelling; using proper writing formats.

    ISLLC Relationships

    Standard 1 (Vision), Standard 2 (Instruction), Standard 4 (Community), Standard 5 (Ethics), Standard 6 (Context)

    NPBEA Relationships

    Domain 2 (Programmatic), Domain 4 (Contextual)

    Performance Indicators

    - Expressing ideas clearly

    - Writing with no errors in spelling

    - Writing with no errors in grammar

    - Using appropriate forms of written communications (e.g., notes, letters, memos, proposals, news releases, plans, charts, graphs)

11. ORAL PRESENTATION

    Capsule Definition: Expressing ideas clearly, effectively; using correct grammar, diction, pronunciation; using visual aids effectively.

    ISLLC Relationships

    Standard 1 (Vision), Standard 3 (Management), Standard 4 (Community)

    NPBEA Relationships

    Domain 3 (Interpersonal), Domain 4 (Contextual)

    Performance Indicators

    - Standing for formal presentations

    - Using appropriate volume, tone, rate of speech

    - Using pauses when speaking

    - Varying pitch when speaking

    - Making no errors in grammar

    - Making enthusiastic presentations

14 SKILLS CLUSTERS *continued*

- Demonstrating a confident manner: eye contact, gestures, word emphasis, and so on

- Clearly presenting facts and ideas

- Presenting supportive reasons for recommendations

- Expressing well-organized thoughts

- Maintaining eye contact with the audience

- Making opening statements to audience

- Making closing statements to audience

IV. Personal Characteristics Cluster

12. EXPRESSING PROFESSIONAL VALUES

Capsule Definition: Expressing professional values; sharing vision for improving curriculum, instruction.

ISLLC Relationships — Standard 1 (Vision), Standard 2 (Instruction), Standard 4 (Community), Standard 5 (Ethics), Standard 6 (Context)

NPBEA Relationships — Domain 2 (Programmatic), Domain 4 (Contextual)

Performance Indicators — *Strongly held values or beliefs about*

- Schools and education-related issues

- Curriculum and instruction

- Teaching and learning

- Schools and education

- School leadership and management

- School safety and security

- Student and teacher behavior

- Educational policy and policymaking

- Parents and community

- Finance and schools

A personal vision for

- Teaching and learning

- Schools and education

- Curriculum and instruction

- Issues of importance to education

- Finance and schools

13. RANGE OF INTERESTS

Capsule Definition: Actively participating in a broad range of professional and non-professional experiences, activities.

ISLLC Relationship — Standard 6 (Context)

NPBEA Relationships — Domain 3 (Interpersonal), Domain 4 (Contextual)

Performance Indicators — *Range of*

- Part-time and full-time jobs

- Electives taken in school or college

14 SKILLS CLUSTERS *continued*

- Extracurricular activities in school or college

- Outside activities currently engaged in

- Outside interests actively pursued

14. PROFESSIONAL MOTIVATION	*Capsule Definition:* Pursuing clear goals, actively engaging in personal and professional growth.
ISLLC Relationships	Standard 1 (Vision), Standard 2 (Instruction), Standard 4 (Community), Standard 6 (Context)
NPBEA Relationship	Domain 3 (Interpersonal)
Performance Indicators	

- History of steady advancement and growth in job responsibilities

- History of voluntarily participating in a variety of professional development activities

- History of accepting new challenges

- History of making needed changes in work situations

- Expressing clear career goals

- History of volunteering for new assignments

- History of seeking feedback on performance

- Expressing personal work standards

- Expressing a personal skill improvement plan

- History of actively building support for ideas

SOURCE: Adapted with permission from Council of Chief State School Officers (1996); National Association of Secondary School Principals (1988); S. D. Thomson, S. Hill, & B. M. Conny (1993).

Improving Performance

The leadership skill clusters, performance areas, capsule definitions, relationships to national standards, and the performance indicators presented in the 14 Skills Clusters lay the foundation for the activities later (that follow) in this book. The effectiveness of these activities relies on reflective practice and discussion of the activities.

For maximum success with this program, you will need to choose a reliable partner who is as interested in leadership development as you are. You will complete the activities together. Although it is possible to complete the activities in this book on your own, maximum benefit comes from sharing the activities with a partner. It is easy to gloss over elements of the activities when completing them by yourself, to take shortcuts, or to not clarify or examine your reasons for making certain choices. Taking the easy way is not possible when you have to explain your positions, reasons, and actions to a partner.

Although this is a do-it-yourself project, a better way to think of it would be as a do-it-together project. After studying and completing each activity, you will exchange your responses with your partner. Your completed responses are referred to as *artifacts*. The word *artifacts* seems to suggest something dug up from the site of an ancient civilization, perhaps some kind of tool or a water jug or a doll—evidence of what life was like in a distant time and place. But artifacts are not necessarily ancient; right now your own artifacts surround you, and most of us create new artifacts almost daily. In this chapter's activity, you will both create and interpret artifacts, which is what we call the evidence that remains when the activity is completed.

Artifacts in this book include your case study analyses, school improvement plans, deskwork, group problem solving and personal interviews, and videotapes of you and your partner making school board presentations and solving problems in a group.

Discussions between you and your partner should resolve any differences between you in the actions taken during the simulations. We'll discuss more about the selection of your partner later in this chapter.

The documentation activities in this book use a similar process:

- Checking for the presence or absence of specific performance indicators grouped by competency areas
- Noting examples and quoting comments
- Reflecting on reasons that prompted choices
- Discussing the differences between partners' choices in completing activities

Rating Performance

After activity artifacts have been examined and the presence of performance indicators verified through documentation, you will find a page at the end of each documentation form for summarizing your demonstrated performance levels. Examine the symbols used and their interpretations. They represent levels of skill demonstrated by your partner. After examining the completed documentation form and noting particular performance areas and their indicators (analyzing problems, exercising judgment, etc.), decide on the rating for each performance area documented. In the performance summary ratings, rate the performance areas listed on a scale from very low skill to very high skill.

When you complete rating performance on individual summary rating forms for an activity, complete your Overall Performance Summary. Later, you will summarize performance in all activities on a final rating form in each chapter. After agreeing on assigned ratings, you will use this information for drafting your professional development plan.

Development Processes

The processes used in this leadership development book are organized in several stages. We remind you to read this entire chapter before completing any of the activities. In fact, we encourage you to read the entire book before beginning the activities—just so there are no surprises. We want you to be as prepared as possible, so you will do your best in all the activities.

We believe that leadership development is a personal responsibility, and we have done everything possible to reduce any threat by putting your final performance documentation in the hands of a partner you trust.

In brief, this leadership development program requires that you do the following:

- Identify a partner.
- Complete job simulation activities.
- Summarize individual activity performance levels.
- Reflect on your decisions, the belief systems and reasons for your choices, and what you have learned from each activity.
- Summarize overall performance levels across all activities.
- Develop a personal professional growth plan.

Subsequent chapters explain in detail what is involved in meeting each of the requirements just cited.

CASE STUDY

The case study you will work with, which is in Chapter 2, lays the foundation for the set of simulations to follow in other chapters. The first task in the case study is to read about and study the existing circumstances in Normal School, a fictitious school in a fictitious community. The second task is to identify and prioritize strengths, weaknesses, and the urgent problems facing you, as a new principal at Normal School. You will note that professional values is one of the performance areas you document in this activity and in some activities in later chapters.

We emphasize that *you will not attempt to judge* the worth of expressed values but instead will check the activity artifacts to see if your partner actually did express them in writing or speaking.

Case Study Performance Areas

Analyzing Problems	Written Communication
Exercising Judgment	Expressing Professional Values
Making Decisions	

Improvement Plan

Following analysis of the case study in Chapter 2, you will prepare, in Chapter 3, a school improvement plan for one of the urgent problems. To prepare a high-quality plan, you may need to spend as long as 1 week.

School Improvement Plan Performance Areas

Analyzing Problems	Making Decisions
Exercising Judgment	Interpersonal Sensitivity
Organizing and Planning	Written Communication

Office Deskwork

The deskwork activity in Chapter 4 simulates the tasks new principals might face at their desk the first day on the job in a new community and school. The overall task is to review, prioritize, and handle a set of realistic, school-related issues and problems. The items reflect the breadth of issues that typically face a newly assigned principal: writing letters and memos, planning and making telephone calls, drafting e-mail, and planning for anticipated conversations. The need for effective time-management skills and maintenance of quality responses when handling a volume of paperwork over a relatively short period of time becomes evident when completing this activity.

Deskwork Performance Areas

Analyzing Problems	Delegating Effectively
Exercising Judgment	Interpersonal Sensitivity
Organizing and Planning	Written Communication
Making Decisions	Expressing Professional Values

Oral Presentation

The oral presentation activity in Chapter 5 has four parts: analyzing a problem situation facing a newly assigned principal, identifying key information about the situation, drafting a formal report to a school board, and orally presenting the report. This simulation is video recorded for later analysis.

Oral Presentation Performance Areas

Analyzing Problems	Managing Stress
Exercising Judgment	Oral Communication
Organizing and Planning	Oral Presentation
Making Decisions	Expressing Professional Values

Group Discussion

The group problem-solving discussion in Chapter 6 is in two parts. In the first part, you will rank three school improvement plans, present and defend a preassigned plan, and participate in a discussion with your partner and a colleague to arrive at a consensus on the best plan for district recognition. The second part of the simulation involves preparation of a consensus report to the superintendent detailing the processes you, your partner and a colleague used for arriving at your recommendation.

Group Discussion Performance Areas

Analyzing Problems	Managing Stress
Exercising Judgment	Oral Communication
Group Leadership	Oral Presentation
Interpersonal Sensitivity	Expressing Professional Values

Group Discussion Interview

The first interview in Chapter 7 is limited to performance in the problem-solving discussion. It gives you and your partner an opportunity to reflect on your performance in the group discussion. One of you will ask the other a set of questions, and then you will exchange roles. An important part of the interview activity is learning how to conduct fair and impartial structured interviews.

Group Discussion Interview Performance Reporting Areas

Analyzing Problems	Group Leadership
Exercising Judgment	Interpersonal Sensitivity
Organizing and Planning	Managing Stress
Making Decisions	Oral Communication

Personal Interview

The personal interview in Chapter 7 is also structured but more personal in nature. It gives you and your partner an opportunity to answer thoroughly questions about your background, career, goals, and professional life. As with the preceding problem-solving discussion, important skills to learn are how to listen and how to conduct fair and impartial interviews. Again, you will take turns asking the same set of questions in the same sequence, without added comments or explanations.

Personal Interview Performance Reporting Areas

Analyzing Problems	Managing Stress
Exercising Judgment	Oral Communication
Organizing and Planning	Expressing Professional Values
Making Decisions	Range of Interests
Group Leadership	Professional Motivation
Interpersonal Sensitivity	

NINE-STEP DEVELOPMENT PROCESS

In conclusion, we have learned from experience that you can effectively improve your leadership skills if the following steps are taken:

1. Become familiar with the entire book before starting the activities.

2. Complete the leadership simulations and related activities.

3. Reflect on the completed activity, your choices, and the beliefs and reasons underlying your choices.

4. Share with your partner your reflections on your choices.

5. With your partner, review any differences between your choices and underlying belief systems.

6. In each chapter, complete your performance summary forms and the overall form for all activities.

7. Review the final outcomes and compare with your self-inventory, which you completed earlier.

8. Based on the summary performance form, as well as the entire experience, write your targeted, professional leadership development plan—your action plan.

9. Share your action plan with others; implement it and evaluate your growth in leadership skills.

Choosing a Partner

When choosing a partner for completing the activities in this book, you should use the following guidelines. Both of you should

- Have prior knowledge about each other
- Agree to become familiar with the processes and program goals
- Agree to study a copy of this book (each partner should have their own copy).
- Be comfortable working together
- Have voluntarily chosen to complete activities together
- Have similar work ethics, such as punctuality
- Have similar jobs
- Live in the same geographic area
- Be at similar educational levels

Video Technology

This development program requires the use of video technology for documenting your performance and the performance of your partner. To analyze and develop you oral-orientation and group leadership skills, you will need a video camera, tripod, playback unit, and blank videotape. You will each need your own video tape, but the other technology may be shared.

You will use a video camera for the board presentation and the problem-solving discussion. Replaying portions of the videotapes enhances accuracy and performance analysis for both partners.

THE LEADERSHIP SELF-INVENTORY

Before going further, be sure you have learned the 14 capsule definitions in the 14 Skills Clusters. After learning these leadership definitions, and before beginning the activities in this book, you should complete the self-inventory of your leadership skills (Form 1.1). Answer each question the way someone who has often observed your behavior would answer it. The questions help you evaluate the relative frequency with which you demonstrate a specific behavior. The inventory serves two purposes: (a) to allow you to consider how others around you are likely to see your leadership, and (b) to provide information you will use to create a professional development plan after you've completed the activities with your partner. Reflect on how others may judge your abilities. Examine each leadership dimension listed on Form 1.1. Then reflect on your performance in terms of when and how others may see you performing on the job. Circle the number representing the relative frequency with which you think others may see you demonstrating one of the skills. To get the most out of this activity, be as objective as you possibly can. Use the following guidelines for Form 1.1: 1—very seldom, 2—seldom, 3—occasionally, 4—as often as not, 5—often, and 6—very often. Note: Extreme ratings (1 and 6) are exceptional; use them only in truly exceptional instances.

Add the ratings. The nearer your total is to 84, the more likely you are to be doing things that contribute in an important way to your effectiveness as a leader. The performance areas and skills indicated in this profile may get you started on further enhancing your leadership effectiveness. If you have time, complete Form 1.1 by identifying things you do best—or your best practices.

Form 1.1 **Leadership Self-Inventory**

Performance Areas   *Ratings*

1. **Analyzing Problems** ------- 1 2 3 4 5 6
   Skill Capsule: Seeking relevant background information to solve problems, following directions, analyzing information

2. **Exercising Judgment** ------- 1 2 3 4 5 6
   Skill Capsule: Setting priorities, showing appropriate caution, not fabricating information, making quality decisions

3. **Organizing and Planning** ------- 1 2 3 4 5 6
   Skill Capsule: Completing tasks, organizing information, planning solutions to problems

4. **Making Decisions** ------- 1 2 3 4 5 6
   Skill Capsule: Taking prompt action to resolve problems; showing confidence; making clear, decisive presentations

5. **Group Leadership** ------- 1 2 3 4 5 6
   Skill Capsule: Setting the direction for groups, keeping groups on task, assisting with the accomplishment of group tasks

6. **Delegating Effectively** ------- 1 2 3 4 5 6
   Skill Capsule: Clearly assigning responsibilities, clarifying expectations, providing prompt feedback

7. **Interpersonal Sensitivity** ------- 1 2 3 4 5 6
   Skill Capsule: Acknowledging others' viewpoints, taking actions promptly and tactfully on concerns of others

8. **Managing Stress** ------- 1 2 3 4 5 6
   Skill Capsule: Remaining outwardly calm under pressure, not expressing criticism strongly, coping successfully with professional challenges

9. **Oral Communication** ------- 1 2 3 4 5 6
   Skill Capsule: Orally expressing ideas clearly and effectively; using appropriate eye contact; using correct grammar, diction, pronunciation

10. **Written Communication** ------- 1 2 3 4 5 6
    Skill Capsule: Expressing ideas clearly and effectively in writing; using correct grammar, syntax, and spelling; using proper writing formats

11. **Oral Presentation** ------- 1 2 3 4 5 6
    Skill Capsule: Expressing ideas clearly, effectively; using correct grammar, diction, pronunciation; using visual aides effectively

12. **Expressing Professional Values** ------- 1 2 3 4 5 6
    Skill Capsule: Expressing professional values, expressing vision for improving curriculum and instruction

13. **Range of Interests** ------- 1 2 3 4 5 6
    Skill Capsule: Actively participating in a broad range of interests, experiences, and activities

14. **Professional Motivation** ------- 1 2 3 4 5 6
    Skill Capsule: Pursuing clear goals, actively engaging in personal and professional growth

1. Performance area: _____

What I do best:

_____

_____

2. Performance area: _____

What I do best:

_____

_____

3. Performance area: _____

What I do best:

_____

_____

4. Performance area: _____

What I do best:

_____

_____

Your Best Practices

Examine the results of the inventory you just completed. Work alone for a few minutes and list three or four performance areas that you believe categorize your strongest skills. Think about the skill capsules in the inventory and things that you do to be effective. After you have written down your best leadership performance areas, think about how you would describe your actions. Then make notes in the space below to use to explain your strengths to your partner.

The chapters that follow present a series of simulations designed around the demands of the job of a principal. After summarizing your performance in each activity, you will be able to prepare your own professional development plan using the entire experience and your own conclusions from comparing your performance with your partner's.

Professional growth is not complete until you put your plans into practice. When specific behaviors are included in the plan, it will make for highly specific skill development. As with the work of any performer, mastery comes from knowing what to practice and then practicing, practicing, practicing.

2

Analyzing a Case Study

OVERVIEW

In this chapter, you and your partner will complete the first job-related activity in the leadership development series. You will analyze a case study about a fictitious school and community. In this case, *analyzing* refers to developing lists of issues that you, as the new principal, determine need to be acknowledged and addressed. Links to key performance aspects of the Interstate School Leaders Licensure Consortium's (ISLLC) Standards are provided in Resources (Table R.17).

ARTIFACTS

The particular kinds of artifacts you'll deal with in this first leadership-building activity will be paper and pencil responses that you and your partner produce (see Chapter 1 for an explanation of how the term *artifacts* is used in this book). These artifacts provide the substance for performance documentation, analysis, and reflection. After completing the activity, you and your partner exchange artifacts and document each other's work first, and then you'll each focus on your own performance. As you analyze, reflect on, and document the artifacts, you'll already have begun strengthening your leadership skills.

In this chapter, before you begin the actual case study, you will need to prepare three blank sheets each with the headings Strengths, Weaknesses, and Urgent Problems. After you read the case study: (a) You and your partner, using the self-prepared sheets, each make a list of strengths, weaknesses, and urgent problems; (b) you exchange lists, and each of you documents what's on the other's lists, using the documentation forms provided; (c) you again exchange lists so you each have your own lists plus your partner's documentation of the lists; (d) after discussion, you rate your own performance using the symbols provided.

ABOUT THE CASE STUDY

The case study provides a foundation for other activities in this program and is used in conjunction with the school improvement planning activity in Chapter 3. In this case study you are introduced to a fictitious school where you will serve as the new principal. Strengths, weaknesses, and urgent problems facing the school and community are presented in narrative form. After identifying strengths, you will then want to give special attention to identifying urgent problems; in most cases, they are not the same as weaknesses. Your first task is to acquaint yourself with the case study. As the new principal, you will be unfamiliar with the school and the community. The case study conserns a K-6 elementary school. Similar strengths, weaknesses, and urgent problems found in the elementary school can also be found in secondary schools.

Your second task is to produce lists of strengths, weaknesses, and urgent problems facing the school; prioritize the urgent problems. They may be problems such as teacher morale, declining test scores, vandalism, or rumors of drugs, etc.

Case Study Performance Areas

The activity provides opportunities for you to demonstrate your skills in

- Analyzing Problems
- Exercising Judgment
- Making Decisions
- Written Communication
- Expressing Professional Values

Two questions arise: What performance aspects in the ISLLC Standards are related to the performance areas for the case study? What skills are needed in order to be successful in meeting the standards? The activities in this book provide a bridge to the performance aspects of the ISLLC Standards.

Standards, Performance Areas, and Aspects

Each of the related standards below is presented as an abbreviated statement followed by program skill areas and the number of related performance aspects. In some instances, the activity calls for skills not found in the ISLLC Standards. Because of space limitations, specific performance aspects are not included here but may be found in Resources (Form R.17).

The information shows the linkages between the case study and performance aspects of the ISLLC's Standards.

STANDARD 1:
Developing, articulating, implementing, and stewarding a shared vision of learning
Analyzing Problems
        7 ISLLC performance aspects related to analyzing problems
Exercising Judgment
        No other ISLLC-related performance aspects

STANDARD 2:
Advocating, nurturing, and sustaining a school culture and effective instructional program conducive to student learning and staff professional growth
Analyzing Problems
        6 ISLLC performance aspects related to analyzing problems
Exercising Judgment
        1 ISLLC performance aspect related to exercising judgment
        No other ISLLC-related performance aspects
Professional Motivation
        4 ISLLC performance aspects related to professional motivation
Expressing Professional Values
        10 ISLLC performance standards related to professional values

STANDARD 3:
Ensuring management of the organization, operations, and resources for a safe, efficient, and effective learning environment
Analyzing Problems
        10 ISLLC performance aspects related to analyzing problems
Effective Delegation
        2 ISLLC performance aspects related to effective delegation
Expressing Professional Values
        2 ISLLC performance aspects related to expressing professional values

STANDARD 4:
Collaborating with families and community members, responding to diverse community interests and needs, and mobilizing community resources
Analyzing Problems
        6 ISLLC performance aspects related to analyzing problems
Exercising Judgment
        5 ISLLC performance aspects related to exercising judgment

STANDARD 5:
Promoting success of all students through integrity, fairness, and an ethical manner
Analyzing Problems
        No ISLLC-related performance aspects
Expressing Professional Values
        19 ISLLC performance aspects related to expressing professional values

STANDARD 6:
Promoting the success of all students by understanding, responding to, and influencing the larger political, social, economic, legal, and cultural context
Analyzing Problems
        7 ISLLC performance aspects related to analyzing problems
Expressing Professional Values
        6 ISLLC performance aspects related to expressing professional values

---

Note: Linkages were identified by the principal author and verified by education experts.
SOURCE: Adapted from Council of Chief State School Officers (1996).

Reflective Practice

You, no doubt, have some strong feelings about certain things in education. Often, depending on our job assignments, we think we cannot express our feelings and beliefs to others, and yet strong leadership involves being able to show and articulate them. A priority listing is one way of expressing professional values. In other activities, where you or your partner might write or say, "It's important . . ., I believe . . ., I have strong feelings about . . ., Let me emphasize . . .," it will be easy to identify expressions of professional values. Developing the habit of reflective practice—examining how one's belief systems inform one's decisions—is essential to becoming an effective leader. Reflective practice is a key component of every activity in this book.

Instructions for Completing the Case Study

You should allow approximately 45 minutes to read the case study about our hypothetical school and to complete your blank rating sheets, which profile your view of the school's strengths, weaknesses, and urgent problems. Although this is an elementary school case study, the performance indicators are the same as those for a secondary school case study.

A committee of principals, central office administrators, and higher education faculty members reviewed and agreed on the lists of performance indicators. As you read about Normal School, you will probably feel that you want more information. In a real situation, additional information would probably be available to you from other sources, but for the purposes of this activity, you have to rely only on what you already have in your own head—no further information will be available to you. One aspect of being an administrator is that we seldom have all the information we would like to have before making decisions. Thus the challenge is to make as much sense as possible using the information that is available.

Just as there never seems to be enough information with which to make a decision, there never seems to be enough time to carefully think through the decisions that need to be made. And yet the decisions must be made with the information at hand and within the time allowed. That is part of the challenge built into this activity. We have all experienced the frustration of working with an administrator who cannot make a decision in a timely fashion. You will need to structure the available time so that you can read the material, study it, and try to complete all three stages, if possible, within 45 minutes. As in real life, administrators often report that they feel rushed and do not have the time they would like to have. You will, no doubt, experience that same feeling from this activity and others with time limits.

Steps for Development

You and your partner begin by completing the case study. The developmental tasks consist of the following steps, all of which should be completed in 45 minutes:

1. Read about the case study—its performance areas and instructions for completing it.

2. Complete the case study.

3. Exchange completed rating sheets.

4. Document your partner's artifacts using the case study documentation forms.

5. Exchange completed documentation forms.

6. Review and compare your documented performances with your partner's; discuss and reach consensus, if you can, on the results. In some cases, you may not agree with your partner's analyses.

7. After discussing documentation results, rate your own performance in this activity. Use the rating symbols that we provide.

You may want to use a highlighter or pencil for keeping track of the information as you read. Before you begin, you will want to note the beginning and ending time.

NORMAL SCHOOL CASE STUDY

Introduction

Your assignment is to read, study, and draw conclusions about the strengths, weaknesses, and urgent problems of a hypothetical school in a fictitious city. Although the school, the city, and the community are not real, the information presented in this case study is typical for many schools that actually exist—schools that have a history, unique qualities, and problems. When completing this activity, feel free to make notes in the book.

Background Information

Normal Elementary School is a public school currently serving kindergarten through Grade 6. It has been in existence for more than 60 years. The school has a good reputation for instilling the basics, and the teachers are proud of its activity-centered learning programs. Over the years, the school has served as an important institution in the community.

Normal School is stable, but there are certain conditions that are compelling school officials to seriously reconsider policies, goals, and practices followed for many years. One problem is that the dropout rate, resulting in part from transient and at-risk students, is steadily increasing, and average daily attendance is declining. This is due largely to continuing changes in the socioeconomic nature of the neighborhood. Most children actually want to complete school. There is, however, a growing belief among some children, particularly in the upper grades, that school is not important.

Normal Elementary School is in Normal City. The city has a population of approximately 225,000 residents. Normal City's economic base is government, light industry, and small businesses. Several corporate offices have recently moved to Normal City. A university, an endowed library, several historic sites, and government agencies are within the city limits.

Normal City is typical of many of our cities: It is becoming more culturally and ethnically diverse. The current ethnic composition of Normal City is 25% African American, 30% Caucasian, 25% Hispanic, and 20% Asian and other minorities. The workforce is about one-fourth blue-collar, one-half managerial and professional, and one-fourth clerical and service-related. Half the adults in the Normal School community work in civil service occupations, small businesses, and education. Other adults are either unemployed or work in low-paying jobs.

Tax revenues are diminishing, but due to a sincere belief that the system could operate more efficiently, the Normal City School Board has decided to implement a districtwide, site-based management program beginning next year. The board's decision has caused school officials to change the traditional role expectations of its principals. The current principal of Normal Elementary School feels threatened by the decision to start site-based management. There are no plans to provide inservice programs for the principal or staff.

Normal School serves best those children who come from middle- to upper-income families, whose parents are well educated and work in professional or managerial positions; children from low-income families feel left out. The current enrollment at Normal Elementary is 465:

- Kindergarten: 60 students
- Grade 1: 66 students
- Grade 2: 68 students
- Grade 3: 63 students
- Grade 4: 72 students
- Grade 5: 67 students
- Grade 6: 69 students

The ratio of boys to girls is about even; the racial and ethnic mix of the student body is representative of the community. The staff is concerned about the welfare of the children. The primary functions of the guidance program are testing, record keeping, and scheduling.

The Normal Elementary School faculty consists of 27 full-time elementary teachers plus itinerant music, speech, vocal music, and art teachers. There is one librarian and a half-time guidance counselor. The physical education (PE) teacher serves as a part-time administrative assistant to the principal. There is a typical balance of female and male teachers: 20 females and 7 males. The average age of the teachers is 37: 39 for females and 35 for males. Because of the school's focus on quality teaching, many teachers have master's degrees. Thirty percent of the faculty is African-

American; 70% is Caucasian and other minority races and ethnic groups. Faculty leadership comes from a small group of teachers who have served the school for the past 20 years or longer.

As for teaching experience, the staff includes extreme age and experience differences. Many seasoned teachers are burned-out. Younger faculty members have expressed resentment that older teachers are assigned smaller classes and better students.

Though a relatively small school, Normal Elementary has had a reputation for outstanding afterschool programs. The school has a good PE program—Normal has won the regional fitness championship three times and the district championship five times. However, few children are now attending afterschool activities.

There is a marked contrast in the quality of some programs. Traditionally, Normal Elementary School has had a strong band and strings program. The band has competed successfully on a regional level, winning several awards. But the English as a second language (ESL) program is weak due to a lack of faculty leadership. In spelling, there have been occasional spelling bee winners, largely due to the interest of individual parents. Teachers have provided no help in preparing children for the spelling bees.

The school's parent teacher organization (PTO) is weak, yet some parents, though not active in the PTO, work hard to support their favorite school programs. They recognize these programs' importance for the future of their own children. One or two special-interest programs are presented annually for the general PTO membership. PTO meetings are poorly attended. Teachers only casually support the PTO. There has been little cause for broad-based support for the PTO, as parents have not felt the need to rally around a major problem or school issue. However, a disturbing rumor exists: the school board is planning a total renovation of the school. Another problem relates to neighborhood drug wars near the school.

Overall, the school is adequately supplied with textbook materials and the necessary equipment for operating a quality academic program. Some funds, though limited, are earmarked to allow the principal to attend conferences. The media center is well stocked and equipped for a school of Normal's size, and books are added regularly. The school building is well maintained, although vandalism in the school is increasing. For the first time in recent years, graffiti has been reported in the girls' lavatories.

Current Issues and Events

Several issues and events are having an influence on Normal Elementary School. Many teachers are interested in computers and other instructional technology. Some upper-grade classrooms have been provided with computers. But at a recent staff meeting, a grade-level chairperson spoke out and complained that teachers do not get support for needed instructional technology. The chairperson further stated that children are not being taught to use the basic technology needed for success in the secondary school. Some teachers are demanding to know what the principal is going to do about it.

At the same staff meeting, other grade-level chairpersons reported that there were too many public address system interruptions during the school day. They complained that too much instructional time is lost to assemblies and other special events. The teachers unanimously agreed that they were being continually interrupted by disruptive intercom messages, often to the amusement of the children.

The student roundtable recently reported that children were upset because the dress policy is unfairly administered. Some students are allowed to violate the code in some classrooms, but others are directed to the office and then sent home to change clothes. The president of the student roundtable lodged a formal complaint with the administration charging that the dress code was out of date.

At a recent PTO meeting, several key parents informed the principal that they had written the school board about a drop in test scores at Normal Elementary School. Reportedly, over the past 2 years, composite scores in several academic subjects have dropped significantly. Additionally, test scores for the last two promoted sixth-grade classes are below the school's historic average. Parents are demanding to know what the principal and staff are going to do to improve test scores.

Although some children do well in secondary school, parents are concerned that the school's reputation will be affected by declining basic-skills test results. Recently, basic-skills test scores have dropped significantly.

Although student test scores are declining, teachers at Normal Elementary School are not interested in curriculum review and revision. Their major concern is the planned use of a new evaluation procedure that was piloted in some other schools in Normal City during the current school year. Part of the procedure includes a reporting format that places an emphasis on identifying development needs of the teachers. The plan calls for semiannual evaluations of both tenured and nontenured teachers along with pre- and post-observation conferences. An evaluation of the pilot is currently under development by the school district administration. The report will be presented to the superintendent soon.

Tenured teachers at Normal Elementary definitely do not like the new teacher evaluation procedures; they are convinced that the principal is not competent to evaluate their teaching. Other teachers share a different concern, namely, that some of their colleagues' teaching skills are not satisfactory. They believe that the central office is not informed of how much inadequacy prevails among them. With a possible reduction in force (RIF), evaluation practices and procedures are real concerns.

Your Reactions

Now that you have read the case materials, you should spend the balance of the 45 minutes compiling three lists. If you haven't already done so, take three blank sheets of paper and write one of the following three headings on each separate sheet: (a) Normal School's Strengths, (b) Normal School's Weaknesses, and (c) Normal School's Urgent Problems. Then:

1. List Normal School's strengths.

2. List Normal School's weaknesses.

3. Create a 1–to–10 priority listing of Normal School's urgent problems (if you have more than 10 problems, that doesn't change the rating scale), with 1 the most urgent and 10 the least urgent.

Your listing of weaknesses and urgent problems may be similar. You may want to develop a combined list on another piece of paper, and then sort out the urgent problems. See Box R.1 in Resources for an example of these three lists.

After you have finished analyzing the case study, exchange your listings of strengths, weaknesses, and urgent problems with your partner. To gain the most from this activity, you should follow the steps for development previously listed in this chapter. It's important that you review and apply them consistently.

You are now ready to document your partner's listings or artifacts. Your partner will document yours.

Case Study Documentation Form—Strengths

Instructions

After examining your partner's list of strengths, place a check mark (✓) in the blank in front of each strength listed below for each matching identified strength on your partner's list. Do not give credit for broad, general statements. **Look for specific responses. If more than one strength is included in a single listing, give credit for each strength by placing check marks in front of all appropriate items. If a strength is listed in the artifacts, and is not on the list below, just ignore it and go on.** When you finish deciding and numbering the strengths, place dots (•) in the remaining spaces. **This helps to assure your partner that you made a specific decision concerning each statement.**

ANALYZING PROBLEMS—EXERCISING JUDGMENT—EXPRESSING PROFESSIONAL VALUES

_____ 1. The School has a good reputation for instilling the basics.

_____ 2. There are activity-centered learning programs.

_____ 3. The racial and ethnic mix of the student body is representative of the community.

_____ 4. The staff is concerned about the welfare of the children.

_____ 5. Most children want to complete school.

_____ 6. There is a satisfactory balance of male and female teachers.

_____ 7. Many teachers have master's degrees.

_____ 8. The school has had a reputation for outstanding afterschool programs.

_____ 9. The school has a good physical education program.

_____ 10. The school has had a strong band and strings program.

_____ 11. Some parents work hard to support favorite programs.

_____ 12. The school is adequately supplied.

_____ 13. Some funds are earmarked for the principal to attend conferences.

_____ 14. The media center is well stocked and equipped.

_____ 15. The school building is well maintained.

_____ 16. Many teachers are interested in computers and instructional technology.

_____ 17. Some upper-grade classrooms have been provided with computers.

_____ 18. Some children do very well in secondary schools.

_____ 19. Evaluation procedures call for semiannual evaluations of all staff.

_____ 20. Pre- and post-observation conferences are held.

_____ 21. A number is written beside each listed strength.

_____ 22. The listing of strengths differs from the order listed above. Examine the sequence.

_____ Record here the total number of strengths in the list above that corresponds with your partner's listing.

WRITTEN COMMUNICATION

_____ 23. The strengths are clearly written. If they are not, write examples:

_____ 24. There are no errors in spelling. If there are, write examples:

_____ 25. There are no errors in grammar. If there are, write examples:

Case Study Documentation Form—Strengths (continuted)

Rating Performance

Examine the symbols and their interpretations below. Use the symbols below to represent demonstrated levels of skill. Once you are familiar with them they are easy to use. After studying the completed documentation form, count the number of matches between your list of strengths and the list of strengths identified by a committee of experienced school administrators and university faculty. Rate each performance area (Analyzing Problems, Exercising Judgment, Written Communication, and Expressing Professional Values) and record the Rates in the Performance Ratings area below. In some instances several performance indicators may be attributed to more than one skill area.

When you have completed rating your partner's lists of strengths, weaknesses, and urgent problems, you will be ready to transfer your ratings to the Overall Performance Summary on the last page of this section.

Use the symbols and interpretations to determine performance summary ratings for the skill areas in this activity.

Symbols	Interpretations	Ranges
$\oplus$	Very high skill shown	= 17-19
+	More than moderate skill	= 14-16
(+)	Moderate skill shown	= 11-13
(−)	Less than moderate skill	= 8-10
−	Little skill shown	= 5-7
$\ominus$	Very little skill shown	= 1-4

Performance Summary Ratings: Strengths

Performance Areas	Rating Symbols
Analyzing Problems Performance Rating: _____	_____
Exercising Judgment Performance Rating: _____	_____
Making Decisions Performance Rating: _____	_____
Written Communication Performance Rating: _____	_____

Since little writing is called for in the Case Study, most participants receive a Moderate (+).
Enter a + if the spelling/vocabulary is more than moderate.
If there is more than one error in spelling you would enter a − or (−), showing a need for improvement.

Expressing Professional Values _____
Performance Rating: _____

Note: *Extreme ratings $\oplus$ or $\ominus$ are seldom appropriate.*

Reflective Practice

You, no doubt, have some strong feelings about certain things in education. Often, depending on our job assignments, we think we cannot express our feelings to others, and yet leadership involves being able to show and articulate them. A priority listing is one way of expressing professional values. In other activities, where you or your partner might write or say, "It's important . . ., I believe . . ., I have strong feelings about . . ., Let me emphasize . . .," it will be easy to identify expressions of professional values. Developing the habit of reflective practice—examining how one's belief systems inform one's decisions—is essential to becoming an effective leader. Reflective practice is a key component of every activity in this book.

Case Study Documentation Form—Weaknesses

Instructions

After examining your partner's list of weaknesses, place a check mark (✓) in the blank in front of each weakness listed below for each weakness that you partner identified. Do not give credit for broad, general statements. **Look for specific responses. If more than one weakness is included in a single listing, give credit for each weakness by placing check marks in front of all appropriate items. If a weakness is listed in the artifacts, and is not on the list below, just ignore it and go on.** When you finish deciding and numbering the weaknesses, place dots (•) in the remaining spaces. **This helps to assure your partner that you made a specific decision concerning each statement.**

ANALYZING PROBLEMS—EXERCISING JUDGMENT—EXPRESSING PROFESSIONAL VALUES

_____ 1. There is a growing belief among some upper-grade children that school is not important.

_____ 2. Children from low-income families feel left out.

_____ 3. The primary functions of the guidance program are testing, record keeping, and scheduling.

_____ 4. Faculty leadership comes from a small group of teachers who served the school 20 years or more.

_____ 5. Few children are now attending afterschool programs.

_____ 6. The ESL program is weak due to lack of faculty leadership.

_____ 7. Teachers have provided no help for spelling bees.

_____ 8. The school's PTO is weak.

_____ 9. The PTO is only casually supported by teachers.

_____ 10. Teachers are not interested in curriculum review and revision.

_____ 11. A number is written beside each listed weakness.

_____ 12. The listing of weaknesses differs from the order listed above. Examine the sequence.

_____ Total and record weaknesses in the list above that correspond with your partner's listing.

WRITTEN COMMUNICATION

_____ 13. The weaknesses are clearly written. If they are not, write examples:

_____ 14. There are no errors in spelling. If there are, write examples:

_____ 15. There are no errors in grammar. If there are, write examples:

Case Study Documentation Form—Weaknesses (continued)

Rating Performance

Examine the symbols and their interpretations below. You will use these symbols to represent demonstrated levels of skill. After studying the completed documentation form, count the number of matches between your list of weaknesses and the list of weaknesses identified by a committee of experienced school administrators and university faculty. Rate each performance area (Analyzing Problems, Exercising Judgment, Written Communication, and Expressing Professional Values) and record the rates in the Performance Ratings area below. In some instances several performance indicators may be attributed to more than one skill area.

When you have completed rating your partner's lists of strengths, weaknesses, and urgent problems, you willl be ready to complete the Overall Performance Summary on the last page of this chapter.

Use the symbols and interpretations below to determine performance summary ratings for the skill areas in this activity.

Symbols	Interpretations		Ranges
⊕	Very high skill shown	=	9-10
+	More than moderate skill	=	7-8
(+)	Moderate skill shown	=	5-6
(−)	Less than moderate skill	=	3-4
−	Little skill shown	=	1-2
⊖	Very little skill shown	=	0

Performance Summary Ratings: Weaknesses

Performance Areas	Rating Symbols
Analyzing Problems Performance Rating: ____	____
Exercising Judgment Performance Rating: ____	____
Written Communication Performance Rating: ____	____

Since little writing is called for in the Case Study, most participants receive a Moderate (+).
Enter a + if the spelling/vocabulary is more than moderate.
If there is more than one error in spelling you would enter a − or (−), showing a need for improvement.

Expressing Professional Values ____
Professional Value: ____

Note: *Extreme ratings ⊕ or ⊖ are seldom appropriate.*

Case Study Documentation Form—Urgent Problems

Instructions

After examining your partner's prioritized list of urgent problems, write the number on the line beside each problem. Do not give credit for broad, general statements. The listings here have been developed by committees of practicing school administrators; not everyone will agree with their consensus listings of urgent problems and weaknesses. Remember, this is not a test. The results should produce good discussions with your partner. **Look for specific responses. If more than one problem is included in a single listing, give credit for each by repeating the number beside the second problem. If an urgent problem is listed in the artifacts, and is not on the list below, just ignore it. Note:** *Do not give credit for "solutions" to problems.* **The 10 most urgent problems identified by the committee are listed in bold.** When you finish deciding and numbering the urgent problems, place dots (•) in the remaining spaces. **This helps to assure your partner that you made a specific decision concerning each statement.** A sample completed form may be found in the resource section (Form R.1).

ANALYZING PROBLEMS—EXERCISING JUDGMENT—
EXPRESSING PROFESSIONAL VALUES—MAKING DECISIONS

_____ **1. The dropout rate is steadily increasing.**

_____ **2. There is a steadily declining average daily attendance.**

_____ **3. The school board has decided to implement districtwide, site-based management without inservice.**

_____ **4. The current principal feels threatened by the decision to start site-based management.**

_____ 5. Many seasoned teachers are burned out.

_____ **6. Resentment expressed by younger faculty over class assignments.**

_____ 7. PTO programs are poorly attended by parents and teachers.

_____ 8. There is a disturbing rumor that the school board is planning total renovation.

_____ **9. There are drug wars in the neighborhood of the school.**

_____ **10. There is increasing vandalism in the school.**

_____ 11. Teachers are not getting support for needed instructional technology.

_____ 12. Children are not taught the technology needed for success in secondary school.

_____ 13. There are too many public address system interruptions during the school day.

_____ 14. There is too much instructional time lost to assemblies and other special events.

_____ 15. Children upset because dress policy is unfairly administered.

_____ **16. Parents demand to know what will be done to improve test scores.**

_____ **17. Basic skills test scores have dropped significantly.**

_____ 18. Tenured teachers do not like the new evaluation procedures.

_____ **19. Teachers are convinced the principal is not competent to evaluate their teaching.**

ANALYZING PROBLEMS—EXERCISING JUDGMENT—EXPRESSING PROFESSIONAL VALUES

_____ 20. Your partner listed 10 urgent problems as directed.

_____ 21. Your partner's listing of urgent problems differs from the order listed above.

Case Study Documentation Form—Urgent Problems (continued)

_____ 22. Your partner identified some of the most urgent problems
(those identified in bold type).

_____ Total the number of most urgent problems identified in bold on the preceeding list.

WRITTEN COMMUNICATION

_____ The problems are clearly written. If they are not, write examples:

_____ There are no errors in spelling. If there are, write examples:

_____ There are no errors in grammar. If there are, write examples:

Rating Performance

Examine the symbols and their interpretations below. You will use these symbols to represent demonstrated levels of skill. After studying the completed documentation form, count the number of matches between your list of urgent problems and the list of urgent problems identified by the committee (those items printed in bold lettering). Rate each performance area (Analyzing Problems, Exercising Judgment, Making Decisions, and Expressing Professional Values) in the Performance Ratings area below. In some instances several performance indicators may be attributed to more than one skill area.

When you have completed rating your partner's lists of strengths, weaknesses, and urgent problems, you will be ready to complete the Overall Performance Summary on the last page of this section.

Use the symbols and interpretations to determine performance summary ratings for the skill areas in this activity.

Symbols	Interpretations		Ranges
$\oplus$	Very high skill shown	=	9-10
+	More than moderate skill	=	7-8
(+)	Moderate skill shown	=	5-6
(−)	Less than moderate skill	=	3-4
−	Little skill shown	=	1-2
$\ominus$	Very little skill shown	=	0

**Performance Summary Ratings:
Urgent Problems**

Performance Areas	Rating Symbols
Analyzing Problems
Performance Rating: ____	____
Exercising Judgment
Performance Rating: ____	____
Making Decisions
Performance Rating: ____	____

Since little writing is called for in the Case Study, most participants receive a Moderate (+).
Enter a + if the spelling/vocabulary is more than moderate.
If there is more than one error in spelling you would enter a − or (−), showing a need for improvement.

Expressing Professional Values ____
Performance Rating: ____

Note: *Extreme ratings $\oplus$ or $\ominus$ are seldom appropriate.*

Case Study Documentation Form—Urgent Problems (continued)

Rating Overall Performance Summary: Case Study

On the Overall Performance Summary form below, rate each performance area on a scale of ⊖ to ⊕ (very little skill shown to very high skill shown). This information is summarized here and later used on the final performance summary chart in the resource section of this book. After viewing the final chart you will reach consensus with your partner on areas of strength and areas for improvement. A sample completed overall rating form (Form R.2) for the Case Study may be found in the resource section.

Symbols	Interpretations
⊕	Very high skill shown
+	More than moderate skill
(+)	Moderate skill shown
(−)	Less than moderate skill
−	Little skill shown
⊖	Very little skill shown

Overall Performance Summary
Case Study
(use ratings on pages 33, 36 and 38)

Performance Areas	Overall Rating Symbols
Overall Rating for Analyzing Problems Performance Ratings: ____, ____, ____	_____
Overall Rating for Exercising Judgment Performance Ratings: ____, ____, ____	_____
Overall Rating for Making Decisions Performance Rating: ____	_____
Overall Rating for Written Communication Performance Ratings: ____, ____, ____	_____
Overall Rating for Expressing Professional Values Performance Ratings: ____, ____, ____	_____

Note: *Extreme ratings of ⊕ or ⊖ are seldom appropriate.*

REFLECTIVE PRACTICE

You have now had the opportunity to compare your choices to those of your partner and those of the committee of experienced administrators and university faculty who helped to develop our lists. There are undoubtedly differences.

Go through each of your scoring sheets again and highlight your choices that differ from choices the others made. For each item highlighted, ask yourself the questions in the bulleted list that follows. On a clean piece of paper, make notes on your responses to these questions. When you have completed the task, share your responses with your partner. Discuss the differences in your responses; do not attempt to persuade your partner to your point of view. There is more than enough educational theory and research to support almost any point of view, and this activity is not intended to create arguments. The purpose of this task is for you to clarify for yourself what your beliefs are and to recognize how they influence your decisions.

- In what ways does your response differ from that of your partner?

- Why do you think the responses are different? Do you each have a different interpretation of the information presented in the case study? Or are your differences grounded in the differences in your basic beliefs about education?

- Which of your decisions were influenced by what you believe to be the purpose of education?

- Which of your decisions were influenced by what you believe about how children learn and about the ability of children to learn?

- Which of your decisions were influenced by your beliefs about the roles of teachers, administrators, counselors, students, parents, the community, the government, and other regulatory agencies?

- What has the case study activity revealed to you about your skills in analyzing problems, exercising judgment, making decisions, expressing personal values, and written communications?

- If you were to repeat the activity, would you make any choices differently? Why or why not?

In this chapter, you were asked to read a case study of a school, to make some decisions about its strengths and weaknesses, and to identify its most urgent problems. In the next chapter, you will be asked to take one of the urgent problems and develop a school improvement plan to address the problem. During this activity, you will have opportunities to practice more of the skills identified in the four main skill clusters: Problem Solving, Interpersonal Sensitivity, Communications, and Personal Characteristics.

3

Developing School Improvement Plans

OVERVIEW

In this chapter, you will complete the second activity in this leadership development series. You will become acquainted with an existing school improvement plan and the process for developing one. You will also gain further experience with analysis and performance documentation. Links to key performance aspects of the Interstate Leadership Licensure Consortium (ISLLC) Standards are provided in Resources (Table R.17).

ANALYZE, REFLECT, AND DOCUMENT

Analyze, reflect, and document: These are the three habits of leadership you will practice several times as you proceed with this program. As with the case study in the previous chapter, the school improvement planning activity in this chapter will result in paper and pencil performance artifacts. It is these artifacts that will provide the substance for peer analysis, reflection, and performance documentation. After completing the activity, you will use the artifacts as a focus of examination and study, first on your partner's work and then on your own. As with all activities in this book, leadership development results not only from completing an activity but also from analyzing, reflecting, and accurately documenting its artifacts.

This chapter uses a rating process similar to the one used in Chapter 2. You will make use of the same symbols to complete the rating form at the end of each activity in this series. During this planning activity, you will also develop a high-quality improvement plan to address a problem presented to you as a new principal—a problem that arises out of the urgent problems you documented in the previous chapter.

Steps for Development

You and your partner complete the school improvement planning activity. The developmental tasks for this activity consist of the following steps:

1. Read about the planning activity and its performance areas; familiarize yourself with the instructions for completing the activity.

2. Examine the sample improvement plan (artifact) included later in this chapter.

3. Complete your school improvement plan.

4. Exchange your completed plans with your partner.

5. Using the forms in this chapter, document your partner's performance artifacts.

6. Exchange completed documentation forms with your partner.

7. Review and compare your documented performances; discuss and reach consensus on the results.

8. After completing and discussing documentation results, you will want to rate your performance in this activity.

About Planning

Many school districts require their principals to develop annual school improvement plans. The ability to create an improvement plan is essential to good leadership. If you are unfamiliar with this type of planning, you may wish to examine models in your professional library or talk with administrators in your school district. The sample included in this chapter is typical of improvement plans developed by participants in this program. It has both strengths and weaknesses.

This school improvement planning activity builds on the foundation of the case study and uses one of the problems drawn from it. Using that problem, you will now develop a 10-month school improvement plan that should illustrate your best work. We have provided a specific set of plan requirements for you to follow.

Planning Performance Areas

This planning activity provides opportunities for you to demonstrate your skill in the following:

- Analyzing Problems
- Exercising Judgment
- Making Decisions
- Organizing and Planning
- Interpersonal Sensitivity
- Expressing Professional Values
- Written Communication

As in the previous chapter, the answers to questions regarding ISLLC performance aspects and the skills needed to be successful in meeting the standards are found in the linkages made in this book. You will find the performance aspects of the standards relating to each of the performance areas in the school improvement planning activity.

STANDARDS, PERFORMANCE AREAS, AND ASPECTS

Each of the related standards is presented below as an abbreviated statement followed by program skill areas and the number of related performance aspects. In some instances, as in the case study, an activity calls for some skills not identified in the ISLLC Standards. Because of space limitations, specific details that define performance aspects are not included here (but may be found in Resources in Table R.18). The information below shows the linkages between the school improvement planning activity and the performance aspects of ISLLC's standards.

STANDARD 1
Developing, articulating, implementing, and stewarding a shared vision of learning
Analyzing Problems
> 7 ISLLC performance aspects related to analyzing problems
Exercising Judgment
> No ISLLC-related performance aspects
Organizing and Planning
> 13 ISLLC performance aspects related to organizing and planning
Delegating Effectively
> No ISLLC-related performance aspects
Interpersonal Sensitivity
> 3 ISLLC performance aspects related to interpersonal sensitivity
Professional Motivation
> 5 ISLLC performance aspects related to professional motivation
Expressing Professional Values
> 8 ISLLC performance aspects related to professional values
Written Communication
> 4 ISLLC performance aspects related to written communication

STANDARD 2
Advocating, nurturing, and sustaining a school culture and effective instructional program conducive to student learning and staff professional growth
Analyzing Problems
> 6 ISLLC performance aspects related to analyzing problems |

ISLLC STANDARDS (Continued)
Exercising Judgment
    1 ISLLC performance aspect related to exercising judgment
Organizing and Planning
    10 ISLLC performance aspects related to organizing and planning
Delegating Effectively
    No ISLLC-related performance aspects
Interpersonal Sensitivity
    6 ISLLC performance aspects related to interpersonal sensitivity
Expressing Professional Values
    10 ISLLC performance aspects related to professional values
Written Communication
    No ISLLC-related performance aspects

STANDARD 3
Ensuring management of the organization, operations, and resources for a safe, efficient, and effective learning environment
Analyzing Problems
    10 ISLLC performance aspects related to analyzing problems
Exercising Judgment
    7 ISLLC performance aspects related to exercising judgment
interpersonal sensitivity
    8 ISLLC performance aspects related to interpersonal sensitivity
professional motivation
    No ISLLC-related performance aspects
Expressing Professional Values
    2 ISLLC performance aspects related to professional values
Written Communication
    1 ISLLC performance aspect related to written communication

STANDARD 4
Collaborating with families and community members, responding to diverse community interests and needs, and mobilizing community resources
Analyzing Problems
    6 ISLLC performance aspects related to analyzing problems
exercising judgment
    5 ISLLC performance aspects related to exercising judgment
organizing and planning
    11 ISLLC performance aspects related to organizing and planning
Effective Delegation
    No ISLLC-related performance aspects
Interpersonal Sensitivity
    11 ISLLC performance aspects related to interpersonal sensitivity
professional motivation
    8 ISLLC performance aspects related to professional motivation
Expressing Professional Values
    11 ISLLC performance aspects related to professional values
Written Communication
    4 ISLLC performance aspects related to written communication

STANDARD 5
Promoting success of all students through integrity, fairness, and an ethical manner
Analyzing Problems
    No ISLLC-related performance aspects
Exercising Judgment
    10 ISLLC performance aspects related to exercising judgment
Organizing and Planning
    No ISLLC-related performance aspects
Effective Delegation
    No ISLLC-related performance aspects

ISLLC STANDARDS (Continued)

Interpersonal Sensitivity
>   9 ISLLC performance aspects related to interpersonal sensitivity

Professional Motivation
>   No ISLLC-related performance aspects

Expressing Professional Values
>   19 ISLLC performance aspects related to professional values

Written Communication
>   No ISLLC-related performance aspects

STANDARD 6
Promoting the success of all students by understanding, responding to, and influencing the larger political, social, economic, legal, and cultural context

Analyzing Problems
>   7 ISLLC performance aspects related to analyzing problems

Exercising Judgment
>   4 ISLLC performance aspects related to exercising judgment

Organizing and Planning
>   2 ISLLC performance aspects related to Organizing and planning

Effective Delegation
>   No ISLLC-related performance aspects

Group Leadership
>   No ISLLC-related performance aspects

Interpersonal Sensitivity
>   No ISLLC-related performance aspects

Expressing Professional Values
>   6 ISLLC performance aspects related to professional values

Written Communication
>   No ISLLC-related performance aspects

Note: Linkages were identified by the principle author and verified by education experts.
SOURCE: Adapted from Council of Chief State School Officers (1996).

There are many performance areas that bridge the ISLLC Standards. This book attempts to bring clarity to the skills needed for implementing the standards. Detailed performance aspects of the ISLLC Standards relating to this activity are found in the Resources (Table R.18).

Instructions for the Planning Activity

You should give yourself at least 1 week to develop your school improvement plan. It should represent your best work. Although you will complete your plan on your own, you may consult other professionals for assistance. As you recall, Normal Elementary School has several urgent problems. We have selected one of them for you to develop. That is, you are to prepare a statement of the problem and explain its importance. You are also to prepare goals and measurable objectives. If you do not know how to state measurable objectives, you should check with other professionals or the professional literature in order to be certain yours are measurable.

Your school improvement plan should include appropriate references from research or professional literature. It should also include a timeline but be limited to four pages plus a cover page. As an administrator, it is especially important to get feedback and commitment from others; be sure to explain how you plan to involve others in modifying and finalizing the plan.

SAMPLE SCHOOL IMPROVEMENT PLAN FOR BOOSTING STUDENT TEST SCORES

Planning Task

School administrators need to plan well. In this activity related to the case study, you are to assume the role of the principal of Normal School. As the principal, you are to develop your own 10-month plan for dealing with one of Normal School's most urgent problems. In this case, we have selected for you *declining test scores*.

For your plan, state the problem, explain its importance, and state the goals and objectives for remedying the problem. Cite appropriate references from the professional literature. The plan is to include a timeline and clearly measurable outcomes.

You should explain how others will be involved in further development and implementation. Your plan should be as detailed as possible given the time limitations. It should use standard margins, be produced on a word processor or typewriter, and not exceed four pages plus a cover page. The plan you submit should be an example of your best individual effort.

Use the following Normal School Improvement Plan as a model for your own improvement plan documentation and rating. Remember, when you document and analyze your partner's plan, you will both be resolving differences in in-depth discussions of both of your performances.

Authors' note: The School Improvement Plan that follows was prepared by a student to address one of the problems at Normal School. Care has been taken to retain the original flavor, language, and structure of the plan. **No corrections were made in spelling, grammar, or syntax.**

SAMPLE SCHOOL IMPROVEMENT PLAN FOR IMPROVING STUDENT TEST SCORES

NORMAL SCHOOL IMPROVEMENT PLAN

Problem Identification Statement

Overall student performance on both norms referenced and standardized achievement tests have dropped significantly over the past few years. This may be symptomatic of a number of factors. An analysis of our current situation reveals that:

- The curriculum and instructional delivery system has not been reviewed, revised, or modified in 15 years even though the student population has changed dramatically.

- English is a second language for many students. Some students come from home backgrounds that are not language rich, some lack background experiences that hamper their understanding of content, and many are dealing with emotional and social issues that create barriers to learning.

- Teachers are teaching according to old paradims that are not working with our current student body. This has resulted in frustration, confusion, and "burnout." At this point our students do not have equitable access to a challenging and appropriate instructional program using curricula that reflects their cultures and future needs.

These situations must be corrected before student achievement scores can improve.

Goals and Objectives

A school has two goals (or purposes) for existing: productivity (attainment of knowledge and skills), and satisfaction (sense of value, esteem and belonging). Currently, our students are not being productive and, in some cases, do not feel satisfied within their school. It is imperative that we change this situation so that we can become a viable institution again. Goal: Become a productive and satisfying school for students, staff, and parents. Objectives:

- Improve the instructional delivery system so that students will master the skills and concepts taught and be able to demonstrate competency in all areas of the curriculum.

- Increase staff opportunities to improve their skills and participate in decisions made about the school organization.

Evaluation Indicators

- In June, report card grades for all students will verify that they were legitimately promoted to the next grade.

- Ninety percent of all students tested by the [Iowa Test of Basic Skills] ITBS will score above the 50th percentile on all subtests.

- In January, log entries will show that 100% of the teachers participated in scheduled staff development and 80% integrated the strategies learned into their instructional planning.

- Student performance on all three sections of the State Literacy Test and on all seven strands of the Program of studies mathematics test will show a 50% increase when compared to the most recent scores.

- Baseline data on the number of hours parents volunteer in the classroom will be collected for the first marking period of the year. Data collected for the second and third marking periods will show a 25% increase each period when compared to the previous marking period. Data collected for the second and third marking periods will show a 25% increase each period when compared to the previous marking period. Data collected in June will show a 100% increase when compared with November.

- A school climate/attitudinal survey administered to the staff, students and parents in June will show a 75% increase in satisfaction with school when compared to the one previously administered in September.

10-Month Work Plans

- August: Schedule a 2-hour faculty meeting to discuss status, goals, issues, concerns, instructional and climatic factors related to student performance. During this session, collaboratively plan a staff retreat for the first weekend in September. The school system will find this retreat. (primary responsibility: principal and counselor.)

- September: Conduct a 2-day retreat to review fifth-grade student data and records. The objective will be to find ways to "level the playing field" for all students and to improve overall student performance. The review should help staff determine what experiences perceived successful students have had that perceived unsuccessful students have not had. Records of 20 fifth grade students will be studied.

Criteria for Selection of Student Samples

Fifth grade students perceived by staff as, and whose reported cards identify, achievers and underachievers. These definitions include students who are socially, emotionally, and academically well and successful, and students who have experienced difficulty socially, emotionally, and academically. Ten students in each category will be selected.

Data to Be Reviewed

The student review will include cumulative records, child study reports, At-Risk Students List, records of special programs and services provided.

What to Look For

- Positive or negative expectations articulated in teacher comments
- Pacing and placement
- Actions taken to assist child when trouble was noted
- Instructional modifications
- Parent/school communication
- Enrichment/assessment of interests
- Applications of test data to instructional decisions
- Progress trends and reactions if achievement declined
- Monitoring processes

Anticipated Outcomes

It is anticipated that old assumptions are challenged or affirmed, expectations will be validated or questioned, and practices and processes when scrutinized will either prove worthy or lay sound pedagogical foundations. Teachers should discover which nonacademic factors are powerful mediators of success and failure. These insights will lead to recommendations for improving the learning environment and, ultimately, result in greater student achievement.

Staff will record a summary of findings indicating what was learned and suggest next steps to correct for problem areas. (primary responsibility: principal, team leaders, and counselor.)

- October: Create a Collaborative School Team to assist with the implementation of "next steps" identified at the retreat and to develop and monitor implementation of the school plan. The composition shall include parents, teaches, and support staff. Each grade level will select a representative to serve on the team. Parents' selection will reflect the student population. The group will appoint a chair. Members of the superintendent's office will train the team in the collaborative process. Following the training, the collaborative team will meet monthly. (primary responsibility: principal and appointed chair.)

- October: Begin the process of developing a school mission statement of shared values. Staff, parents, and students will participate. Hire an outside consultant to facilitate these sessions. Sessions should begin not later than October 15. Sessions will be held on the second and fourth Mondays each month until the mission and shared values are completed. The Collaborative Team will develop a Likert Scale measurement instrument to be administered to the parents and teachers in the spring to determine how well we acted upon our beliefs. (primary responsibility: faculty advisory committee, collaborative team, and PTO board.)

- November: Create an advisory board consisting of Parents, teachers, sixth grade students, business and industry personnel for the purpose of obtaining support for academic programs, locating enrichment experiences for staff and students, improving communication and creating good public relations for the school. The first meeting will take place the first week in November. (primary responsibility: principal, FAC, and PTO board.)

- November-April: Schedule staff development in areas identified at the staff retreat. Two staff development days will be set aside per month for teachers to improve their repertoire or strategies for teaching in heterogeneous classrooms. Fifty percent of the staff will participate on the fist day and 50% on the second day of training. All training will be conducted from a multi cultural perspective. Training is mandatory. (primary responsibility: collaborative team.)

- November: Establish a student achievement task force who will:

    1. Identify student experiencing learning difficulties and/or who scored in the lower quartiles on a standardized test. Create a monitoring list of those students.

    2. Meet monthly with teachers to monitor student progress and make recommendations for instructional modifications for targeted students.

    3. Monitor and collect achievement data on the targeted students, report findings, and recommend staff development initiatives. (primary responsibility: chair appointed by the collaborative team.)

- May: Schedule a staff retreat for the purpose of reflecting on the progress made during the school year and implications for school planning. All data collected for the evaluation will be reviewed and analyzed by the total staff. Recommendations for additional initiatives will be made. (primary responsibility: collaborative team.)

SCHOOL IMPROVEMENT PLAN PERFORMANCE DOCUMENTATION

Part I

After you and your partner complete your own school improvement plans, you should exchange your plans. Using the appropriate form, each of you should document your partner's school improvement plan after carefully studying the instructions.

Improvement Plan Documentation Form

Instructions for Completing the Documentation Form

Examine the performance indicators below. Place a check (✓) to the left of each true statement. Do not check false statements. Make comments to the right for any statement that does not accurately describe the completed plan.

ANALYZING PROBLEMS—EXERCISING JUDGMENT—ORGANIZING AND PLANNING—MAKING DECISIONS—INTERPERSONAL SENSITIVITY— EXPRESSING PROFESSIONAL VALUES

The school improvement plan for declining test scores: *Comments:*

_____ 1. Adheres to the specified number of pages.   _____

_____ 2. Includes a clear statement of the problem.   _____

_____ 3. Includes a clear explanation of importance.   _____

_____ 4. Cites references from the professional literature.   _____

_____ 5. Includes clearly stated goals.   _____

_____ 6. Includes clearly stated objectives.   _____

_____ 7. Covers the prescribed 10 months.   _____

_____ 8. Clearly outlines steps to be taken.   _____

_____ 9. Sets completion dates for major events.   _____

_____ 10. Pages are numbered.   _____

_____ 11. Includes a cover page.   _____

_____ 12. Page margins are at least one inch wide on all sides.   _____

_____ 13. Is neat in appearance; no typeovers, smudges, etc.   _____

_____ 14. Is clearly based on information from the case study.   _____

_____ 15. Involves other ideas for further development.   _____

_____ Total the matches (checks) in this column

Rating Performance

Examine the following symbols and their interpretations. You will use these symbols to represent demonstrated levels of skill. After studying the documentation form, count the number of matches between your partner's school improvement plan and the 15 items on the documentation form. Rate each performance area (Analyzing Problems, Exercising Judgment, Making Decisions, Organizing and Planning, Interpersonal Sensitivity, and Expressing Professional Values) in the *Performance Ratings*. In some instances several performance indicators may be attributed to more than one skill area.

When you have completed scoring your lists of strengths, weaknesses, and urgent problems, you are ready to complete the *Overall Performance Summary* on the last page of this chapter. Use the symbols and interpretations to determine performance summary ratings for the skill areas in this activity.

Improvement Plan Documentation Form (continued)

Symbols	Interpretations	Total Match Ranges
⊕	Very high skill shown	= 13-15
+	More than moderate skill	= 10-12
(+)	Moderate skill shown	= 7-9
(–)	Less than moderate skill	= 4-6
–	Little skill shown	= 2-3
⊖	Very little skill shown	= 0

Performance Summary Ratings: School Improvement Plan

Performance Areas	Rating Symbols
Analyzing Problems	_____
Exercising Judgment	_____
Making Decisions	_____
Organizing and Planning	_____
Interpersonal Sensitivity	_____
Expressing Professional Values	_____

Note: *Extreme ratings ⊕ or ⊖ are seldom appropriate.*

Instructions

Place a check (✓) to the left of each true statement below. Do not check false statements. A sample of this completed form may be found in the resources section (Form R.3).

ANALYZING PROBLEMS

The goals and objectives of the plan relate directly to:

_____ 1. Afterschool programs

_____ 2. Attendance and absenteeism rates

_____ 3. Community involvement

_____ 4. Curriculum development

_____ 5. First language of students

_____ 6. Guidance and counseling program

_____ 7. Improving instruction

_____ 8. Inservice and staff development

_____ 9. Leadership

_____ 10. Mentoring and tutoring

_____ 11. Parent involvement

_____ 12. Research and evaluation

_____ 13. Scheduling

_____ 14. School climate

_____ 15. Student demographics

_____ 16. Student morale

_____ 17. Teacher burnout

_____ 18. Teacher involvement

_____ 19. Teacher morale

_____ 20. Test results and student achievement

_____ 21. Test-taking preparation

Total matches (checks) in this column: ____

EXERCISING JUDGMENT

The plans include measurable outcomes that relate to:

_____ 1. Absenteeism

_____ 2. Curriculum

_____ 3. Emphasis placed on test results

_____ 4. GPA

_____ 5. Information given to parents concerning the testing program

_____ 6. Language of students taking tests

_____ 7. Preparing students for taking tests

_____ 8. Promotion rates

_____ 9. Scheduling tests

_____ 10. Student demographics

_____ 11. Teacher morale

_____ 12. Test results

_____ 13. The plan for improving scores does not include outcomes stated in *measurable terms*

Total matches (checks) in this column: _____

Improvement Plan Documentation Form (continued)

Rating Performance

Examine the symbols and their interpretations below. You will use these symbols to represent demonstrated levels of skill. After studying the documentation form, count the number of matches between your partner's school improvement plan and the lists for Analyzing Problems and Exercising Judgment. Rate each performance area (Analyzing Problems and Exercising Judgment) in the *Performance Ratings* below. In some instances several performance indicators may be attributed to more than one skill area.

Use the symbols and interpretations to determine performance summary ratings for the skill areas in this activity.

Symbols	Interpretations	Total Match Ranges
⊕	Very high skill shown	= 19-21
+	More than moderate skill	= 15-18
(+)	Moderate skill shown	= 11-14
(−)	Less than moderate skill	= 7-10
−	Little skill shown	= 4-6
⊖	Very little skill shown	= 0

Performance Summary Ratings:
School Improvement Plan

Performance Areas	Rating Symbols
Analyzing Problems	_____
Exercising Judgment	_____

Note: *Extreme ratings* ⊕ *or* ⊖ *are seldom appropriate.*

WRITTEN COMMUNICATION

Place a check (✓) to the left of each true statement below. Do not check a false statement.

_____ 1. **The school improvement plan is not clearly written.**

Examples:

Clarity refers to whether or not the expression of ideas in writing is easily understood, overall. A rating lower than moderate requires justification with examples.

Check (✓) the most appropriate descriptor below. Place a dot beside the others.

___ Very High Clarity
___ More than Moderate Clarity
___ Moderate Clarity
___ Less than Moderate Clarity
___ Little Clarity
___ Very Little Clarity

_____ 2. **There are errors in spelling.**

Examples:

Improvement Plan Documentation Form (continued)

Spelling refers to correctly spelled words. A rating lower than moderate requires justification with examples. Check (✓) the most appropriate descriptor below. Place a dot (•) beside the others.

_____	0 errors:	Very high skill in spelling (difficult vocabulary)
_____	0 errors:	More than moderate skill in spelling (average vocabulary)
_____	1 error:	Moderate skill in spelling
_____	2 errors:	Less than moderate skill in spelling
_____	3 errors:	Poor skill in spelling
_____	4+ errors:	Very poor skill in spelling

_____ 3. **There are errors in grammar.**

Examples:

Grammar refers to conformity to accepted grammatical rules of expression in writing. A rating lower than moderate requires justification with examples.

Check (✓) the most appropriate descriptor below.

_____	0 errors:	Very high skill in grammar (difficult construction)
_____	0 errors:	More than moderate skill in grammar (average construction)
_____	1 error:	Moderate skill in grammar
_____	2 errors:	Less than moderate skill in grammar
_____	3 errors:	Poor skill in grammar
_____	4+ errors:	Very poor skill in grammar

Rating Performance

Examine the symbols and their interpretations below. You will use these symbols to represent demonstrated levels of skill. After studying the documentation form, rate the written communication performance area in the *Performance Summary Ratings* box below. In some instances several performance indicators may be attributed to more than one skill area.

When you have completed scoring your lists of strengths, weaknesses, and urgent problems, you are ready to complete the *Overall Performance Summary* on the last page of this chapter.

Use the symbols and interpretations to determine performance summary ratings for the skill areas in this activity.

Symbols	Interpretations
⊕	Very high skill shown
+	More than moderate skill
(+)	Moderate skill shown
(–)	Less than moderate skill
–	Little skill shown
⊖	Very little skill shown

Performance Summary Ratings: School Improvement Plan

Performance Areas	Rating Symbols
Written Communication	
1. Clarity	_____
2. Spelling	_____
3. Grammar	_____

Note: *Extreme ratings ⊕ or ⊖ are seldom appropriate.*

Improvement Plan Documentation Form (continued)

Rating Overall School Improvement Plan Performance

When you have completed rating the performance indicators in the *Improvement Plan,* you are ready to complete the *Overall Performance Summary* below.

On the Performance Summary form below, rate each performance area on a scale of ⊖ to ⊕ (very little skill shown to very high skill shown). This information is summarized here and later used on the final performance summary chart in the last section of this handbook. After viewing the final chart you will reach consensus with your partner on areas of strength and areas for improvement. A sample of a completed summary rating form for this activity (Form R.4) may be found in the resources section.

Use the symbols and interpretations from the previous summary rating forms to determine the *Overall Performance Summary Ratings* for the School Improvement Plan activity.

Symbols	Interpretations
⊕	Very high skill shown
+	More than moderate skill
(+)	Moderate skill shown
(−)	Less than moderate skill
−	Little skill shown
⊖	Very little skill shown

Overall Performance Summary
School Improvement Plan
(Use Ratings on Pages 52, 53, and 54)

Performance Areas	Rating Symbols
Overall Rating for Analyzing Problems Performance Ratings: ____, ____	_____
Overall Rating for Exercising Judgment Performance Ratings: ____, ____	_____
Overall Rating for Organizing and Planning Performance Ratings: ____	_____
Overall Rating for Making Decisions Performance Ratings: ____	_____
Overall Rating for Interpersonal Sensitivity Performance Ratings: ____	_____
Overall Rating for Written Communication Performance Ratings: ____	_____
Overall Rating for Expressing Professional Values Performance Ratings: ____	_____

Note: *Extreme ratings ⊕ or ⊖ are seldom appropriate.*

REFLECTIVE PRACTICE

You have now had the opportunity to prepare a school improvement plan, to compare your plan with your partner's plan, and to evaluate both plans against the items that were deemed important by the committee of experienced administrators and university faculty who helped develop the lists in the tables. There are undoubtedly differences.

Go through each of your rating sheets again and highlight any of your choices that differ from the others' choices. For each highlighted item, answer the questions listed below. On a clean piece of paper, make notes on your responses to the questions. When you have completed the task, share your responses with your partner. Discuss the differences in your responses; do not attempt to persuade your partner to your point of view. There is more than enough educational theory and research to support almost any point of view, and this activity is not intended to create arguments. Your purpose in this task is to clarify for yourself what your beliefs are and to recognize how they influence your decisions.

- In what ways does your response differ from that of your partner?

- Why do you think the responses are different? Are your differences grounded in the differences in your basic beliefs about education and about how children learn?

- Which of your decisions were influenced by what you believe to be the purpose of education?

- Which of your decisions were influenced by how you believe children learn and by your views about the ability of children to learn?

- Which of your decisions were influenced by your beliefs about the roles of teachers, administrators, counselors, students, parents, the community, government, and other regulatory agencies?

- What has the school improvement plan activity revealed to you about your skills in analyzing problems, exercising judgment, making decisions, organizing and planning, interpersonal sensitivity, expressing personal values, and written communications?

- If you were to repeat the activity, would you alter your school improvement plan in any way? Why or why not?

In this chapter, you were asked to develop a school improvement plan to address the urgent need to raise declining test scores. You had an extended period of time to gather information and develop a plan. In Chapter 4, you will be asked to confront a task faced daily by every administrator—wading through the mountain of seemingly unrelated paperwork that appears on your desk as if by magic. During this activity, you will have many opportunities to practice more of the skills identified in the four main skill clusters: problem solving, interpersonal skills, communications, and personal characteristics.

4

Office Deskwork

OVERVIEW

In this chapter, you will complete the third activity in this leadership development series: deskwork. Along with development tasks and performance indicators, you will encounter a stimulating range of deskwork items to handle. You will respond to typical items you are likely to find awaiting your arrival at the fictitious Normal School in the Normal City community. Links to key performance aspects of the Interstate School Leaders Licensure Consortium's (ISLLC) Standards are provided in the resource section (Table R.17).

YOUR FIRST DAY ON THE JOB

Will it be a honeymoon or will you be swamped with paperwork? If your experience is anything like what most principals experience, this chapter will help prepare you for it. By completing the deskwork activity, you will produce paper and pencil artifacts that provide substance for analysis, reflection, and performance documentation. Your responses to the deskwork items will become the focus of examination and study as you and your partner exchange artifacts and document them. Throughout this process, you will grow in leadership as you clarify your strengths and improvement needs.

STEPS FOR DEVELOPMENT

Study the entire chapter before starting the simulation. The developmental tasks for this activity consist of the following steps:

1. Study the deskwork materials provided.

2. Complete the simulation.

3. Exchange your deskwork artifacts with your partner.

4. Study the instructions on the documentation forms.

5. Use the blank documentation and rating forms to document your partner's artifacts.

6. Return the completed documentation forms to your partner.

7. Review and compare each other's documented performance; discuss and reach consensus on the results.

8. After completing and discussing documentation results, rate your performance in this activity.

9. Complete the reflective practice activity, and share your responses with your partner.

ABOUT THE DESKWORK ACTIVITY

This paper and pencil activity builds on the foundation resulting from completing the previous two activities: case study and school improvement planning. Now you will tackle some items that might appear on your desk the first day on the job. Read the deskwork items and respond as you would if you were actually on the job. You will not be familiar with the persons sending you memos and letters, but you will have to do the best you can. Write your responses on the copies you make of the forms supplied here.

Deskwork Performance Areas

The deskwork simulation requires skill in the following:

- Analyzing Problems
- Exercising Judgment
- Organizing and Planning
- Making Decisions
- Delegating Effectively
- Interpersonal Sensitivity
- Managing Stress
- Expressing Professional Values
- Written Communication

The answers to questions regarding ISLLC performance aspects can be found in the linkages made in this book. There are performance areas that bridge the ISLLC Standards. This book attempts to bring clarity to the skills needed for implementing the standards. A listing of performance aspects of ISLLC Standards as well as relevant National Policy Board for Educational Administration (NPBEA) Domains and Dimensions (Form R.18) are found in Resources.

Standard, Performance Areas, and Aspects

The related standards are presented below as an abbreviated statement followed by program skill areas and the number of related performance aspects. In some instances the activity calls for skills not identified in the ISLLC Standards. The following information is presented to show the linkages between the office deskwork activity and the performance aspects of ISLLC Standards.

STANDARD 1
Developing, articulating, implementing, and stewarding a shared vision of learning
Analyzing Problems
      7 ISLLC performance aspects related to analyzing problems
Exercising Judgment
      No ISLLC-related performance aspects
Organizing and Planning
      13 ISLLC performance aspects related to organizing and planning
Delegating Effectively
      No ISLLC-related performance aspects
Making Decisions
      No ISLLC-related performance aspects
Interpersonal Sensitivity
      3 ISLLC performance aspects related to interpersonal sensitivity
Expressing Professional Values
      8 ISLLC performance aspects related to professional values
Written Communication
      4 ISLLC performance aspects related to written communication

STANDARD 2
Advocating, nurturing, and sustaining a school culture and effective instructional program conducive to student learning and staff professional growth
Analyzing Problems
      6 ISLLC performance aspects related to analyzing problems
Exercising Judgment
      1 ISLLC performance aspect related to exercising judgment
Organizing and Planning
      10 ISLLC performance aspects related to organizing and planning
Delegating Effectively
      No ISLLC-related performance aspects
Making Decisions
      No ISLLC-related performance aspects
Interpersonal Sensitivity
      6 ISLLC performance aspects related to interpersonal sensitivity
Professional Motivation
      4 ISLLC performance aspects related to professional motivation

ISLLC STANDARDS (Continued)

Expressing Professional Values
> 10 ISLLC performance aspects related to professional values

Written Communication
> No ISLLC-related performance aspects

STANDARD 3

Ensuring management of the organization, operations, and resources for a safe, efficient, and effective learning environment

Analyzing Problems
> 10 ISLLC performance aspects related to analyzing problems

Exercising Judgment
> 7 ISLLC performance aspects related to exercising judgment

Analyzing Problems
> 15 ISLLC performance aspects related to analyzing problems

Effective Delegation
> 2 ISLLC performance aspects related to effective delegation

Making Decisions
> 3 ISLLC performance aspects related to making decisions

Interpersonal Sensitivity
> 8 ISLLC performance aspects related to interpersonal sensitivity

Expressing Professional Values
> 2 ISLLC performance aspects related to professional values

Written Communication
> 1 ISLLC performance aspect related to written communication

STANDARD 4

Collaborating with families and community members, responding to diverse community interests and needs, and mobilizing community resources

Analyzing Problems
> 6 ISLLC performance aspects related to analyzing problems

Exercising Judgment
> 5 ISLLC performance aspects related to exercising judgment

Organizing and Planning
> 11 ISLLC performance aspects related to organizing and planning

Effective Delegation
> No ISLLC-related performance aspects

Making Decisions
> No ISLLC-related performance aspects

Interpersonal Sensitivity
> 11 ISLLC performance aspects related to interpersonal sensitivity

Expressing Professional Values
> 11 ISLLC performance aspects related to professional values

Written Communication
> 4 ISLLC performance aspects related to written communication

STANDARD 5

Promoting success of all students through integrity, fairness, and an ethical manner

Analyzing Problems
> No ISLLC-related performance aspects

Exercising Judgment
> 10 ISLLC performance aspects related to exercising judgment

Organizing and Planning
> No ISLLC-related performance aspects

Effective Delegation
> No ISLLC-related performance aspects

ISLLC STANDARDS (Continued)

Making Decisions
     No ISLLC-related performance aspects
Interpersonal Sensitivity
     9 ISLLC performance aspects related to interpersonal sensitivity
Expressing Professional Values
     19 ISLLC performance aspects related to professional values
Written Communication
     No ISLLC-related performance aspects

STANDARD 6
Promoting the success of all students by understanding, responding to, and influencing the larger political, social, economic, legal, and cultural context

Analyzing Problems
     7 ISLLC performance aspects related to analyzing problems
Exercising Judgment
     4 ISLLC performance aspects related to exercising judgment
Organizing and Planning
     2 ISLLC performance aspects related to organizing and planning
Effective Delegation
     No ISLLC-related performance aspects
Making Decisions
     No ISLLC-related performance aspects
Interpersonal Sensitivity
     No ISLLC-related performance aspects
Expressing Professional Values
     6 ISLLC performance aspects related to professional values
Written Communication
     No ISLLC-related performance aspects

Note: Linkages were identified by the principal author and verified by education experts.
SOURCE: Adapted from Council of Chief State School Officers (1996).

Complete the entire deskwork simulation. It will probably take you a little more than an hour to respond to all parts of the activity. Later, documenting your partner's work may seem a bit tedious, but it is important to take the time to follow all the steps.

Background for the Activity

You will have about 60 minutes to read over and respond to the Normal School deskwork items. Additional tasks will probably take 15 more minutes. You have blank copies of supplies such as a calendar, memo forms, school stationery, information request forms, and e-mail and fax forms. After writing on the copies, you may want to staple or clip together your responses to each deskwork item. Use only these materials; it makes it much easier for your partner to document what you did from a set of standard materials.

As with the previous simulations, you will probably feel that you need more information than we make available to you. That is intentional. The deskwork you will complete here assumes that you are not familiar with the personalities or situations; it is, after all, your first day on the job.

NORMAL SCHOOL DESKWORK

Deskwork Instructions

You will play the role of Page Turner, new principal in the Normal City Public Schools. Today is October 9. You have approximately 60 minutes to take care of some of the work that has accumulated since your employment. At the end of this time, you are scheduled to meet with the superintendent concerning your assignment. You will not be able to return to your office until tomorrow morning. There is no clerical assistance available for the next few days, so you will have to prepare all memos, letters, and so on, yourself.

You have been employed to fill the position of a former principal who has not been on the job for several weeks. Thomas Jung, assistant principal, has been the acting principal. Because the school board members were increasingly concerned about declining instructional programs at this school, they decided to hire you from outside the school system. They stated that they wanted someone who would be free of local biases and who would bring a fresh approach to problem solving and program implementation. Believing that you could return the school to its former prominence, the superintendent has asked that you begin immediately, even though you are not familiar with past practices, procedures, or policies of the Normal City Public Schools.

Your immediate task is to read the deskwork materials and take appropriate action. Write down everything that you decide to do or plan to do. Make notes to yourself about things you want to do later. Outline plans and prepare agendas. Draft letters for your secretary, who will return to work in a few days, to complete. If you plan to hold meetings, write down agendas. It is important that you staple your written responses to each deskwork item as you proceed.

Remember that everything you decide to do must be in writing. If you fail to record something, your partner, examining your responses, will not be able to document your intentions. If you plan to call, e-mail, fax, or talk to someone, write down what you intend to say to them. Be careful to use only the information available to you in this deskwork activity. Do not make up or fabricate things.

Most of the materials have come to you in anticipation of your arrival. Remember that you are a new principal in both a school and school district with which you are unfamiliar. Be yourself and show what you can do! Do not merely describe actions you plan to take at some later time. Do exactly what you would and could do while you are actually sitting at your desk reading your mail.

Deskwork Items

Before beginning, you will want to duplicate each item in your deskwork (Figures 4.1 through 4.13). These will result in some of your deskwork artifacts; others will be written on office forms supplied here. After duplicating the pages you will be working with, read all 13 deskwork items.

Figure 4.1 Deskwork Item #1

NORMAL SECONDARY SCHOOL

MEMORANDUM

DATE: October 8

TO: Page Turner, Principal

FROM: Clarice Jackson, Guidance   *Clare*

SUBJECT: Memorial Service for David Jones

As you may have heard, the shooting death of David Jones has caused great concern among the student body and the community. It is a very tragic symbol of the way the drug conflicts in the neighborhood are affecting our children's lives, even outstanding students like David.

I have worked with David's brother and the SCA President, Bobby Fisher, to originate a Memorial Service for David. We would like to hold it in the school auditorium the last hour of the day, Friday, October 12. Will this be all right?

Although you are new to Normal School and did not know David personally, we think it is appropriate for you, as principal, to say a few words at the service.

How would you like to handle excusing the students to attend? Should we invite David's family and friends in his church and neighborhood who might like to attend?

Obviously the school must respond in a way that will help children deal with their grief and their own fears.

Figure 4.2 Deskwork Item #2

AFL/CIO * * * Yours for Results

October 6

Dr. Joseph Miller
Superintendent of Schools
Normal City Public Schools
Normal City

Dear Dr. Miller:

This is to inform you that the Normal City AFL/CIO Executive Committee voted today to support the NEA resolution that all elementary and secondary teachers cease to work with special interest clubs or perform extracurricular duties after regular hours, without additional pay.

The effective date of this action is Monday, October 29.

Sincerely,

Bill

William Smith
President

cc: Page Turner, Principal

Figure 4.3 Deskwork Item #3

NORMAL SECONDARY SCHOOL

MEMORANDUM

DATE: October 8

TO: Page Turner, Principal

FROM: Thomas Jung, Assistant Principal   *Tom*

SUBJECT: Holiday Dance for Graduating Seniors

Welcome aboard!

You may not be aware of the School Board's decision to pilot a mid-year graduation ceremony, January 18, for Normal City students, who have been promoted last June, but failed to meet requirements. Many of the students attended summer school or returned this year to finish up and will be eligible in January, when the Board wants to recognize their special effort with a formal graduation ceremony.

We are holding an interschool Holiday Graduation Ball, December 21, at the Columbia Hotel for all matriculating seniors to celebrate the occasion. There are a number of related issues that I need to discuss with you ASAP. Can we set up a time?

Figure 4.4 Deskwork Item #4

October 6

Dear Dr. Turner,

Welcome to our school!

Last month students formally complained to the principal that the dress code is too strict. Mr. Binder, our former principal, never replied.

On behalf of the students, I am writing to you to ask you to review the dress code. We don't understand what's wrong with tank tops? In fact, many of us wear T-shirts with the sleeves removed. We don't understand the difference.

We hope that you will take the time to hear our concerns and have the courtesy to answer us.

Sincerely,

Bobby Fisher

SCA President

Figure 4.5 Deskwork Item #5

NORMAL CITY TEACHERS ASSOCIATION
1000 South Mall
Route 66
Normal City

October 8

Dear Page Turner
Normal Secondary School
Normal City

Dear Dr. Turner:

At the first meeting of the executive council of the local affiliate of the NEA, the question of teachers' covering and/or sponsoring extra-curricular activities without supplemental pay was discussed. Several of those present expressed strong personal feelings against this practice. They feel that in order to do outstanding instruction in the classroom they are unwilling to take on the burden of non-instructional duties that do not contribute directly to the quality of teaching. The Executive Committee, therefore, voted to recommend to the membership that they refuse to perform extra-curricular duties or work with special interest clubs without adequate supplemental pay.

The staff at Normal Secondary has met, and they support the recommendations of the Executive Committee. I must, therefore, inform you that we will no longer assume extra curricular responsibilities this year, after the end of the fourth week in October while under the standard contract.

Very truly yours,

Ted

Theodore Fleisher

NCTA/NEA Building Representative

Figure 4.6 Deskwork Item #6

Normal City First Baptist Church

October 5

Dear Dr. Turner,

On behalf of our community, let me welcome you. I am sure you will find this a fine place to live.

I am, however, appalled by what I see young people wearing on the streets these days. They are not decent!

I checked the school handbook that says that hot pants, shorts, short skirts, and pants more than 6" above the ankles are not allowed. If this is the case, why are all the students wearing them on the way home from school?

I would like to meet with you to discuss how we can do something about his. Unless I hear from you, I will be in your office on Friday afternoon at 3:20 P.M.

Respectfully,

T. Abernathy

Rev. Thomas Abernathy, III

Figure 4.7 Deskwork Item #7

NORMAL CITY PUBLIC SCHOOLS
Normal City

TO: All Principals

FROM: Dr. Joyce Gloeckler, Deputy Superintendent

SUBJECT: Attendance Records

DATE: October 5

The Normal City Schools have been under attack recently for alleged discrepancies between actual and reported enrollment. As a result, Superintendent Miller has directed an internal audit.

Preliminary to the audit team's visit to your school, please verify the accuracy of the information already in the system. Check the past three fiscal years (7/1 to 6/30) up to the present. Your verification of the accuracy of the information is to be completed by 9:00 A.M. Monday, October 15.

Figure 4.8 Deskwork Item #8

NORMAL CITY PUBLIC SCHOOLS
Normal City

DATE: October 5

TO: All Principals

FROM: A. Harriman, Director of Procurement   *Harriman*

SUBJECT: Inventory of Instructional Supplies

Before we begin the procurement process for the next FY, we want to update the current system-wide computer inventory of instructional supplies. We ask that you "clean up" the supplies inventory using data entry Form No. I-C-802. In the column marked "Number of Units," enter the number of each item on hand as of 10/15.

Please complete by 10/19 and verify completion in writing.

Figure 4.9 Deskwork Item #9

Dear Principle -

Lennie Mathias has a locker near me and he has a gun wrapped up in a sweatshirt in it. I think he stole it because I heard him bragging on it.

ANONIMOUS

Figure 4.10   Deskwork Item #10

October 8

Dear Dr. Turner,

We need to do something about the girls' locker room. Lately, paper
goods and other items have clogged toilets. Mirrors have been cracked
and pieces taken. Also, things written on the walls are disgusting. I
can't keep things cleaned
up if I have to be a plumber too. Please help!

Sorry to bother you with this problem on your first day...we need to talk.

Jake

Head Custodian

Figure 4.11   Deskwork Item #11

---

8 de Octubre

Estimado Director:

El viernes, mi hijo Tommy, fué mandado a casa desde la escuela porque Mr. Jung dijo que no puede llevar puesto un tank top a la escuela. Hay una niña que vive cerca que los usa todo el tiempo cuando va a la escuela.

No comprendo por qué la maestra lo atormenta. El ha tenido problemas con ella antes. Yo le aseguro que Tommy no va a volver a pelear con ella.

Favor de llámarme por teléfono cuando reciba esta nota.

Sinceramente,

Señora Aida Zig

¡Una madre preocupada!

Figure 4.12 Deskwork Item #12

The Small Business Association of Normal City
3592 Parkway Drive
Normal City

October 4

Dear Dr. Turner,

There is a problem you should be made aware of. Shoplifting has become a serious problem to businesses in the community.

Last week in my store, I saw two boys wearing Normal School sweatshirts, looking at fishing knives. In a flash, I noticed that two knives were missing. My sources tell me that the boys were Lennie Mathias and Tony Valdez.

Several of my friends and I would like to come to Normal as soon as possible because there is a strong possibility that these knives are in the school. We want to help you search for them.

I know students are not allowed to bring weapons to school, but if they would steal, I bet they would do that too.

Please contact me immediately and maybe we can teach these guys a lesson.

Sincerely,

Tom

Thomas Pillar, Vice President

October 4

Figure 4.13   Deskwork Item #13

Dear Dr. Turner,

Welcome to our school. I volunteered to help students prepare for the debate competition this year. As a new teacher here, I was delighted to take on this responsibility because I have a minor in Speech and have also had experience in debate and public speaking.

I really want to help these students, who have lots of potential and enthusiasm. The curriculum objectives for the year include the integration of speaking and writing across the curriculum while emphasizing Standards. The debate competition would give us the opportunity to meet these objectives and organize learning around a theme.

I am very sad about the teachers' organization voting not to work with students after contract hours. I really want to keep working with the students, but I am afraid to get the more experienced teachers angry with me, and I don't know what to do. I see the debate competition as a natural part of the curriculum and clearly support the instructional objectives this year.

Could I see you to discuss the matter further?

Sincerely,

Glenda Moore

English Teacher

Preparing Your Responses

Now, prepare responses to the preceding deskwork items on the blank forms that follow. Before doing that, make 3 or 4 copies of Normal School stationary, the Information Request form, Memorandum, and E-mail or Fax Transmission form. If you wish, you may make 1 copy each of the Calendar, Summary of Actions Taken form and the Performance Reflection Form.

Your written responses to the deskwork items become the artifacts for analysis, reflection, and documentation. To make it easier for your partner to document your work, do not use tablets, scratch paper, Post-it notes, and so on. Use only the forms that follow.

Form 4.1   Information Request

NORMAL CITY SCHOOLS

Information requested:

1.

2.

3.

(*Note:* Add as many numbered points as you need.)

Office from which the information is requested (If information is requested from several different offices, complete a separate form for each office.):

Date information needed:

Form 4.2   Memorandum

NORMAL SECONDARY SCHOOL

MEMORANDUM

DATE:
TO:
FROM:
SUBJECT:

Form 4.3 E-Mail or Fax

E-MAIL or FAX TRANSMISSION
Normal School

Office of the Principal

To: _____

Date: _____

E-mail address: _____

Fax number: _____

Pages: _____

From: _____

Subject: _____

Form 4.4   October Calendar

October

Sunday	Monday	Tuesday	Wednesday	Thursday	Friday	Saturday
	1	2	3	4	5	6
7	8 Columbus Day	9	10	11	12	13
14	15	16	17	18	19 End of 1st 6 weeks	20
21	22	23 Professional Day	24	25	26	27
28 Daylight Savings – Set clock back 1 hour	29	30	31 Halloween			

Form 4.4   November Calendar

November

Sun	Mon	Tue	Wed	Thu	Fri	Sat
				1	2	3
4	5 Professional Day	6 Election Day	7	8	9 End of 1st 9 weeks	10
11	12	13	14	15 Evening Parent Conferences	16 Professional Day	17
18	19	20	21	22 Thanksgiving Holidy	23 Thanksgiving Holiday	24
25	26	27	28	29	30 Professional Day	

You may want to use more than one type of form for responding to a particular item.

Blank Office Deskwork Response Forms

You will need to structure the time yourself and take an additional 15 minutes, after responding to the items, to complete the next two forms before exchanging your artifacts with your partner.

Summary of Actions Taken

On a duplicate copy of Form 4.5, describe what you did on each deskwork item and briefly explain why. If you did not get to an item because of time, write *did not handle*. If you got to an item but decided not to do anything about it just now, write *took no action*.

Performance Reflection Form

Fill in a duplicate copy of Form 4.6 as you reflect on the deskwork you just did.

Form 4.5   Summary of Actions Taken

ITEM	WHAT I DID	WHY I DID IT
DW #1: Memo from Guidance re memorial service Friday		
DW#2: Copy of letter to supt. re cessation of after-school duties		
DW#3: Memo from AP re: midyear graduation and holiday graduation ball		
DW #4: Letter from SCA president re: dress code		
DW#5: Letter from building representative re: after-school extra-duties stoppage		
DW#6: Letter from pastor re: student dress. Coming to school Friday at 2:30 p.m.		
DW#7: Memo from dep. supt. re: attendance record verification. Due Monday, October 15.		

Form 4.5   Summary of Actions Taken (continued)

ITEM	WHAT I DID	WHY I DID IT
DW#8: Memo from director of procurement re: updating instructional supplies inventory; due October 15.		
DW#9: Anonymous note re: alleged gun in a student locker		
DW#10: Note from head custodian re: vandalism in girls' locker room		
DW#11: Letter from Spanish-speaking parent re: son and dress code		
DW#12: Letter from small-business association re: shoplifting near school		
DW#13: Letter from teacher re: extra duties after school		

Note: Refer to deskwork (DW) item numbers. For example, Figure 4.1 is DW#1.
SOURCE: Adapted from National Association of Secondary School Principals (1988).

Form 4.6 Performance Reflection Form

PERFORMANCE REFLECTION FORM

1. What approach did you use to handle the deskwork tasks?

2. Did you complete all deskwork tasks? If not, how did you choose the items that you handled?

3. How well do you think you handled the deskwork tasks?

4. If you could repeat this activity again immediately, what, if anything, would you do differently?

OFFICE DESKWORK PERFORMANCE DOCUMENTATION AND RATING

In order to document your partner's deskwork artifacts, you will want to study the steps that follow and take particular note of the interpretation of some the standard performance indicators:

1. Examine the completed deskwork items and locate the following:
    *   Original items (Figures 4.1-4.13) and responses (Forms 4.1-4.4) to them
    *   Calendars (Form 4.4)
    *   Summary of Actions Taken (Form 4.5)
    *   Performance Reflection Table (Form 4.6)

2. Read all artifacts carefully and, using a highlighter, mark any problems with spelling, grammar, or clarity. Most people using the program in this book usually do not write many notes on the original items. They use more stationary, memos, and so on.

3. Label responses related to other items using the deskwork item number (e.g., DW #1, DW #5). The steps below are helpful for getting ready to analyze the artifacts. For example:
    *   If several deskwork responses are referred to on a note to self, an agenda, a things-to-do list, a calendar entry, or the like, label each response with the deskwork item number (e.g., DW #7, DW #13).
    *   Cross-referencing deskwork responses found on another action-taken record (e.g., calendar entry) helps to organize the information you need with documenting *all* deskwork response actions taken.
    *   Use a colored pen or pencil for labeling your deskwork responses. Use the Summary of Actions Taken (Form 4.5) as a guide for determining the item number for a referenced item (e.g., DW #10).
    *   If several items are stapled together, list them on the top page of the grouping (e.g., DW #2, DW #8).

Stack all completed deskwork artifacts in numerical sequence to the extent possible (DW #1 through DW #13). Write the numbers of items that are in the stack on the cover page. This makes it easier for you to keep track of the responses when documenting them. Keep the calendar (Form 4.4), Summary of Actions Taken (Form 4.5), and Performance Reflection Form (Form 4.6) separate from the stapled responses to locate them more easily when documenting your partner's responses.

Performance Definitions

Handled means that there is evidence that the participant actually read the item and decided whether or not to take some action. Examine your partner's Summary of Actions Taken (Form 4.5) if you are not sure how to document this action. If there is no tangible evidence that the item was read, leave blank, and go on to the next item to document. This is an exception to the rule of checking or dotting all statements.

Took some action means that there is evidence that the participant did something more than file the item or leave it for later action. The participant must write a letter, outline a plan of action, write a memo, plan a meeting, seek background information, prepare a call to someone, and so on. If no action was taken, leave blank, and go on to the next deskwork item to document. This is an exception to the rule of always checking or dotting all statements.

Sought more information means that there is evidence that the participant requested additional information related to the item. This is a generic statement related to the overall item or issue. (Requests for specific kinds of information are asked for later.)

Agreed with or *to* something means that the participant said, in one way or another, that the other person was right. If there is evidence of agreement, enter a check mark and explain and quote the statement.

Prepared a plan means that there is evidence of at least a two-step plan. Steps in plans are often but not always numbered. There must be tangible evidence of a plan. Just stating that there is a plan is not enough behavioral evidence to give credit for a plan. Occasionally, your partner may list the plan's steps in the Summary of Actions Taken (Form 4.5).

Showed tact means that there is delicate and considerate perception of what is appropriate. *A lack of tact* implies untimely or inconsiderate remarks regarding the concerns or interests of the other party. Give an example or quote from the participant's response. If no contact was made with another person, leave blank. This is an exception to the rule of always checking or dotting a statement.

Tied items means that the participant acknowledges, in some way, a relationship between one or more deskwork items to another item (tied) by making reference to them in a note, memo, things-to-do list, agenda, and so on. You may also find evidence on the calendar of tying.

Committed means agreeing to do something. If there is a commitment, explain and quote from the participant's deskwork response. If there is no commitment, place a large dot on the line to the left. If no contact was made with another person, leave blank. This is another exception to the rule of always checking or dotting a statement.

Prepared for a call means that there is evidence of what is going to be said in the telephone call. Merely saying that a call would be made is not enough evidence of having prepared a call. If in doubt, review your partner's Summary of Actions Taken (Form 4.5).

Prepared for a meeting means there is evidence of what the meeting will cover. Preparing an agenda is one kind of evidence. Making notes about the substance of the meeting is another kind. If there is no evidence other than a statement of intent, place a dot on the line.

Stated a strong value means that there is no doubt about what the participant believes about a particular professional issue. The statement must be very clear to get a check. Usually such strong value statements begin with, "I believe . . . It is important that . . . Let me emphasize . . . " and so on.

Showed this is a priority refers to an action by the participant that shows an item is important. Actions might include putting the item on the calendar, developing a plan to handle the item, responding to the person presenting the issue, or simply stating somewhere that the item is very important. This type of statement may sometimes appear on the Summary of Actions Taken (Form 4.5).

Delegated means that a task is assigned to someone else. Note what is delegated, to whom it is delegated, whether it is the appropriate person to delegate the task to, and whether the task is clearly defined and stated. Also note whether a deadline is given and follow-up specified.

Completing Deskwork Documentation Forms

1. After reviewing Step 2 in the previous Instructions, document positive and negative written communication examples on the last page of the following form.
   - Note clarity, spelling, and grammar.

2. If a participant takes some action of major significance that is not listed, write it down under *Unique Behaviors* on the last page of the form and designate the item number (e.g., DW #2).

3. Answer the statements on the documentation form using the following guidelines:
   - Use a check (✓) if a behavior on the list is in evidence.
   - Use a dot (•) if an item is not in evidence.
   - Leave blank only those statements with a shaded box when no evidence is available (i.e., *Handled, Took Action, Tact, Committed*).

4. Whenever appropriate, record additional examples to illustrate actions taken.

5. When giving examples opposite items on the documentation form, use the following abbreviations to identify the source of the example. These abbreviations help to convince your partner that your documentation is accurate.

NOO	Note on original	MEMO	Memo
TTD	Things-to-do list	LTR	Letter
IRF	Information request form	SAT	Summary-of-actions-taken form
CE	Calendar entry	PRF	Performance reflection form

SOURCE: National Association of Secondary School Principals (1988).

About Delegation

If something is delegated, make brief comments on the second page of each item's performance documentation answering four aspects of delegation tasks bulleted in Form 4.7. Most often a yes or no is sufficient. If an item is delegated to another person, note the person's position (e.g., secretary, teacher), and then comment on the appropriate form (see Form 4.7).

Form 4.7 Delegation

If an item is delegated to another person, note the person's position (e.g. secretary, teacher), and then comment on each of the four bullets that follow.

Name and position of delegatee: _____

- The information gathering task and authority for the task are appropriate for the person and job of the delegatee.

- The item is delegated with control (e.g., set deadline for completion).

- The item is delegated with follow-up (e.g., specific steps for checking on completion or success).

- The instructions given are specific and clear.

Documentation and Rating Forms—Office Deskwork

Form DW #1   Handling of Deskwork Item #1 (Figure 4.1)

GUIDANCE

Review the paragraphs beneath the Deskwork Instructions and Preparing Your Responses headings earlier in this chapter before documenting your partner's work on this form. Mark an item with a check (✓) if the applicable performance indicator is in evidence, with a dot (•) if it is not. Give examples where you can.

Task Completion

ORGANIZING AND PLANNING, and MAKING DECISIONS

_____ 1. Handled the guidance memo   (Read performance definitions)
re: memorial service as a high-priority item.
If not, enter a dot and go on to the next deskwork item.

_____ 2. Took some action.   (Read performance definition)
If not, mark with a dot and go on to the next
deskwork item.

ANALYZING PROBLEMS

_____ 3. Sought more information   (Read performance definition)
on the memorial service issue.

_____ 4. Sought more information on the family.

_____ 5. Sought information on the neighborhood drug situation.

_____ 6. Sought information on scheduling the memorial service.

_____ 7. Sought policy information on holding memorial services at school.

ORGANIZING AND PLANNING

_____ 8. Prepared a plan for the school   (Read performance definition)
memorial service issue.

INTERPERSONAL SENSITIVITY and DELEGATING EFFECTIVELY

_____ 9. Contacted Guidance about the memorial service.

_____ 10. Directly acknowledged the viewpoint held by Guidance.

_____ 11. Shared some memorial service information with Guidance.

_____ 12. Used tact when contacting Guidance.   (Read performance definition)

_____ 13. Had someone else contact Guidance about the memorial service issue.

EXERCISING JUDGMENT

_____ 14. Showed that the memorial service is a priority issue. (Read performance definition)

_____ 15. Committed to having a memorial service at school.   (Read performance definition)

EXPRESSING PROFESSIONAL VALUES

_____ 16. Stated strong personal value about the memorial service.   (Read performance definition)

_____ 17. Stated a strong value about the memorial being held at school.

_____ 18. Stated a strong value about excusing students to attend a school memorial service.

_____ 19. Stated another strong value. Describe here:

Documentation and Rating Forms—Office Deskwork (continued)

ORGANIZING AND PLANNING

_____ 20. Prepared a to-do list for something in this issue.

_____ 21. Made a calendar entry for something in this issue.

_____ 22. Prepared an agenda for addressing this issue.

_____ 23. Wrote a note to self on the original item.

_____ 24. Wrote a note to self on paper other than on the original item.

_____ 25. Wrote a note to someone else on the original item.

_____ 26. Wrote a note to someone else other than on the original item.

INTERPERSONAL SENSITIVITY and EXERCISING JUDGMENT

_____ 27. Wrote a memo or e-mail to Guidance.

_____ 28. Wrote a letter to Guidance.

ORGANIZING AND PLANNING and INTERPERSONAL SENSITIVITY

_____ 29. Prepared for a call to Guidance.   (Read performance definition)

_____ 30. Prepared for a meeting with Guidance.   (Read performance definition)

Delegation

If an item is delegated to another person, note the person's position (e.g., secretary, teacher), and then comment on each of the four bullets that follow. A Yes or No is usually sufficient.

Name and position of delegatee: _____   **Comments**

- The information gathering task and authority for the task   _____
  are appropriate for the person and job of the delegatee.

- The item is delegated with control   _____
  (e.g., set deadline for completion).

- The item is delegated with follow-up   _____
  (e.g., specific steps for checking on completion or success).

- The instructions given are specific and clear.   _____

Documentation and Rating Forms—Office Deskwork (continued)

Rating Performance

The symbols below are used to represent demonstrated levels of skill. After studying the completed documentation form, with particular attention to the skill areas and frequency of checked performance indicators, rate each performance area in the Performance Ratings below. In some instances several of the performance indicators may be attributed to more than one skill area.

When you have completed rating the individual deskwork items, complete the Overall Performance Summary on the last page of this chapter.

Symbols	Interpretations
⊕	Very high skill shown
+	More than moderate skill
(+)	Moderate skill shown
(−)	Less than moderate skill
−	Little skill shown
⊖	Very little skill shown

Performance Summary Ratings—DW# Item #1

Performance Areas	Rating Symbols
Analyzing Problems Performance Ratings: ____, ____	_____
Exercising Judgment Performance Ratings: ____, ____	_____
Organizing and Planning Performance Ratings: ____, ____, ____	_____
Making Decisions Performance Rating: ____	_____
Delegating Effectively Performance Rating: ____	_____
Interpersonal Sensitivity Performance Ratings: ____, ____, ____	_____
Written Communication *Since only a moderate amount of writing is required, most participants receive a modesate (+).* *Enter + if the spelling and vacabulary are more than moderate. If there is more than one error in spelling, enter − or (−) showing a need for improvement.*	_____
Expressing Professional Values Performance Rating: ____	_____

Note: *Extreme ratings of ⊕ or ⊖ are seldom appropriate.*

Documentation and Rating Forms—Office Deskwork (continued)

Form DW #2   Handling of Deskwork Item #2 (Figure 4.2)

ORGANIZATION PRESIDENT

Review the paragraphs beneath the Deskwork Instructions and Preparing Your Responses headings earlier in this chapter before documenting your partner's work on this form. Mark an item with a check (✓) if the applicable performance indicator is in evidence, with a dot (●) if it is not. Give examples where you can.

Task Completion

ORGANIZING AND PLANNING and MAKING DECISIONS

_____ 1. Handled the organization president's letter as a high-priority item.
If not, mark with a dot and go on to the next deskwork item.

_____ 2. Took some action.

ANALYZING PROBLEMS

_____ 3. Sought more information on performing duties without pay.

_____ 4. Sought information on the executive committee.

_____ 5. Sought policy information on extracurricular duty without pay.

_____ 6 Sought information on the union president.

_____ 7. Tied item to the building representative's issue.   (Read performance definition)
(Deskwork Item #5)

_____ 8. Tied item to the English teacher's issue. (Deskwork Item #13)

EXERCISING JUDGMENT

_____ 9. Showed this is a priority issue.   (Read performance definition)

_____ 10. Agreed with the union president's conclusion.   (Read performance definition)

_____ 11. Informed supervisor about the union's letter.

EXPRESSING PROFESSIONAL VALUES

_____ 12. Stated a strong value about extra duties without pay.

_____ 13. Stated a strong value about special interest clubs.

_____ 14. Stared a strong value about extra duty activities.

_____ 15. Stated a strong value about duties after regular hours.

_____ 16. Stated a strong value about teachers' unions.

_____ 17. Stated a strong value about retracting resolutions.

_____ 18. Stated a strong value about accepting resolutions.

ORGANIZING AND PLANNING

_____ 19. Prepared a to-do list for something in this issue.

_____ 20. Made a calendar notation for something in this issue.

_____ 21. Prepared an agenda for addressing this issue.

_____ 22. Wrote a note to self on the original item.

_____ 23. Wrote a note to self on paper other than the original item.

Documentation and Rating Forms—Office Deskwork (continued)

_____ 24. Wrote a note to someone else on the original item.

_____ 25. Wrote a note to someone else on paper other than the original item.

INTERPERSONAL SENSITIVITY and EXERCISING JUDGMENT

_____ 26. Wrote a memo or e-mail to the union president.

_____ 27. Wrote a letter to the union president.

ORGANIZING AND PLANNING and INTERPERSONAL SENSITIVITY

_____ 28. Prepared for a call to the union president.   (Read definition)

_____ 29. Prepared for a meeting with the union president.   (Read definition)

Delegation

If an item is delegated to another person, note the person's position (e.g., secretary, teacher), and then comment on each of the four bullets that follow. A Yes or No is usually sufficient.

Name and position of delegatee: _____   **Comments**

- The information gathering task and authority for the task are appropriate for the person and job of the delegatee.   _____

- The item is delegated with control (e.g., set deadline for completion).   _____

- The item is delegated with follow-up (e.g., specific steps for checking on completion or success).   _____

- The instructions given are specific and clear.   _____

Documentation and Rating Forms—Office Deskwork (continued)

Rating Performance

The symbols below are used to represent demonstrated levels of skill. After studying the completed documentation form, with particular attention to the skill areas and frequency of checked performance indicators, rate each performance area in the Performance Ratings below. In some instances several of the performance indicators may be attributed to more than one skill area.

When you have completed rating the individual deskwork items, complete the Overall Performance Summary on the last page of this section.

Symbols	Interpretations
⊕	Very high skill shown
+	More than moderate skill
(+)	Moderate skill shown
(–)	Less than moderate skill
–	Little skill shown
⊖	Very little skill shown

Performance Summary Ratings—DW# Item #2

Performance Areas	Rating Symbols
Analyzing Problems Performance Rating: ___	____
Exercising Judgment Performance Ratings: ____, ____	____
Organizing and Planning Performance Ratings: ____, ____, ____	____
Making Decisions Performance Rating: ____	____
Delegating Effectively Performance Rating: ____	____
Interpersonal Sensitivity Performance Ratings: ____, ____	____
Written Communication *Since only a moderate amount of writing is required, most participants receive a moderate (+).* *Enter + if the spelling and vacabulary are more than moderate. If there is more than one error in spelling, enter – or (–) showing a need for improvement.*	____
Expressing Professional Values Performance Rating: ____	____

Note: *Extreme ratings of ⊕ or ⊖ are seldom appropriate.*

Documentation and Rating Forms—Office Deskwork (continued)

Form DW #3   Handling of Deskwork Item #3 (Figure 4.3)

ASSISTANT PRINCIPAL

Review the paragraphs beneath the Deskwork Instructions and Preparing Your Responses headings earlier in this chapter before documenting your partner's work on this form. Mark an item with a check (✓) if the applicable performance indicator is in evidence, with a dot (●) if it is not. Give examples where you can.

Task Completion

ORGANIZING AND PLANNING and MAKING DECISIONS

_____ 1. Handled the graduation dance memo from the assistant principal.
       If not, mark with a dot and go on to the next deskwork item.

_____ 2. Took some action.

ANALYZING PROBLEMS

_____ 3. Sought more information on the graduation dance issue.

_____ 4. Sought policy information on school dances.

_____ 5. Sought information on the number of students affected.

_____ 6. Sought information on critical issues around graduation.

INTERPERSONAL SENSITIVITY and DELEGATING EFFECTIVELY

_____ 7. Contacted assistant principal regarding dance concerns.

_____ 8. Had someone else contact the assistant principal about dance concerns.

_____ 9. Directly acknowledged the assistant principal's concerns.

_____ 10. Shared information with the assistant principal regarding concerns.

_____ 11. Used tact when contacting the assistant principal.

ORGANIZING AND PLANNING

_____ 12. Prepared a to-do list for something in this issue.

_____ 13. Made a calendar notation for something in this issue.

_____ 14. Prepared an agenda for addressing this issue.

_____ 15. Wrote a note to self on the original item.

_____ 16. Wrote a note to self on paper other than the original item.

_____ 17. Wrote a note to someone else on the original item.

_____ 18. Wrote a note to someone else other on paper than the original item.

INTERPERSONAL SENSITIVITY and EXERCISING JUDGMENT

_____ 19. Wrote a memo to the assistant principal.

_____ 20. Wrote a letter to the assistant principal.

ORGANIZING AND PLANNING and INTERPERSONAL SENSITIVITY

_____ 21. Prepared for a call to the assistant principal.

_____ 22. Prepared for a meeting with the assistant principal.

Documentation and Rating Forms—Office Deskwork (continued)

Delegation

If an item is delegated to another person, note the person's position (e.g., secretary, teacher), and then comment on each of the four bullets that follow. A Yes or No is usually sufficient.

Name and position of delegatee: _____   **Comments**

- The information gathering task and authority to do so is appropriate for the person and job of the delegatee.   _____

- The item is delegated with control (e.g., set deadline for completion).   _____

- The item is delegated with follow-up (e.g., specific steps for checking on completion or success).   _____

- The instructions given are specific and clear.   _____

Rating Performance

The symbols below are used to represent demonstrated levels of skill. After studying the completed documentation form, with particular attention to the skill areas and frequency of checked performance indicators, rate each performance area in the Performance Ratings below. In some instances several of the performance indicators may be attributed to more than one skill area.

When you have completed rating the individual deskwork items, complete the Overall Performance Summary on the last page of this chapter.

Symbols	Interpretations
⊕	Very high skill shown
+	More than moderate skill
(+)	Moderate skill shown
(–)	Less than moderate skill
–	Little skill shown
⊖	Very little skill shown

Performance Summary Ratings—DW# Item #3

Performance Areas	**Rating Symbols**
Analyzing Problems Performance Ratings: ____, ____	_____
Exercising Judgment Performance Rating: ____,	_____
Organizing and Planning Performance Ratings: ____, ____	_____
Making Decisions Performance Rating: ____	_____
Delegating Effectively Performance Rating: ____	_____
Written Communication (*Overall written responses to these items*)	_____

Note: *Extreme ratings of ⊕ or ⊖ are seldom appropriate.*

Documentation and Rating Forms—Office Deskwork (continued)

Form DW #4   Handling of Deskwork Item #4 (Figure 4.4)

STUDENT LEADER
Review the paragraphs beneath the Deskwork Instructions and Preparing Your Responses headings earlier in this chapter before documenting your partner's work on this form. Mark an item with a check (✓) if the applicable performance indicator is in evidence, with a dot (•) if it is not. Give examples where you can.

Task Completion

ORGANIZING AND PLANNING and MAKING DECISIONS

_____ 1. Handled the student council president's letter as a high-priority item.
If not, mark with a dot and go on to the next deskwork item

_____ 2. Took some action.

ANALYZING PROBLEMS

_____ 3. Sought more information about the strictness of the dress code.

_____ 4. Sought the school handbook to review the dress code policy.

_____ 5. Sought history of the dress code policy from staff members.

_____ 6. Sought information on the student president.

_____ 7. Tied item to the pastor's issue. (Deskwork Item #6)

_____ 8. Tied item to the concerned parent's issue. (Deskwork Item #11)

INTERPERSONAL SENSITIVITY and DELEGATING EFFECTIVELY

_____ 9. Contacted the student president regarding the dress code.

_____ 10. Had someone else contact student president about code.

_____ 11. Directly acknowledged student president's dress code concerns.

_____ 12. Shared information with the student president regarding dress code.

_____ 13. Used tact when contacting the student president.

EXERCISING JUDGMENT

_____ 14. Committed to review the dress code.

EXPRESSING PROFESSIONAL VALUES

_____ 15. Stated a strong personal value about dress codes.

_____ 16. State a strong value about student presidents.

ORGANIZING AND PLANNING

_____ 17. Prepared a to-do list for something in this issue.

_____ 18. Made a calendar entry for something in this issue.

_____ 19. Prepared an agenda item for addressing this issue.

_____ 20. Wrote a note to self on the original item.

_____ 21. Wrote a note to self on paper other than the original item.

_____ 22. Wrote a note to someone else on paper other than the original item.

_____ 23. Verbalized a note to someone else other than on the original item.

Documentation and Rating Forms—Office Deskwork (continued)

INTERPERSONAL SENSITIVITY and EXERCISING JUDGMENT

_____ 24. Wrote a memo or e-mail to the student president.

_____ 25. Wrote a letter to the student president.

ORGANIZING AND PLANNING and INTERPERSONAL SENSITIVITY

_____ 26. Prepared for a call to the student president.

_____ 27. Prepared a meeting with the student president.

_____ 28. Agreed to talk further with the student president.

Delegation

If an item is delegated to another person, note the person's position (e.g., secretary, teacher), and then comment on each of the four bullets that follow. A Yes or No is usually sufficient.

Name and position of delegatee: _____   **Comments**

- The information gathering task and authority to do so
  is appropriate for the person and job of the delegatee.   _____

- The item is delegated with control
  (e.g., set deadline for completion).   _____

- The item is delegated with follow-up
  (e.g., specific steps for checking on completion or success).   _____

- The instructions given are specific and clear.   _____

Documentation and Rating Forms—Office Deskwork (continued)

Rating Performance

The symbols below are used to represent demonstrated levels of skill. After studying the completed documentation form, with particular attention to the skill areas and frequency of checked performance indicators, rate each performance area in the Performance Ratings below. In some instances several of the performance indicators may be attributed to more than one skill area.

When you have completed rating the individual deskwork items, complete the Overall Performance Summary on the last page of this chapter.

Symbols	Interpretations
⊕	Very high skill shown
+	More than moderate skill
(+)	Moderate skill shown
(−)	Less than moderate skill
−	Little skill shown
⊖	Very little skill shown

Performance Summary Ratings—DW# Item #4

Performance Areas	Rating Symbols
Analyzing Problems Performance Rating: ____	_____
Exercising Judgment Performance Ratings: ____, ____	_____
Organizing and Planning Performance Ratings: ____, ____, ____	_____
Making Decisions Performance Rating: ____	_____
Delegating Effectively Performance Rating: ____	_____
Interpersonal Sensitivity Performance Ratings: ____, ____, ____	_____
Written Communication (*Overall written responses to these items*)	_____
Expressing Professional Values Performance Rating: ____	_____

Note: *Extreme ratings of ⊕ or ⊖ are seldom appropriate.*

Documentation and Rating Forms—Office Deskwork (continued)

Form DW #5   Handling of Deskwork Item #5 (Figure 4.5)

BUILDING REPRESENTATIVE
Review the paragraphs beneath the Deskwork Instructions and Preparing Your Responses headings earlier in this chapter before documenting your partner's work on this form. Mark an item with a check (✓) if the applicable performance indicator is in evidence, with a dot (•) if it is not. Give examples where you can.

Task Completion

ORGANIZING AND PLANNING and MAKING DECISIONS

_____ 1. Handled the teachers' association representative's letter as a high-priority item. If not, mark with a dot and go on to the next deskwork item.

_____ 2. Took some action.

ANALYZING PROBLEMS

_____ 3. Sought more information.

_____ 4. Sought policy information on pay, extracurricular work, and so on.

_____ 5. Sought information about the NCTA/NEA representative.

_____ 6. Tied item to a teacher's issue. (Deskwork Item #13)

INTERPERSONAL SENSITIVITY and DELEGATING EFFECTIVELY

_____ 7. Contacted NCTA/NEA representative regarding teacher support issues.

_____ 8. Had someone else contact representative about teacher support. Note:

_____ 9. Directly acknowledged NCTA/NEA representative's concerns.

_____ 10. Shared information with representative regarding teacher support.

_____ 11. Used tact when contacting the NCTA/NEA representative.

EXPRESSING PROFESSIONAL VALUES

_____ 12. Stated strong personal value about extracurricular activities/duties.

ORGANIZING AND PLANNING

_____ 13. Prepared a to-do list for something in this issue.

_____ 14. Made a calendar entry for something in this issue.

_____ 15. Prepared an agenda for addressing this issue.

_____ 16. Wrote a note to self on the original item.

_____ 17. Wrote a note to self on paper other than the original item.

_____ 18. Wrote a note to someone else on the original item.

_____ 19. Wrote a note to someone else on paper other than the original item.

INTERPERSONAL SENSITIVITY and EXERCISING JUDGMENT

_____ 20. Wrote a memo or email to the NCTA/NEA representative.

_____ 21. Wrote a letter to the NCTA/NEA representative.

Documentation and Rating Forms—Office Deskwork (continued)

ORGANIZING AND PLANNING and INTERPERSONAL SENSTIVITY

_____ 22. Prepared for a phone call to the NCTA/NEA representative.

_____ 23. Prepared for a meeting with the NCTA/NEA representative.

EXERCISING JUDGMENT

_____ 24. Showed this is an important item.   (Read performance definition)

Delegation

If an item is delegated to another person, note the person's position (e.g., secretary, teacher), and then comment on each of the four bullets that follow. A Yes or No is usually sufficient.

Name and position of delegatee: _____   **Comments**

- The information gathering task and authority to do so
  is appropriate for the person and job of the delegatee.   _____

- The item is delegated with control
  (e.g., set deadline for completion).   _____

- The item is delegated with follow-up
  (e.g., specific steps for checking on completion or success).   _____

- The instructions given are specific and clear.   _____

Documentation and Rating Forms—Office Deskwork (continued)

Rating Performance

The symbols below are used to represent demonstrated levels of skill. After studying the completed documentation form, with particular attention to the skill areas and frequency of checked performance indicators, rate each performance area in the Performance Ratings below. In some instances several of the performance indicators may be attributed to more than one skill area.

When you have completed rating the individual deskwork items, complete the Overall Performance Summary on the last page of this section.

Symbols	Interpretations
⊕	Very high skill shown
+	More than moderate skill
(+)	Moderate skill shown
(–)	Less than moderate skill
–	Little skill shown
⊖	Very little skill shown

Performance Summary Ratings—DW# Item #5

Performance Areas	Rating Symbols
Analyzing Problems Performance Rating: ____	____
Exercising Judgment Performance Ratings: ____, ____	____
Organizing and Planning Performance Ratings: ____, ____, ____	____
Making Decisions Performance Rating: ____	____
Delegating Effectively Performance Rating: ____	____
Interpersonal Sensitivity Performance Ratings: ____, ____, ____	____
Written Communication (*Overall written responses to these items*)	____
Expressing Professional Values Performance Rating: ____	____

Note: *Extreme ratings of ⊕ or ⊖ are seldom appropriate.*

Documentation and Rating Forms—Office Deskwork (continued)

Form DW #6   Handling of Deskwork Item #6 (Figure 4.6)

COMMUNITY REPRESENTATIVE
Review the paragraphs beneath the Deskwork Instructions and Preparing Your Responses headings earlier in this chapter before documenting your partner's work on this form. Mark an item with a check (✓) if the applicable performance indicator is in evidence, with a dot (•) if it is not. Give examples where you can.

Task Completion:

ORGANIZING AND PLANNING and MAKING DECISIONS

_____ 1. Handled the letter from the pastor as a high-priority item.
          If not, mark with a dot and go on to the next deskwork item.

_____ 2. Took some action.

ANALYZING PROBLEMS

_____ 3. Sought more information.

_____ 4. Sought background information on the pastor.

_____ 5. Tied the item to the concerned parent's issue. (Deskwork Item #11)

INTERPERSONAL SENSITIVITY and DELEGATING EFFECTIVELY

_____ 6. Contacted the pastor regarding the student dress code.

_____ 7. Had someone else contact the pastor about the dress code.

_____ 8. Directly acknowledged the pastor's concerns.

_____ 9. Shared information with the pastor regarding dress code concerns.

_____ 10. Used tact when contacting the pastor.

EXPRESSING PROFESSIONAL VALUES

_____ 11. Stated a strong value about enforcement of dress codes.

_____ 12. Stated a strong value about dress codes in general.

_____ 13. Stated a strong value about the school's responsibilities.

_____ 14. Stated a strong value about responding to community leaders.

ORGANIZING AND PLANNING

_____ 15. Prepared a to-do list for something in this issue.

_____ 16. Made a calendar entry for something in this issue.

_____ 17. Prepared an agenda item for addressing this issue.

_____ 18. Wrote a note to self on the original item.

_____ 19. Wrote a note to self on paper other than the original item.

_____ 20. Wrote a note to someone else on the original item.

_____ 21. Wrote a note to someone else on paper other than the original item.

Documentation and Rating Forms—Office Deskwork (continued)

INTERPERSONAL SENSITIVITY and EXERCISING JUDGMENT

_____ 22. Wrote a memo or e-mail to the pastor.

_____ 23. Wrote a letter to the pastor.

ORGANIZING AND PLANNING and INTERPERSONAL SENSITIVITY

_____ 24. Prepared for a call to the pastor.

_____ 25. Prepared for a meeting with the pastor.

EXERCISING JUDGMENT

_____ 26. Agreed with the pastor.   (Read performance definition)

_____ 27. Asked the pastor for more time to investigate.

_____ 28. Showed this is a priority issue.

Delegation

If an item is delegated to another person, note the person's position (e.g., secretary, teacher), and then comment on each of the four bullets that follow. A Yes or No is usually sufficient.

Name and position of delegatee: _____   **Comments**

- The information gathering task and authority to do so
  is appropriate for the person and job of the delegatee.   _____

- The item is delegated with control
  (e.g., set deadline for completion).   _____

- The item is delegated with follow-up
  (e.g., specific steps for checking on completion or success).   _____

- The instructions given are specific and clear.   _____

Documentation and Rating Forms—Office Deskwork (continued)

Rating Performance

The symbols below are used to represent demonstrated levels of skill. After studying the completed documentation form, with particular attention to the skill areas and frequency of checked performance indicators, rate each performance area in the Performance Ratings below. In some instances several of the performance indicators may be attributed to more than one skill area.

When you have completed rating the individual deskwork items, complete the Overall Performance Summary on the last page of this chapter.

Symbols	Interpretations
⊕	Very high skill shown
+	More than moderate skill
(+)	Moderate skill shown
(−)	Less than moderate skill
−	Little skill shown
⊖	Very little skill shown

Performance Summary Ratings—DW# Item #6

Performance Areas	Rating Symbols
Analyzing Problems Performance Rating: ____	____
Exercising Judgment Performance Ratings: ____	____
Organizing and Planning Performance Ratings: ____, ____, ____	____
Making Decisions Performance Rating: ____	____
Delegating Effectively Performance Rating: ____	____
Interpersonal Sensitivity Performance Ratings: ____, ____, ____	____
Written Communication (*Overall written responses to these items*)	____
Expressing Professional Values Performance Rating: ____	____

Note: *Extreme ratings of ⊕ or ⊖ are seldom appropriate.*

Documentation and Rating Forms—Office Deskwork (continued)

Form DW #7   Handling of Deskwork Item #7 (Figure 4.7)

DEPUTY SUPERINTENDENT

Review the paragraphs beneath the Deskwork Instructions and Preparing Your Responses headings earlier in this chapter before documenting your partner's work on this form. Mark an item with a check (✓) if the applicable performance indicator is in evidence, with a dot (●) if it is not. Give examples where you can.

Task Completed

ORGANIZING AND PLANNING and MAKING DECISIONS

_____ 1. Handled the memo from the deputy superintendent as a high-priority item. If not, mark with a dot and go on to the next deskwork item.

_____ 2. Took some action.

ANALYZING PROBLEMS

_____ 3. Sought more enrollment information.

_____ 4. Sought information on prior enrollment discrepancies.

_____ 5. Showed awareness of time limit for ensuring information accuracy.

ORGANIZING AND PLANNING

_____ 6. Prepared a plan to check the enrollment information.

_____ 7. Prepared a timeline for getting enrollment information.

_____ 8. Prepared a to-do list for something in this issue.

_____ 9. Made a calendar entry for something in this issue.

_____ 10. Prepared an agenda item for addressing this issue.

_____ 11. Wrote a note to self on the original item.

_____ 12. Wrote a note to self on other paper other than the original item.

_____ 13. Wrote a note to someone else on the original item.

_____ 14. Wrote a note to someone else on paper other than the original item.

INTERPERSONAL SENSITIVITY and EXERCISING JUDGMENT

_____ 15. Wrote a memo to the deputy superintendent.

_____ 16. Wrote a letter to the deputy superintendent.

_____ 17. Prepared an e-mail or a fax message to the deputy superintendent.

EXERCISING JUDGMENT

_____ 18. Showed this is a priority issue.

Documentation and Rating Forms—Office Deskwork (continued)

Delegation

If an item is delegated to another person, note the person's position (e.g., secretary, teacher), and then comment on each of the four bullets that follow. A Yes or No is usually sufficient.

Name and position of delegatee: _____

Comments

- The information gathering task and authority for the task are appropriate for the person and job of the delegatee. _____

- The item is delegated with control (e.g., set deadline for completion). _____

- The item is delegated with follow-up (e.g., specific steps for checking on completion or success). _____

- The instructions given are specific and clear. _____

Rating Performance

The symbols below are used to represent demonstrated levels of skill. After studying the completed documentation form, with particular attention to the skill areas and frequency of checked performance indicators, rate each performance area in the Performance Ratings below. In some instances several of the performance indicators may be attributed to more than one skill area.

When you have completed rating the individual deskwork items, complete the Overall Performance Summary on the last page of this chapter.

Symbols	Interpretations
⊕	Very high skill shown
+	More than moderate skill
(+)	Moderate skill shown
(−)	Less than moderate skill
−	Little skill shown
⊖	Very little skill shown

Performance Summary Ratings—DW# Item #7

Performance Areas	Rating Symbols
Analyzing Problems Performance Rating: _____	_____
Exercising Judgment Performance Ratings: _____, _____	_____
Organizing and Planning Performance Ratings: _____, _____	_____
Making Decisions Performance Rating: _____	_____
Interpersonal Sensitivity Performance Rating: _____	_____
Written Communication (*Overall written responses to these items*)	_____

Note: *Extreme ratings of ⊕ or ⊖ are seldom appropriate.*

Documentation and Rating Forms—Office Deskwork (continued)

Form DW #8   Handling of Deskwork Item #8 (Figure 4.8)

DIRECTOR

Review the paragraphs beneath the Deskwork Instructions and Preparing Your Responses headings earlier in this chapter before documenting your partner's work on this form. Mark an item with a check (✓) if the applicable performance indicator is in evidence, with a dot (•) if it is not. Give examples where you can.

Task Completion

ORGANIZING AND PLANNING and MAKING DECISIONS

_____ 1. Handled the memo from the director as a high-priority item.
If not, mark with a dot and go on to the next item.

_____ 2. Took some action.

ANALYZING PROBLEMS

_____ 3. Sought more information on the instructional supplies inventory.

_____ 4. Sought information on the computer inventory system procedures.

_____ 5. Showed information on the current inventory levels.

ORGANIZING AND PLANNING

_____ 6. Prepared a plan to get the instructional supplies information.

_____ 7. Prepared a to-do list for something in this issue.

_____ 8. Made a calendar entry for something in this issue.

_____ 9. Prepared an agenda item for addressing this issue.

_____ 10. Wrote a note to self on the original item.

_____ 11. Wrote a note to self on paper other than the original item.

_____ 12. Wrote a note to someone else on the original item.

_____ 13. Wrote a note to someone else on paper other than the original item.

INTERPERSONAL SENSITIVITY and EXERCISING JUDGMENT

_____ 14. Wrote a memo to the director.

ORGANIZING AND PLANNING

_____ 15. Prepared an e-mail or a fax message to the director.

Documentation and Rating Forms—Office Deskwork (continued)

Delegation

If an item is delegated to another person, note the person's position (e.g., secretary, teacher), and then comment on each of the four bullets that follow. A Yes or No is usually sufficient.

Name and position of delegatee: _____   **Comments**

* The information gathering task and authority to do so
  is appropriate for the person and job of the delegatee.   _____

* The item is delegated with control
  (e.g., set deadline for completion).   _____

* The item is delegated with follow-up
  (e.g., specific steps for checking on completion or success).   _____

* Whether or not the instructions given are specific and clear.   _____

Rating Performance

The symbols below are used to represent demonstrated levels of skill. After studying the completed documentation form, with particular attention to the skill areas and frequency of checked performance indicators, rate each performance area in the Performance Ratings below. In some instances several of the performance indicators may be attributed to more than one skill area.

When you have completed rating the individual deskwork items, complete the Overall Performance Summary on the last page of this chapter.

Symbols	Interpretations
⊕	Very high skill shown
+	More than moderate skill
(+)	Moderate skill shown
(−)	Less than moderate skill
−	Little skill shown
⊖	Very little skill shown

Performance Summary Ratings—DW# Item #8

Performance Areas	Rating Symbols
Analyzing Problems Performance Rating: ____	____
Exercising Judgment Performance Rating: ____	____
Organizing and Planning Performance Ratings: ____, ____, ____	____
Making Decisions Performance Rating: ____	____
Interpersonal Sensitivity Performance Rating: ____	____
Written Communication (*Overall written responses to these items*)	____

Note: *Extreme ratings of ⊕ or ⊖ are seldom appropriate.*

Documentation and Rating Forms—Office Deskwork (continued)

Form DW #9   Handling of Deskwork Item #9 (Figure 4.9)

ANONYMOUS NOTE

Review the paragraphs beneath the Deskwork Instructions and Preparing Your Responses headings earlier in this chapter before documenting your partner's work on this form. Mark an item with a check (✓) if the applicable performance indicator is in evidence, with a dot (•) if it is not. Give examples where you can.

Task Completion

ORGANIZING AND PLANNING and MAKING DECISIONS

_____ 1. Handled the anonymous note as a high-priority item.
If not, mark with a dot and go on to the next deskwork item.

_____ 2. Took some action.

ANALYZING PROBLEMS

_____ 3. Sought more information about locker searches.

_____ 4. Sought more information on alleged student with a gun.

_____ 5. Informed staff of possible student with a gun.

_____ 6. Sought policy information on weapons in school buildings.

_____ 7. Tied item to the small business association's issue. (Deskwork Item #12)

ORGANIZING AND PLANNING

_____ 8. Prepared a plan for addressing the locker search issue.

EXPRESSING PROFESSIONAL VALUES

_____ 9. Stated a strong value about searches.

_____ 10. Stated a strong value about anonymous notes.

_____ 11. Stated a strong value about follow-up actions.

ORGANIZING AND PLANNING

_____ 12. Prepared a to-do list for something in this issue.

_____ 13. Made a calendar entry for something in this issue.

_____ 14. Prepared an agenda item for addressing this issue.

_____ 15. Wrote a note to self on the original item.

_____ 16. Wrote a note to self on paper other than the original item.

_____ 17. Wrote a note to someone else on the original item.

_____ 18. Wrote a note to someone else on paper other than the original item.

INTERPERSONAL SENSITIVITY and EXERCISING JUDGMENT

_____ 19. Wrote a memo or e-mail to someone within the organization concerning the issue.

_____ 20. Wrote a letter to someone outside the organization concerning this issue.

_____ 21. Showed this is a priority issue.

_____ 22. Delayed contacting the student.

Documentation and Rating Forms—Office Deskwork (continued)

ORGANIZING AND PLANNING and INTERPERSONAL SENSITIVITY

_____ 23. Prepared for a phone call to someone who needs to know.

Delegation

If an item is delegated to another person, note the person's position (e.g., secretary, teacher), and then comment on each of the four bullets that follow. A Yes or No is usually sufficient.

Name and position of delegatee: _____   **Comments**

- The information gathering task and authority to do so
  is appropriate for the person and job of the delegatee.   _____

- The item is delegated with control
  (e.g., set deadline for completion).   _____

- The item is delegated with follow-up
  (e.g., specific steps for checking on completion or success).   _____

- The instructions given are specific and clear.   _____

Rating Performance

The symbols below are used to represent demonstrated levels of skill. After studying the completed documentation form, with particular attention to the skill areas and frequency of checked performance indicators, rate each performance area in the Performance Ratings below. In some instances several of the performance indicators may be attributed to more than one skill area.

When you have completed rating the individual deskwork items, complete the Overall Performance Summary on the last page of this section.

Symbols	Interpretations
⊕	Very high skill shown
+	More than moderate skill
(+)	Moderate skill shown
(−)	Less than moderate skill
−	Little skill shown
⊖	Very little skill shown

Performance Summary Ratings—DW# Item #9

Performance Areas	Rating Symbols
Analyzing Problems Performance Rating: _____	_____
Exercising Judgment Performance Rating: _____	_____
Organizing and Planning Performance Ratings: _____, _____, _____, _____	_____
Making Decisions Performance Rating: _____	_____
Interpersonal Sensitivity Performance Rating: _____	_____
Written Communication (*Overall written responses to these items*)	_____
Expressing Professional Values Performance Rating: _____	_____

Note: *Extreme ratings of ⊕ or ⊖ are seldom appropriate.*

Documentation and Rating Forms—Office Deskwork (continued)

Form DW #10   Handling of Deskwork Item #10 (Figure 4.10)

HEAD CUSTODIAN

Review the paragraphs beneath the Deskwork Instructions and Preparing Your Responses headings earlier in this chapter before documenting your partner's work on this form. Mark an item with a check (✓) if the applicable performance indicator is in evidence, with a dot (•) if it is not. Give examples where you can.

Task Completion

ORGANIZING AND PLANNING and MAKING DECISIONS

_____ 1. Handled the note from the head custodian as a high-priority item. If not, mark with a dot and go on to the next deskwork item.

_____ 2. Took some action.

ANALYZING PROBLEMS

_____ 3. Sought more information about the girls' locker room.

_____ 4. Sought information on prior locker room problems.

_____ 5. Sought information on past vandalism problems.

INTERPERSONAL SENSITIVITY and DELEGATING EFFECTIVELY

_____ 6. Contacted the head custodian regarding vandalism.

_____ 7. Had someone else contact head custodian about vandalism.

_____ 8. Directly acknowledged head custodian's concerns.

_____ 9. Shared information with the head custodian regarding vandalism.

_____ 10. Used tact when contacting the custodian.

EXPRESSING PROFESSIONAL VALUES

_____ 11. Stated a strong personal value about vandalism.

_____ 12. Stated a strong value about health of students.

_____ 13. Stated a strong value about safety of students.

_____ 14. Stated a strong value about prompt correction of problems.

ORGANIZING AND PLANNING

_____ 15. Prepared a to-do list for something in this issue.

_____ 16. Made a calendar entry for something in this issue.

_____ 17. Prepared an agenda item for addressing this issue.

_____ 18. Wrote a note to self on the original item.

_____ 19. Wrote a note to self on paper other than the original.

_____ 20. Wrote a note to someone else on the original item.

_____ 21. Wrote a note to someone else on paper other than the original item.

Documentation and Rating Forms—Office Deskwork (continued)

INTERPERSONAL SENSITIVITY and EXERCISING JUDGMENT

_____ 22. Wrote a memo or e-mail to the head custodian.

_____ 23. Wrote a letter to the head custodian.

ORGANIZING AND PLANNING and INTERPERSONAL SENSITIVITY

_____ 24. Prepared for a call to the head custodian.

_____ 25. Prepared for a meeting with the head custodian.

EXERCISING JUDGMENT

_____ 26. Showed this is a priority issue.

_____ 27. Agreed to fix the locker room problem.

Delegation

If an item is delegated to another person, note the person's position (e.g., secretary, teacher), and then comment on each of the four bullets that follow. A Yes or No is usually sufficient.

Name and position of delegatee: _____   **Comments**

- The information gathering task and authority to do so   _____
  is appropriate for the person and job of the delegatee.

- The item is delegated with control   _____
  (e.g., set deadline for completion).

- The item is delegated with follow-up   _____
  (e.g., specific steps for checking on completion or success).

- The instructions given are specific and clear.   _____

Documentation and Rating Forms—Office Deskwork (continued)

Rating Performance

The symbols below are used to represent demonstrated levels of skill. After studying the completed documentation form, with particular attention to the skill areas and frequency of checked performance indicators, rate each performance area in the Performance Ratings below. In some instances several of the performance indicators may be attributed to more than one skill area.

When you have completed rating the individual deskwork items, complete the Overall Performance Summary on the last page of this chapter.

Symbols **Interpretations**

⊕ Very high skill shown
+ More than moderate skill
(+) Moderate skill shown
(−) Less than moderate skill
− Little skill shown
⊖ Very little skill shown

Performance Summary Ratings—DW# Item #10

Performance Areas	Rating Symbols
Analyzing Problems Performance Rating: ____	____
Exercising Judgment Performance Ratings: ____, ____	____
Organizing and Planning Performance Ratings: ____, ____, ____	____
Making Decisions Performance Rating: ____	____
Delegating Effectively Performance Rating: ____	____
Interpersonal Sensitivity Performance Ratings: ____, ____, ____	____
Written Communication (*Overall written responses to these items*)	____
Expressing Professional Values Performance Rating: ____	____

Note: *Extreme ratings of ⊕ or ⊖ are seldom appropriate.*

Documentation and Rating Forms—Office Deskwork (continued)

Form DW #11   Handling of Deskwork Item #11 (Figure 4.11)

CONCERNED PARENT

Review the paragraphs beneath the Deskwork Instructions and Preparing Your Responses headings earlier in this chapter before documenting your partner's work on this form. Mark an item with a check (✓) if the applicable performance indicator is in evidence, with a dot (●) if it is not. Give examples where you can.

Task Completion

ORGANIZING AND PLANNING and MAKING DECISIONS

_____   1. Handled the Spanish-speaking parent's note as a high-priority item. If not, mark with a dot and go on to the next deskwork item.

_____   2. Took some action.

ANALYZING PROBLEMS

_____   3. Sought more information on the fairness of the tank top policy.

_____   4. Sought information from the assistant principal about suspensions for dress code violations.

_____   5. Sought information on the son of the concerned parent.

_____   6. Tied the item to the pastor's letter. (Deskwork Item #06)

ORGANIZING AND PLANNING

_____   7. Prepared a plan for responding to the parent.

INTERPERSONAL SENSITIVITY and DELEGATING EFFECTIVELY

_____   8. Contacted the concerned parent regarding the dress code.

_____   9. Had someone else contact the parent about the dress code.
Note:

_____   10. Directly acknowledged the parent's concerns.

_____   11. Shared information with the parent about the dress code fairness.

_____   12. Used tact when contacting the parent.

EXPRESSING PROFESSIONAL VALUES

_____   13. Stated a strong personal value about dress code suspensions.

_____   14. Stated a strong value about the fairness of dress code enforcement.

_____   15. Stated a strong value about the importance of dress codes.

_____   16. Stated a strong value about the student's behavior.

_____   17. Stated a strong value about concerned parent(s).

ORGANIZING AND PLANNING

_____   18. Prepared a to-do list for something in this issue.

_____   19. Made a calendar entry for something in this issue.

_____   20. Prepared an agenda item for addressing this issue.

_____   21. Wrote a note to self on the original item.

Documentation and Rating Forms—Office Deskwork (continued)

ORGANIZING AND PLANNING (continued)

_____ 22. Wrote a note to self on paper other than the original.

_____ 23. Wrote a note to someone else on the original item.

_____ 24. Wrote a note to someone else on paper other than on the original item.

INTERPERSONAL SENSITIVITY and EXERCISING JUDGMENT

_____ 25. Wrote a memo or e-mail to the concerned parent.

_____ 26. Wrote a letter to the concerned parent.

ORGANIZING AND PLANNING and INTERPERSONAL SENSITIVITY

_____ 27. Prepared for a call to the concerned parent.

_____ 28. Prepared for a meeting with the concerned parent.

ANALYZING PROBLEMS and INTERPERSONAL SENSITIVITY

_____ 29. Sought translation of the parent's letter.

Delegation

If an item is delegated to another person, note the person's position (e.g., secretary, teacher), and then comment on each of the four bullets that follow. A Yes or No is usually sufficient.

Name and position of delegatee: _____   **Comments**

- The information gathering task and authority to do so   _____
  is appropriate for the person and job of the delegatee.

- The item is delegated with control   _____
  (e.g., set deadline for completion).

- The item is delegated with follow-up   _____
  (e.g., specific steps for checking on completion or success).

- The instructions given are specific and clear.   _____

Documentation and Rating Forms—Office Deskwork (continued)

Rating Performance

The symbols below are used to represent demonstrated levels of skill. After studying the completed documentation form, with particular attention to the skill areas and frequency of checked performance indicators, rate each performance area in the Performance Ratings below. In some instances several of the performance indicators may be attributed to more than one skill area.

When you have completed rating the individual deskwork items, complete the Overall Performance Summary on the last page of this chapter.

Symbols	Interpretations
⊕	Very high skill shown
+	More than moderate skill
(+)	Moderate skill shown
(−)	Less than moderate skill
−	Little skill shown
⊖	Very little skill shown

Performance Summary Ratings—DW# Item #11

Performance Areas — **Rating Symbols**

Analyzing Problems
Performance Ratings: ____, ____   ____

Exercising Judgment
Performance Rating: ____   ____

Organizing and Planning
Performance Ratings: ____, ____, ____, ____, ____   ____

Making Decisions
Performance Rating: ____   ____

Delegating Effectively
Performance Rating: ____   ____

Interpersonal Sensitivity
Performance Ratings: ____, ____, ____, ____   ____

Written Communication
(Overall written responses to these items)   ____

Expressing Professional Values
Performance Rating: ____   ____

Note: *Extreme ratings of ⊕ or ⊖ are seldom appropriate.*

Documentation and Rating Forms—Office Deskwork (continued)

Form DW #12   Handling of Deskwork Item #12 (Figure 4.12)

HEAD CUSTODIAN

Review the paragraphs beneath the Deskwork Instructions and Preparing Your Responses headings earlier in this chapter before documenting your partner's work on this form. Mark an item with a check (✓) if the applicable performance indicator is in evidence, with a dot (•) if it is not. Give examples where you can.

Task Completion

ORGANIZING AND PLANNING and MAKING DECISIONS

_____ 1. Handled the Small Business Association letter as a high-priority item. If not, mark with a dot and go on to the next deskwork item.

_____ 2. Took some action.

ANALYZING PROBLEMS

_____ 3. Sought more information.

_____ 4. Sought information about policy on locker searches.

_____ 5. Sought information on the Small Business Association representative.

_____ 6. Sought information on history of shoplifting in the neighborhood.

_____ 7. Sought information on those accused of shoplifting.

_____ 8. Tied the item to anonymous student's note. (Deskwork Item #9)

ORGANIZING AND PLANNING

_____ 9. Prepared a plan for handling the shoplifting situation.

INTERPERSONAL SENSITIVITY and DELEGATING EFFECTIVELY

_____ 10. Contacted the Small Business Association about shoplifting.

_____ 11. Had someone else contact the Small Business Association.

_____ 12. Directly acknowledged the Small Business Association's concerns.

_____ 13. Shared information with the Small Business Association about shoplifting.

_____ 14. Used tact when contacting the Small Business Association.

ORGANIZING AND PLANNING

_____ 15. Prepared a to-do list for something in this issue.

_____ 16. Made a calendar entry for something in this issue.

_____ 17. Prepared an agenda item for addressing this issue.

_____ 18. Wrote a note to self on the original item.

_____ 19. Wrote a not to self on paper other than the original.

_____ 20. Wrote a note to someone else on the original item.

_____ 21. Wrote a note to someone else on paper other than the original item.

Documentation and Rating Forms—Office Deskwork (continued)

INTERPERSONAL SENSITIVITY and EXERCISING JUDGMENT

_____ 22. Wrote a memo or e-mail to the Small Business Association.

_____ 23. Wrote a letter to the Small Business Association.

ORGANIZING AND PLANNING and INTERPERSONAL SENSITIVITY

_____ 24. Prepared for a phone call to the Small Business Association.

_____ 25. Prepared for a meeting with the Small Business Association.

EXERCISING JUDGMENT

_____ 26. Called in the students named by the Small Business Association.

_____ 27. Agreed to let Small Business Association come to school to investigate situation.

_____ 28. Requested, from the Small Business Association, more time to investigate.

EXPRESSING PROFESSIONAL VALUES

_____ 29. Stated that shoplifting and/or having weapons in school is not good.

Delegation

If an item is delegated to another person, note the person's position (e.g., secretary, teacher), and then comment on each of the four bullets that follow. A Yes or No is usually sufficient.

Name and position of delegatee: _____   **Comments**

- The information gathering task and authority to do so
  is appropriate for the person and job of the delegatee.   _____

- The item is delegated with control
  (e.g., set deadline for completion).   _____

- The item is delegated with follow-up
  (e.g., specific steps for checking on completion or success).   _____

- The instructions given are specific and clear.   _____

Documentation and Rating Forms—Office Deskwork (continued)

Rating Performance

The symbols below are used to represent demonstrated levels of skill. After studying the completed documentation form, with particular attention to the skill areas and frequency of checked performance indicators, rate each performance area in the Performance Ratings below. In some instances several of the performance indicators may be attributed to more than one skill area.

When you have completed rating the individual deskwork items, complete the Overall Performance Summary on the last page of this chapter.

Symbols	Interpretations
⊕	Very high skill shown
+	More than moderate skill
(+)	Moderate skill shown
(−)	Less than moderate skill
−	Little skill shown
⊖	Very little skill shown

Performance Summary Ratings—DW# Item #12

Performance Areas	Rating Symbols
Analyzing Problems Performance Rating: ____	____
Exercising Judgment Performance Ratings: ____, ____	____
Organizing and Planning Performance Ratings: ____, ____, ____, ____	____
Making Decisions Performance Rating: ____	____
Delegating Effectively Performance Rating: ____	____
Interpersonal Sensitivity Performance Ratings: ____, ____, ____	____
Written Communication (*Overall written responses to these items*)	____
Expressing Professional Values Performance Rating: ____	____

Note: *Extreme ratings of ⊕ or ⊖ are seldom appropriate.*

Documentation and Rating Forms—Office Deskwork (continued)

Form DW #13   Handling of Deskwork Item #13 (Figure 4.13)

ENGLISH TEACHER
Review the paragraphs beneath the Deskwork Instructions and Preparing Your Responses headings earlier in this chapter before documenting your partner's work on this form. Mark an item with a check (✓) if the applicable performance indicator is in evidence, with a dot (•) if it is not. Give examples where you can.

Task Completion

ORGANIZING AND PLANNING and MAKING DECISIONS

_____ 1. Handled the English teacher's letter as a high-priority item.
If not, mark with a dot and go on to the next item.

_____ 2. Took some action.

ANALYZING PROBLEMS

_____ 3. Sought more information.

_____ 4. Sought information on the English teacher.

_____ 5. Sought information on how many teachers want to volunteer for extracurricular duties.

INTERPERSONAL SENSITIVITY and DELEGATING EFFECTIVELY

_____ 6. Contacted the teacher about extracurricular duties.

_____ 7. Had someone else contact the teacher.

_____ 8. Directly acknowledged the teacher's concerns.

_____ 9. Shared plans with the teacher about afterschool duties.

_____ 10. Used tact when contacting the teacher.

EXPRESSING PROFESSIONAL VALUES

_____ 11. Stated a strong value about teachers helping after school.

_____ 12. Stated a strong value about volunteerism among teachers.

_____ 13. Stated a strong value about peer pressures.

ORGANIZING AND PLANNING

_____ 14. Prepared a to-do list for something in this issue.

_____ 15. Made a calendar entry for something in this issue

_____ 16. Prepared an agenda item for addressing this issue.

_____ 17. Wrote a note to self on the original item.

_____ 18. Wrote a note to self on paper other than the original.

_____ 19. Wrote a note to someone else on the original item.

_____ 20. Wrote a note to someone else on paper other than the original item.

INTERPERSONAL SENSITIVITY and EXERCISING JUDGMENT

_____ 21. Wrote a memo or e-mail to the English teacher.

Documentation and Rating Forms—Office Deskwork (continued)

ORGANIZING AND PLANNING and INTERPERSONAL SENSITIVITY

_____ 22. Prepared for a meeting with the English teacher.

EXERCISING JUDGMENT

_____ 23. Agreed to let the teacher work with students after school.

Delegation

If an item is delegated to another person, note the person's position (e.g., secretary, teacher), and then comment on each of the four bullets that follow. A Yes or No is usually sufficient.

Name and position of delegatee: _____   **Comments**

- The information gathering task and authority to do so
  is appropriate for the person and job of the delegatee.   _____

- The item is delegated with control
  (e.g., set deadline for completion).   _____

- The item is delegated with follow-up
  (e.g., specific steps for checking on completion or success).   _____

- The instructions given are specific and clear.   _____

Documentation and Rating Forms—Office Deskwork (continued)

Rating Performance
The symbols below are used to represent demonstrated levels of skill. After studying the completed documentation form, with particular attention to the skill areas and frequency of checked performance indicators, rate each performance area in the Performance Ratings below. In some instances several of the performance indicators may be attributed to more than one skill area.

When you have completed rating the individual deskwork items, complete the Overall Performance Summary on the last page of this chapter.

Symbols	Interpretations
⊕	Very high skill shown
+	More than moderate skill
(+)	Moderate skill shown
(–)	Less than moderate skill
–	Little skill shown
⊖	Very little skill shown

Performance Summary Ratings—DW# Item #13

Performance Areas	Rating Symbols
Analyzing Problems Performance Ratings: ____ , ____	_____
Exercising Judgment Performance Ratings: ____ , ____	_____
Organizing and Planning Performance Ratings: ____ , ____	_____
Making Decisions Performance Rating: ____	_____
Delegating Effectively Performance Rating: ____	_____
Interpersonal Sensitivity Performance Ratings: ____ , ____ , ____	_____
Written Communication *(Overall written responses to these items)*	_____
Expressing Professional Values Performance Rating: ____	_____

Note: *Extreme ratings of ⊕ or ⊖ are seldom appropriate.*

Documentation and Rating Forms—Office Deskwork (continued)

Unique Performance

If a participant takes some action of major importance that is not on a list of performance indicators, write it down below with the related deskwork item number (e.g., DW #2).

Item #	Action or Performance
_____	_____
_____	_____
_____	_____

Written Communication Notes

When you have completed documenting all items, consider the overall clarity of writing, overall spelling, and overall grammar and give it a rating. Examine the rating interpretations below.

	Rating	Examples/Justification
Clarity	_____	_____
Spelling	_____	_____
Grammar	_____	_____

Note: *Extreme ratings of ⊕ or ⊖ are seldom appropriate.*

Key to Ratings

⊕	Very high skill shown [0 errors]
+	More than moderate skill [0 errors]
(+)	Moderate skill shown [1 error]
(−)	Less than moderate skill [2 errors]
−	Little skill shown [3 errors]
⊖	Very little skill shown [4+ errors]

Important: If a rating is higher or lower than Moderate (+), give to justify the rating. Moderate (+) does not require examples or justification.

Documentation and Rating Forms—Office Deskwork (continued)

Rating Overall Office Deskwork Performance

Beneath each of the eight skill areas listed in the box below, you will find blank lines on which to copy the rating symbols you assigned to each item, After copying these rating symbols, consider their values and assign an overall rating symbol for each skill area. When rating overall written communication, be sure to factor in ratings given for clarity, spelling, and grammar.

Symbols	Interpretations
⊕	Very high skill shown
+	More than moderate skill
(+)	Moderate skill shown
(−)	Less than moderate skill
−	Little skill shown
⊖	Very little skill shown

Overall Performance Summary—
Office Deskwork Summary Ratings From Forms DW#1–DW#13

Performance Areas	Rating Symbols
Analyzing Problems Performance Ratings: ___, ___, ___, ___, ___, ___, ___, ___, ___, ___, ___, ___, ___	___
Exercising Judgment Performance Ratings: ___, ___, ___, ___, ___, ___, ___, ___, ___, ___, ___, ___, ___	___
Organizing and Planning Performance Ratings: ___, ___, ___, ___, ___, ___, ___, ___, ___, ___, ___, ___, ___	___
Making Decisions Performance Ratings: ___, ___, ___, ___, ___, ___, ___, ___, ___, ___, ___, ___, ___	___
Delegating Effectively Performance Ratings: ___, ___, ___, ___, ___, ___, ___, ___, ___, ___, ___, ___, ___	___
Interpersonal Sensitivity Performance Ratings: ___, ___, ___, ___, ___, ___, ___, ___, ___, ___, ___, ___, ___	___
Written Communication Performance Ratings: ___, ___, ___, ___, ___, ___, ___, ___, ___, ___, ___, ___, ___ *(Overall written response throughout deskwork activity)*	___
Expressing Professional Values Performance Ratings: , ___, ___, ___, ___, ___, ___, ___, ___, ___, ___, ___, ___	___

Note: *Extreme ratings of ⊕ or ⊖ are seldom appropriate.*

The information summarized here will be used again in Chapter 8 when you complete an overall performance rating form.

REFLECTIVE PRACTICE

You have now had the opportunity to compare your handling of everyday deskwork problems with the way that your partner handled the same deskwork problems. In addition, in documenting your partner's artifacts, you have noted what the committee of experienced administrators and university faculty who helped construct this activity deemed important for consideration. There are undoubtedly many differences of opinion.

Go through each of your scoring sheets again and highlight any of your choices that differ from others' choices. For each item highlighted, ask yourself the bulleted questions that follow this paragraph. On a clean piece of paper record your answers. When you have completed the task, share your responses with your partner. Discuss the differences in your responses; do not attempt to persuade your partner to your point of view. There is more than enough education theory and research to support almost any point of view, and this activity is not intended to create arguments. The purpose of this reflective task is for you to clarify for yourself what your beliefs are and to recognize how they influence your decisions. In what ways do your responses differ from those of your partner?

- Why do you think the responses are different? Do you each have a different interpretation of the information presented in the case study? Do you have previous experiences with—and assumptions about—the correspondents (e.g., teachers unions, local merchants, local churches, non-English speakers) and their appropriate role in local schools?

- Which of your decisions were influenced by what you believe to be the purpose of education?

- Which of your decisions were influenced by your beliefs about the roles of teachers, administrators, counselors, students, parents, community, government, and other regulatory agencies? As a principal, you will often have to consider many of your beliefs in responding to a single problem. For example, the issue of whether teachers will perform extracurricular duties goes directly to your beliefs about teachers unions, about the importance or unimportance of extracurricular activities, about "who's the boss here," and about your leadership style.

- What has the deskwork activity revealed to you about your skills in analyzing problems, exercising judgment, organizing and planning, making decisions, delegating effectively, interpersonal sensitivity, expressing professional values, and written communication?

- If your were to repeat the activity, would you make any choices differently? Why or why not?

In this chapter, you were asked to complete a typical morning's task of wading through the memos on your desk, prioritizing them by urgency and importance, and making decisions on how to handle each. In Chapter 5, you will be introduced to making an oral presentation—a frequent requirement for principals.

5

Making Oral Presentations

OVERVIEW

In this chapter you will engage in a powerful activity consisting of a video-taped oral presentation to a hypothetical school board. The activity provides video as well as paper and pencil artifacts. You will use the artifacts for analyzing and documenting your partner's oral presentation skills as well as other skill areas needed for preparing and making oral presentations. Links to key performance aspects of the Interstate School Leaders Licensure Consortium's (ISLLC) standards are provided in Resources (Form R.16).

HOW DO YOU SEE YOURSELF?

Can you see yourself as others see you? With the help of videotape, the activity in this chapter will enable you to see yourself from a new perspective—and help you see with amazing clarity some areas where you can strengthen your oral presentation skills. Watching yourself make a presentation, even to a hypothetical situation, is more powerful than you might suppose. It can also be embarrassing! Suddenly, those little mannerisms that you weren't really aware of become painfully obvious: running your hand distractedly through your hair, rubbing your chin, rapid blinking, frequent pauses filled with "umms" or "y'knows." So you not only have to think about what you are presenting but also the manner—and mannerisms—of your presentation.

The artifacts you will create by completing this activity will be on videotape as well as on paper. As always, these artifacts will provide the substance for performance analysis, reflection, and documentation.

STEPS FOR DEVELOPMENT

The tasks you are to complete for the oral presentation consist of the following:

1. Read about the activity and its performance areas.

2. Study the oral presentation setup, which includes a video camera, a flip chart, felt pens, blank videotapes, and a stand for holding your presentation notes. You and your partner should assist each other in the setup and operation of the camera. Prepare to videotape your presentations.

3. Read Background and Introduction.

4. Have available two pencils or pens of different colors for making notes.

5. You and your partner complete the activity and videotaped oral presentations. Read about the situation and begin.

6. Complete the reflection activity.

7. Exchange artifacts and photocopies of blank documentation and rating forms supplied in this chapter.

8. Study the instructions for completing each documentation and rating form.

9. Document your partner's paper and pencil and videotape artifacts.

10. Return the completed documentation forms to your partner.

11. After completing and discussing documentation results, rate your performance in this activity. Use the rating symbols introduced earlier.

ABOUT THE ORAL PRESENTATION

The board presentation is used for analyzing your presentation skills. The emphasis in this activity is not so much on your ability to uncover factual information as it is on using the information to make a formal videotaped presentation to the hypothetical school board. Based on the information you present, you have an opportunity to make your recommendation and vision for the school.

You will assume the role of a principal new to a secondary school. The school board expects you to gather as much information as you can about the needs for renovating and rejuvenating a historically prominent school. You are to present your views to them, particularly what should be done. Because you don't know much about the school and community, your initial task will be to draft questions you would like to have answers for so you can make a good presentation.

The second task will be to study an information sheet to find all the information that is currently available for getting answers to your prepared questions. The information provided includes data on enrollment, curriculum, staff, the condition of the facilities, and so on.

After you have studied the information, you will see how many answers to your prepared questions are on the information sheet. Your report to the board will cover your findings and recommendations. It also gives you an opportunity to present your vision for the school.

The last task is to actually make a videotape of your presentation. Afterward, you will have an opportunity to reflect on your presentation—particularly the things you did well and the things you might do differently if you could do the activity again. If you choose, you will actually be able to make your presentation a second time.

Oral Presentation Performance Areas

The board presentation activity gives you the opportunity to demonstrate a range of skills in making oral presentations:

- Analyzing Problems
- Exercising Judgment
- Organizing and Planning
- Making Decisions
- Managing Stress
- Oral Communication
- Oral Presentation
- Expressing Professional Values

Standards, Performance Areas, and Aspects

As in the previous chapter, the answers to questions regarding ISLLC performance aspects and the skills needed to be successful in meeting the standards are found in the linkages made in this book. You will find the performance aspects found in the standards relating to each of the performance areas in the school board presentation activity.

STANDARD 1
Developing, articulating, implementing, and stewarding a shared vision of learning
Analyzing Problems
    7 ISLLC performance aspects related to analyzing problems
Exercising Judgment
    No ISLLC-related performance aspects
Organizing and Planning
    13 ISLLC performance aspects related to organizing and planning
Making Decisions
    No ISLLC-related performance aspects
Professional Motivation
    5 ISLLC performance aspects related to professional motivation

ISLLC STANDARDS (Continued)

Expressing Professional Values
> 8 ISLLC performance aspects related to professional values

Managing Stress
> No ISLLC-related performance aspects

Oral Presentation
> 2 ISLLC performance aspects related to oral presentation

Oral Communication
> 3 ISLLC performance aspects related to oral communication

STANDARD 2
Advocating, nurturing, and sustaining a school culture and effective instructional program conducive to student learning and staff professional growth

Analyzing Problems
> 6 ISLLC performance aspects related to analyzing problems

Exercising Judgment
> 1 ISLLC performance aspect related to exercising judgment

Organizing and Planning
> 10 ISLLC performance aspects related to organizing and planning

Making Decisions
> No ISLLC-related performance aspects

Professional Motivation
> 4 ISLLC performance aspects related to professional motivation

Expressing Professional Values
> 10 ISLLC performance aspects related to professional values

Managing Stress
> No ISLLC-related performance aspects

Oral Presentation
> No ISLLC-related performance aspects

Oral Communication
> No ISLLC-related performance aspects

STANDARD 3
Ensuring management of the organization, operations, and resources for a safe, efficient, and effective learning environment

Analyzing Problems
> 10 ISLLC performance aspects related to analyzing problems

Making Decisions
> 3 ISLLC performance aspects related to making decisions

Professional Motivation
> No ISLLC-related performance aspects

Expressing Professional Values
> 2 ISLLC performance aspects related to professional values

Managing Stress
> No ISLLC-related performance aspects

Oral Presentation
> 1 ISLLC performance aspect related to oral presentation

Oral Communication
> 4 ISLLC performance aspects related to oral communication

STANDARD 4
Collaborating with families and community members, responding to diverse community interests and needs, and mobilizing community resources

Analyzing Problems
> 6 ISLLC performance aspects related to analyzing problems

Exercising Judgment
> 5 ISLLC performance aspects related to exercising judgment

ISLLC STANDARDS (Continued)

Organizing and Planning
    11 ISLLC performance aspects related to organizing and planning
Making Decisions
No ISLLC-related performance aspects
Interpersonal Sensitivity
    11 ISLLC performance aspects related to interpersonal sensitivity
Professional Motivation
    8 ISLLC performance aspects related to professional motivation
Expressing Professional Values
    11 ISLLC performance aspects related to professional values
Oral Communication
    4 ISLLC performance aspects related to oral communication

STANDARD 5
Promoting success of all students through integrity, fairness, and an ethical manner

Analyzing Problems
    No ISLLC-related performance aspects
Exercising Judgment
    10 ISLLC performance aspects related to exercising judgment
Organizing and Planning
    No ISLLC-related performance aspects
Making Decisions
    No ISLLC-related performance aspects
Professional Motivation
    No ISLLC-related performance aspects
Managing Stress
    No ISLLC-related performance aspects
Oral Presentation
    No ISLLC-related performance aspects
Oral Communication
    No ISLLC-related performance aspects

STANDARD 6
Promoting the success of all students by understanding, responding to, and influencing the larger political, social, economic, legal, and cultural context

Analyzing Problems
    7 ISLLC performance aspects related to analyzing problems
Exercising Judgment
    4 ISLLC performance aspects related to exercising judgment
Organizing and Planning
    2 ISLLC performance aspects related to organizing and planning
Making Decisions
    No ISLLC-related performance aspects
Expressing Professional Values
    6 ISLLC performance aspects related to professional values
Oral Presentation
    2 ISLLC performance aspects related to oral presentation
Oral Communication
    4 ISLLC performance aspects related to oral communication

---

Note: Linkages were made by the principal author and verified by education experts.
SOURCE: Adapted from Council of Chief State School Officers (1996).

Oral Presentation Setup

You may now begin the board presentation that follows. Consult Figure 5.1 for the setup for an oral presentation. Remember, you will have an opportunity to repeat your presentation if you feel it might be better a second time. It will probably take you an hour to complete all parts of the activity including the optional repetition of your presentation. When your partner is ready to document your school board presentation artifacts, you may ask your partner to document either your first or your second presentation. You will probably choose what you think is your better performance.

Figure 5.1 Setup for Oral Presentation

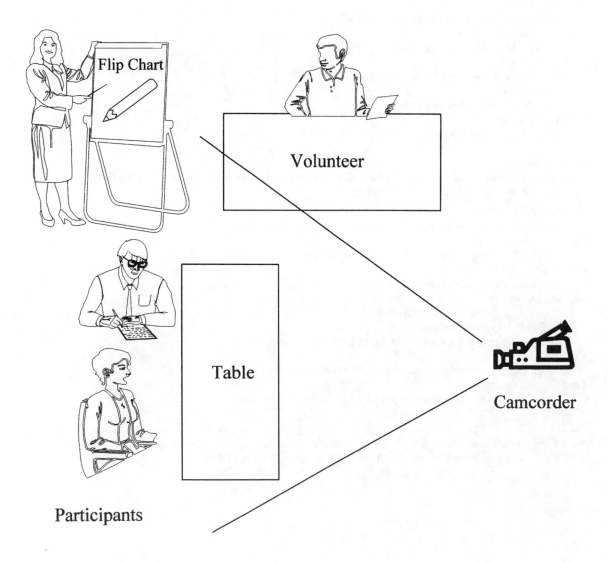

NORMAL SCHOOL BOARD PRESENTATION

Background and Instructions

During the questioning, analyzing, and oral presentation activity, you will have an opportunity to express your personal values and vision for the school. The activity requires approximately 1 hour including reflection and an opportunity to repeat your oral presentation to the school board if you desire. As in other activities in this book, you and your partner will need to help each other keep track of time.

During the time allotted, you are to read, study, and draw conclusions about the school and the community. To complete the stages of this simulation, it is important that you become as familiar as possible with the background material.

We know that you will want more information than we have provided, and we know, also, that in a real situation, additional information would probably be available to you from some other source. But for the purposes of this activity, there is no further information for you to use. One thing about being an administrator is that we seldom have all the information we would like to have before making decisions. Thus the challenge is to make as much sense as possible using the information that is available.

You will need to structure the entire time yourself so that you can read the material, study it, and complete all stages within the time provided. When you're ready, begin by reading the information that follows.

This exercise will provide you with information about your current ability to do the following:

- Analyze problem situations
- Prepare questions and research answers to your questions
- Prepare recommendations based on all information gained from your research
- Make a formal oral presentation on information gained
- Complete a performance reflection form
- Document your partner's performance in this activity
- Rate your own performance

After you finish reading this introduction, you are to read a short description of a problem situation below. In this situation, you will play the role of the newly appointed principal of Normal School. You will have to analyze the situation in detail, make judgments about the information you receive, organize your thoughts, and formally present your findings and recommendations to the board.

After you prepare questions covering the information you want to have for your report, you will read the information provided here, which is all that is available at this time. Now let's go over the schedule:

- You have 10 minutes to read about the situation and prepare questions.
- You will then have 10 minutes to study the information and make notes.
- After that, you will have 10 minutes to review your notes and prepare to present your report.
- Then you will have up to 10 minutes to make a formal presentation to the school board. You or your partner will need to set up the video camera to videotape your presentation.

After the camera and flip chart with felt pens, and so on, are in place, be sure you have two different colored pencils or pens. Changing colors simplifies the documentation task of differentiating between your partner's preparation of questions and the answers provided in the information section.

Jot down the beginning and ending time for this part of the simulation. It should take approximately 40 minutes and is followed by reflection for 5 minutes.

After reflecting, if you have time, you may take 5 minutes to plan a second presentation. Repeat the presentation with any changes you wish to make. This should take another 10 minutes, but it will be time well spent. When you're ready, read the situation below.

The Situation

You are the new principal of Normal School. The school board has been studying the feasibility of extensive curriculum rejuvenation and facilities renovation and enlargement to accommodate an expected increase in enrollment. The board will begin detailed planning after the meeting with you today. Because of their move to site-based management, they have requested that you be at their planning meeting. You are to present your views on what is needed structurally and programmatically to enable Normal School to offer a quality, up-to-date program and to make it a state-of-the-art flagship school again. Due to their schedules, neither the former principal, other principals, nor central office staff are available to assist with your preparation.

You are to present your findings and recommendations in a formal oral presentation to the full school board. Only the information uncovered by you in this activity is considered valid to use in your report.

Prepare Presentation

Take 10 minutes to analyze the problem situation and prepare questions about the situation and any information you would like to have. List your questions on a copy of Form 5.1. If you need additional writing space feel free to use your own notepaper. Set up the paper with the same headings you see in Form 5.1.

Form 5.1 Situation Questions, Answers, and Additional Information

Questions (Color 1)	*Answers (Color 2)*	*Additional Information (Color 3)*
_____	_____	_____
_____	_____	_____
_____	_____	_____
_____	_____	_____
_____	_____	_____
_____	_____	_____
_____	_____	_____
_____	_____	_____
_____	_____	_____
_____	_____	_____
_____	_____	_____
_____	_____	_____
_____	_____	_____
_____	_____	_____
_____	_____	_____
_____	_____	_____
_____	_____	_____
_____	_____	_____

Fact 1a: Projected Enrollment Growth

	Current	Year 1	Year 2	Year 3	Year 4	Year 5
Grade 7	120	145	155	165	175	240
Grade 8	68	120	145	155	165	210
Grade 9	63	67	120	145	155	200
Grade 10	72	78	67	120	145	170
Grade 11	67	65	78	72	120	150
Grade 12	69	59	65	75	72	120
Total:	459	534	630	732	832	1,090

Classrooms in use:	18					
Projected classroom needs:		21	24	28	32	41

Normal School Information

Now *change to a different colored pen or pencil* and go back to your questions, writing down beside your questions any answers you find in the following paragraphs. You should add other information to Form 5.1, from these 2 pages; information that you think is important. By using different colored writing, you simplify your partner's documentation task later. Take 10 minutes to do this.

Fact 1b: Projected Enrollment Growth. Projections for the next 5 years show a substantial increase in enrollments from a current low of 459 to a high of 1,090. An increase of 631 students is anticipated over the next 5 years. There are 20 classrooms. The school currently uses 18 classrooms. There are two vacant classrooms. Beginning a year from now, there is a need for 1 to 9 additional classrooms per year to a maximum of 41 in 5 years. The growth anticipated between years 4 and 5 is the greatest, with nine additional classrooms needed then. Overall, at least 21 additional classrooms are needed. The current student to teacher ratio is 26:1.

Fact 2: Budget and Time Frame. A total budget of $30,000,000 is earmarked for construction, renovation, programs, and inservice. The project is to begin as soon as possible after final specifications are developed and approved and contracts awarded. Once begun, the project is expected to take 18 months to complete.

Fact 3: Age and Condition of Building. The school was built over 60 years ago. With the exception of the heating system, it has had only minor cosmetic renovations since then.

Fact 4: Board Expectations. The board expects to see the entire curriculum and instructional program, including the program for mainstreamed special needs students, enhanced and rejuvenated as a result of the renovations. They want the school to be a flagship school again.

Fact 5: Programs of Study. There are currently eight recognized programs of study including athletics: business education, preengineering, Reserve Officers Training Corps (ROTC) communications, college prep, work-study, music, varsity athletics.

Fact 6: Staffing. There is one full-time principal. One full-time assistant principal and another assistant principal serve half-time as head coaches of the varsity football team. There are currently 24 full-time equivalent (FTE) teachers on staff. Included in FTE staffing are three physical education teachers, two music teachers, one librarian, and two guidance counselors. There are three full-time custodians.

Fact 7: Teacher Morale and Professional Development. Generally, morale is low. The new teacher evaluation procedure has not been met with much teacher support. Most complaining teachers are older and are threatened by the new evaluation process. There is particular concern over the perceived lack of qualifications of the administrators involved in the evaluation of instruction. Sponsoring extracurricular activities after school without extra pay is also a problem. There has been little professional development over the past few years. Little is in the budget for staff development. Most of the budget is usually spent for the administrative staff to attend national conferences and conventions. The school board funds three professional development days that all staff members are required to attend.

Fact 8: Building Floor Plan. The building has three levels: basement, first floor, and second floor.

Basement	*First Floor*	*Second Floor*
1 classroom and 2 music rooms	7 classrooms	6 classrooms
2 vocational education rooms	Main office	Study hall
2 lunchrooms with kitchen	2 administrative offices	2 science labs
Library	Gym	Gym balcony

Fact 9: Physical Plant. There is a 30-year-old heating system. There is no central air conditioning. There are two window air conditioners in the administrative offices. What little insulation there is does not meet current building code standards. There are custodial workrooms and storage rooms. There is one handicapped ramp at the front entrance to the building. There is one restricted-use elevator.

Instructions

Make notes for your presentation. You may use only the questions, answers, and additional information you recorded in Form 5.1. In your presentation, you may present your findings and recommendations as well as your personal vision for the school.

Head a blank piece of paper "Notes for the Formal Oral Presentation" and then take 10 minutes to prepare your presentation using the information you gathered. Be sure you have a flip chart or some other visual aid available should you wish to use it during your presentation. If you have a podium or suitable music stand available, you may use it.

Begin Presentation

After you have prepared for your presentation, it's time to turn on your video camara and begin your presentation to the imaginary school board. You may either operate the camera yourself or have assistance.

You have up to 10 minutes for your presentation—but you may finish early. When you have finished, pause the camera, but don't rewind until you have decided whether or not you wish to make your presentation a second time.

If you wish, you may take 5 minutes to revise your notes and prepare to give a second presentation. If you decide to do so, you may resume videotaping a second school board presentation.

In order to gain the most from this activity, be sure to follow the sequence of steps listed at the beginning of this chapter.

ORAL PRESENTATION PERFORMANCE DOCUMENTATION AND RATING

After videotaping your final presentation, you should take about 5 minutes to complete Form 5.2, the Performance Reflection Form. Thoughtful completion of this instrument will help you reflect and focus on your performance and what you would like to improve in the future. Your questions, presentation notes, videotaped presentation, and the results if your reflection are the artifacts for this activity.

After you and your partner have completed the reflection form (Form 5.2), exchange artifacts and, using the Documentation and Rating Form—School Board Presentation that follows, document each other's paper and pencil artifacts consisting of prepared questions, answers, and other notes as recorded on Form 5.1. In Resources, Form R.7 provides an example of a filled-in School Board Presentation Rating Form.

Form 5.2   Performance Reflection Form

1. What approach did you take to prepare for the school board presentation?

2. Were you able to find the information you wanted? If not, why?

3. Overall, how well do you think you did in this oral presentation simulation?

4. If you could repeat this exercise again immediately, what, if anything, would you do differently?

Documentation and Rating Form— School Board Presentation

Part la: Tallying Prepared Questions and Notes in Form 5.1

Instructions

Study the areas covered below. Then, using your partner's prepared questions, answers and notes for the formal oral presentation, examine and complete Parts la-1c that follow before viewing the videotaped presentation.

Step 1

Review the questions prepared during the preparation period (Form 5.1). Observe the color of the writing. You were asked to change colors for recording the answers to your questions. The different colors now simplify the documentation task of differentiating between your partner's preparation of questions and the answers found on the information sheet.

Place a tally mark (/) on the blank line to the right of the item if it is addressed in a prepared question. If a particular question is not represented in one of the areas, place the tally mark in **Other areas** (#17).

Step 2

Place one check (✓) on the blank line to the left of each numbered item that has at least one tally mark. Do not check an area if it does not have a tally mark; instead, place a large dot (•). Check (✓) **Other areas** (#17) one time only, even if there are several tally marks.

ANALYZING PROBLEMS

Areas Covered   Tally (/)

_____ 1. Board expectations—flagship school, mainstreaming, new
      and enhanced programs, etc.   _____

_____ 2. Budget—amounts for construction, renovation, program development
      and inservice, etc.   _____

_____ 3. Buildings and grounds—age, condition, parking, and space available   _____

_____ 4. Classrooms—media center/library, numbers by grade levels, current
      and projected additional number needed each year, etc.   _____

_____ 5. Climate control—air conditioning and heating.   _____

_____ 6. Community—expectations, involvement, resources, etc.   _____

_____ 7. Enrollment—current and projected   _____

_____ 8. Equipment and technology—materials, supplies, current and projected, etc.   _____

_____ 9. Floor plan—current, classroom and office location, etc.   _____

_____ 10. Inservice and staff development—current and projected needs, etc.   _____

_____ 11. Instruction—teaching, quality, needs, etc.   _____

_____ 12. Programs—extracurricular, curriculum, special, current and projected needs, etc.   _____

_____ 13. Staff—current and projected needs, etc.   _____

_____ 14. Teacher morale—current, contributing causes, etc.   _____

_____ 15. Testing—test results, trends, etc.   _____

_____ 16. Time frame—approval processes, completion, duration, etc.   _____

_____ 17. Other areas   _____

Documentation and Rating Form—School Board Presentation (continued)

ORGANIZING AND PLANNING

Tally of organizing and planning performance indicators:

Total the tally marks (/) to determine the **number of questions** prepared during the information seeking period: _____

Rating Symbols and ranges: 1 = ⊖, 2 = –, 3 = (–), 4 = (+), 5 = + , 6 or more = ⊕

Rating Symbol: _____

ANALYZING PROBLEMS

Check the analyzing problems performance indicators:

Total the check marks (✓) to determine the **number of areas** covered by the questions (1-17): _____

Rating symbols and ranges: 1-2 = ⊖, 3-4 = – , 5-6 = (–), 7-8 = (+), 9-10 = + , 11 or more = ⊕

Rating Symbol: _____

Part Ib: Checking Prepared Questions and Notes in Form 5.1

Instructions

Place a check (✓) to the left of each numbered statement below, if it is true about the way your partner completed Form 5.1. This portion includes all notes prepared by the participant.

Do not place a check (✓) beside a statement if it is not true; instead, place a dot (•) to the left.

ORGANIZING AND PLANNING

_____ 1. Questions drafted are brief.
       Example:

_____ 2. Took notes only on the most important information.
       Explain:

_____ 3. Notes (on either the book or the flip chart) for the formal presentation are
       in outline form.
       Example:

_____ 4. Presentation notes are detailed.
       Explain:

Documentation and Rating Form—School Board Presentation (continued)

_____ 5. Presentation notes include an introductory statement
(e.g., "Members of the Board…," "Good morning, I'm Page Turner,
the new principal…")
Quote:

_____ 6. Presentation notes include general information areas along with major findings.
Example:

_____ 7. Notes include recommendations to the board.
Example:

_____ 8. In summary, presentation notes are well-organized.
Describe:

ORGANIZING AND PLANNING

Check the number of actions taken in preparation for school board presentation:

Total the check marks (✓) to determine the **number of actions** taken in preparation for school board presentation (1-8). _____

Rating symbols and ranges: 1 = ⊖, 2 = –, 3 = (–), 4 = (+), 5 = + , 6 or more = ⊕

Rating Symbol: _____

Part Ic: Prepared Information in Form 5.1

Instructions

As before, study the information in the list that follows. Then, using your partner's notes in Form 5.1, examine and complete the rating section before viewing the videotaped presentation.

Step 1

Review the notes taken during the information-gathering period (Form 5.1). Observe change in the color. You changed colors to distinguish between preparation of questions and answers in the information section. Place a tally mark (/) to the right of an area listed whenever it is added to the initial questions. If the information is not represented in one of the information areas, place the tally mark in **Other areas** (#17). There should be at least one tally mark for each information area covered.

Step 2

Place a check (✓) on the blank line to the left of each numbered item in the preceding list that has at least one tally mark. Do not check an area if it does not have a tally mark; instead, place a large dot (●). Check **Other areas** (#17) one time only, even if there are several tally marks there.

Documentation and Rating Form—School Board Presentation (continued)

ANALYZING PROBLEMS

Noted Information Areas   **Tally (/)**

_____ 1. Board expectations—flagship school, mainstreaming, new
          and enhanced programs, etc.   _____

_____ 2. Budget—amounts for construction, renovation, program development
          and inservice, etc.   _____

_____ 3. Buildings and grounds—age, condition, parking, and space available   _____

_____ 4. Classrooms—media center/library, numbers by grade levels, current
          and projected additional number needed each year, etc.   _____

_____ 5. Climate control—air conditioning and heating, etc.   _____

_____ 6. Community—expectations, involvement, resources, etc.   _____

_____ 7. Enrollment—current and projected   _____

_____ 8. Equipment and technology—materials, supplies, current and projected, etc.   _____

_____ 9. Floor plan—current, classroom and office location, etc.   _____

_____ 10. In-service and staff development—current and projected needs, etc.   _____

_____ 11. Instruction—teaching, quality, needs, etc.   _____

_____ 12. Programs—extracurricular, curriculum, special, current and projected needs, etc.   _____

_____ 13. Staff—current and projected needs, etc.   _____

_____ 14. Teacher morale—current, contributing causes, etc.   _____

_____ 15. Testing—test results, trends, etc.   _____

_____ 16. Time frame—approval processes, completion, duration, etc.   _____

_____ 17. Other areas   _____

ANALYZING PROBLEMS

Tally the analyzing problems performance indicators:

Total the tally marks (/) to determine the **number of facts** noted during
the information-seeking period: _____

Rating symbols and ranges: 1-2 = ⊖, 3-4 = −, 5 -6 = (−), 7-8 = (+), 9-10 = +, 11 or more = ⊕

Rating Symbol: _____

ANALYZING PROBLEMS

Check the analyzing problems performance indicators:

Total the check marks (✓) to determine the **number of areas** covered (1-17): _____

Rating symbols and ranges: 1 = ⊖, 2 = −, 3 = (−), 4 = (+), 5 = +, 6 or more = ⊕

Rating Symbol: _____

Documentation and Rating Form—School Board Presentation (continued)

Rating Oral Presentation Preparation

The symbols in the list that follows represent demonstrated levels of skill. After studying the completed Part IA, Part IB, and Part II of Table 5.6, with particular attention to the skill areas and frequency of checked performance indicators, copy the number of checks in each performance area onto the Summary of Ratings in this section. In some instances, a particular performance indicator may be assigned to more than one skill area.

Symbols	Interpretations
⊕	Very high skill shown
+	More than moderate skill
(+)	Moderate skill shown
(−)	Less than moderate skill
−	Little skill shown
⊖	Very little skill shown

**School Board Presentation Preparation
Summary Ratings
(use ratings on pages 144–147)**

Performance Areas	Rating Symbols
Analyzing Problems
Performance Ratings: ____, ____, ____	____
Organizing and Planning
Performance Ratings: ____, ____	____

Note: *Extreme ratings of ⊕ or ⊖ are seldom appropriate.*

Documentation and Rating Form—School Board Presentation (continued)

Part IIa: Presentation Videotape—First Review

Step 1

Using a VCR and monitor, view the videotape to observe the presentation. You will need to be familiar with the list in this step before viewing the tape.

Place a check (✓) to the left of the findings and conclusions listed below each time your partner mentions something on the list. Check **Other findings and conclusions** (#10) if uncertain of the classification category. Do not check a statement if it is not reported to the school board during the videotaped presentation; instead, place a large dot (•) on the blank line.

The findings and conclusions cited in the presentation to the school board include the following ten items.

EXERCISING JUDGMENT

Findings and Conclusions

_____ 1. **Board expectations**—flagship school, mainstreaming, new and enhanced programs, and so on.

_____ 2. **Budget**—amount allocated for construction, renovation, program development and inservice, and so on (adequate for the job).

_____ 3. **Buildings and grounds**—old building with minor cosmetic renovations since original construction; handicapped ramp; restricted-use elevator; school needs major renovation and expansion.

_____ 4. **Classrooms**—numbers by grade levels, current and projected for the next 5 years; one to nine additional rooms needed per year; little time left to avoid overcrowding.

_____ 5. **Climate control**—no central air conditioning (office units only); old heating system; inadequate for flagship school.

_____ 6. **Enrollment**—numbers by grade levels for next 5 years, current and projected enrollment.

_____ 7. **Programs and curriculum**—extracurricular, special, secondary; programs need major upgrading, and so on.

_____ 8. **Staff**—additional staff will be needed due to program changes and increases in numbers.

_____ 9. **Teacher morale**—confidence in administrators needs to be reestablished; professional development program needs to be upgraded; evaluations need to be reevaluated; pay for extracurricular assignment needs to be revisited.

_____ 10. **Other findings and conclusions**

EXERCISING JUDGMENT

Check the exercising judgment performance indicators:

Total the check marks to determine the **number of conclusions** cited: _____

Rating symbols and ranges: 1-2 = ⊖, 3-4 = − , 5-6 = (−), 7-8 = (+), 9-10 = + , 11 or more = ⊕

Rating Symbol: _____

Documentation and Rating Form—School Board Presentation (continued)

Part IIb: Presentation Videotape—Second Review

Step 2

Study the 6 typical recommendations in the list that follows, then rewind and play the videotape presentation again. Listen for recommendations actually made to the school board. When you hear one, if it's on the list that follows, place a tally mark (/) on the blank line to the right of it. If a particular recommendation to the board is not listed, place the tally mark beside **Other** (#16). When you have finished identifying recommendations, place one check (✓) on the blank line to the left of each listed recommendation having at least one tally mark. Place a dot (●) to the left if there is no corresponding recommendation.

EXERCISING JUDGMENT–EXPRESSING PROFESSIONAL VALUES

Recommendations to the School Board	Tally (/)
Board Expectations	
_____ 1. Upgrade curriculum and programs.	_____
_____ 2. Provide for mainstreaming students.	_____
Budget	
_____ 3. Review expenditure budgets (construction, renovation, program development, inservice).	_____
Buildings and Grounds	
_____ 4. Complete extensive renovation and additions.	_____
_____ 5. Provide facilities for mainstreaming.	_____
_____ 6. Provide temporary classrooms as needed during renovation.	_____
_____ 7. Test for possible asbestos problem.	_____
Classrooms	
_____ 8. Develop a plan for classrooms for implementation of new curriculum and programs.	_____
Climate Control	
_____ 9. Upgrade heating system.	_____
_____ 10. Install air conditioning system.	_____
_____ 11. Improve insulation, lighting, windows, and so on.	_____
Enrollment	
_____ 12. Increase the number of classrooms.	_____
Programs and Curriculum	
_____ 13. Upgrade curriculum and programs.	_____
Staff	
_____ 14. Increase the number of instructional and support staff.	_____
Teacher Morale	
_____ 15. Review and revise the teacher evaluation program.	_____
Other	
_____ 16. Other recommendations	_____

Documentation and Rating Form—School Board Presentation (continued)

EXPRESSING PROFESSIONAL VALUES

Tally the kinds of recommendations to the school board

Total the tally marks (/) on the preceding list to determine the **kinds of recommendations**. Check the participant's notes before making a final decision:_____

Rating symbols and ranges: 1-2 = ⊖, 3-4 = −, 5-6 = (−), 7-8 = (+), 9-10 = +, 11 or more = ⊕

Rating Symbol: _____

EXERCISING JUDGEMENT

Check the number of recommendations to the school board:

Total the checks (✓) on the preceding list to determine the **number of recommendations**. Check the participant's notes before making a final decision:_____

Rating symbols and ranges: 1-2 = ⊖, 3-4 = −, 5-6 = (−), 7-8 = (+), 9-10 = +, 11 or more = ⊕

Rating Symbol: _____

Part IIc: Presentation Videotape—Third Review

Instructions
Place a check (✓) on the blank line to the left of the statements that follow, when they are true. Do not check a statement if it is false; instead, place a dot (•).

EXERCISING JUDGMENT–EXPRESSING PROFESSIONAL VALUES

_____ 1. Gave supporting reasons for most recommendations to the school board.

   Example:

_____ 2. Recommendations to the board are clear.

   Example:

_____ 3. Did not place qualifications on the recommendations made (note example of negative statement) to the school board.

   Example:

Explanation: The participant used qualifications such as: When the school council . . . , May I suggest . . . , With input from . . . , I suggest . . . , These may help . . . , Pending further information . . . . In contrast, a lack of qualifications is shown by saying: I am definitely going to do the following . . . , I assure you that my recommendations will . . . , I will see to it . . . , I will take care of it . . . , I will . . ." and so on.

Documentation and Rating Form—School Board Presentation (continued)

EXERCISING JUDGMENT AND EXPRESSING PROFESSIONAL VALUES

Check the reasons, recommendations, and qualifications performance indicators:

Add the number of checks on the preceding list. Check the participant's presentation notes before making a final decision:_____

Rating symbols and ranges: 1-2 = ⊖, 3-4 = –, 5-6 = (–), 7-8 = (+), 9-10 = +, 11 or more = ⊕

Rating Symbol: _____

Instructions

Place a check (✓) on the blank line to the left of the statements that follow, when they are true. Do not check a statement if it is false; instead, place a dot (•).

MAKING DECISIONS

_____ 4. The manner of delivery is decisive.

Explain:

Rating symbols and ranges: 1 = (+), 0 = (–)

Rating Symbol: _____

MANAGING STRESS

_____ 5. Does not exhibit signs of stress which interfere with the presentation.
If yes, explain and give examples.

Explain:

Rating symbols and ranges: 1 = (+), 0 = (–)

Rating Symbol: _____

Part IId: Overall Rating of Videotaped Presentation

Step 1

If necessary, rewind the tape and play the presentation again to complete this Part. Rate with a plus sign (+) on the blank line to the left of the most appropriate descriptive statements for the six elements of oral communication listed below. If a particular statement is false (no), rate with a minus sign (–). It is important to explain each false statement with a specific example.

ORAL COMMUNICATION

1. Volume

_____ Easy to hear, mark (+). If no (–), explain.

Explain:

Documentation and Rating Form—School Board Presentation (continued)

2. Tone

_____ Pleasant (+). If no (–), explain.

Explain:

3. Rate of speech (choose one of following ratings)

_____ Slow (–)

Explain:

_____ Moderate (+)

_____ Fast (–)

Explain:

4. Pauses (choose one of following ratings)

_____ Few (–)

Explain:

_____ Some (+)

_____ Many (–)

Explain:

5. Pitch variation (choose one of following ratings)

_____ Adequate (+)

_____ Inadequate (–)

Explain:

Documentation and Rating Form—School Board Presentation (continued)

6. Pronunciation (choose one of following ratings)

_____ Acceptable (+)

_____ Not clear (–)
  Explain:

Step 2

Now, place a check (✓) to the left of the statements in the list that follows, when they are true.

Do not check a statement if it is false; instead, place a dot (•) to the left. If a particular statement is false, it is important to explain with specific examples.

ORAL PRESENTATION

_____ 1. Stood while making presentation.

_____ 2. Made an opening statement to the board, e.g., "Ladies and gentlemen of the board, I would like to present my findings, conclusions, and recommendations . . . "
  Quote:

_____ 3. Made a closing statement to the board, e.g., "Thank you for giving me the opportunity to . . . "; "If you have any questions . . . "
  Quote:

_____ 4. Made adequate eye contact with the camera, which represented the audience.
  Explain:

_____ 5. Used visual aids.
  Explain:

_____ 6. Presentation was well organized.
  Explain:

_____ 7. Made a clear presentation of facts and ideas.
  Explain:

Documentation and Rating Form—School Board Presentation (continued)

_____ 8. Showed behaviors of confidence (e.g., relaxed approach, used gestures, focused the presentation on the audience).

Explain:

_____ 9. Gave an enthusiastic presentation.

Explain:

_____ 10. Used correct grammar.

Explain (give examples only if the participant did not use correct grammar):

ORAL PRESENTATION

Check the number of oral presentation performance indicators:

Total the checks (✓) and pluses (+) for the preceding two lists, and determine the number of desirable **oral presentation** performance indicators: _____.

Rating symbols and ranges: 1-2 = ⊖, 3-4 = –, 5 = (–), 6 = (+), 7 = +, 8 or more = ⊕

Rating Symbol: _____

Step 3

Now rate your oral communication skills. Read the components of oral communication listed below and record a rating in the space to the right. The rating range is presented as guidance to help you make a decision regarding the rating you will use. If you assign a rating lower than moderate (+), you must give examples to help the participant.

Symbols	Interpretations
⊕	Very high skill shown
+	More than moderate skill
(+)	Moderate skill shown
(–)	Less than moderate skill
–	Little skill shown
⊖	Very little skill shown

Note: *Extreme ratings of ⊕ or ⊖ are seldom appropriate.*

Documentation and Rating Form—School Board Presentation (continued)

ORAL COMMUNICATION

Components	Rating	Examples
1. Voice volume	_____	
2. Voice quality	_____	
3. Word articulation	_____	
4. Pronunciation	_____	
5. Grammar	_____	
6. Confidence	_____	

OVERALL ORAL COMMUNICATION RATING

First, copy the six component ratings you assigned in Step 1 and the six in Step 3, and then assign an overall rating symbol:

Step 1: _____, _____, _____, _____, _____, _____

Step 3: _____, _____, _____, _____, _____, _____

OVERALL RATING: _____

Documentation and Rating Form—School Board Presentation (continued)

Summary of Ratings

The symbols that follow are used to represent demonstrated levels of skill. After studying the completed preceding forms, with particular attention to the skill areas and frequency of checked performance indicators, rate each performance area. In some instances, a particular performance indicator may be assigned to more than one skill area.

Symbols   **Interpretations**

⊕   Very high skill shown

+   More than moderate skill

(+)   Moderate skill shown

(–)   Less than moderate skill

–   Little skill shown

⊖   Very little skill shown

School Board Presentation
Performance Summary Ratings
(use ratings on pages 149-156)

Performance Areas	Rating Symbols
Exercising Judgment Performance Ratings: ____, ____	_____
Making Decisions Performance Ratings: ____	_____
Oral Communication Performance Ratings: ____	_____
Oral Presentation Performance Rating: ____	_____
Expressing Professional Values Performance Ratings: ____, ____	_____

Note: *Extreme ratings of ⊕ or ⊖ are seldom appropriate.*

Documentation and Rating Form—School Board Presentation (continued)

Rating Overall School Board Performance Summary

On this form, summarize your ratings for each performance area on a scale of ⊖ to ⊕ (very little skill shown to very high skill shown).

You may want to examine a sample overall summary page of a completed documentation for this activity in the Resources section (Form R.8).

Symbols	Interpretations
⊕	Very high skill shown
+	More than moderate skill
(+)	Moderate skill shown
(–)	Less than moderate skill
–	Little skill shown
⊖	Very little skill shown

Overall Rating for School Board Presentation Performance Summary Ratings (Use ratings on pages 148–157)

Performance Areas	Rating Symbols
Analyzing Problems Performance Rating: ____	_____
Exercising Judgment Performance Rating: ____	_____
Organizing and Planning Performance Rating: ____	_____
Making Decisions Performance Rating: ____	_____
Managing Stress Performance Rating: ____	_____
Oral Communication Performance Rating: ____ , ____	_____
Oral Presentation Performance Rating: ____	_____
Expressing Professional Values Performance Rating: ____	_____

Note: *Extreme ratings of ⊕ or ⊖ are seldom appropriate.*

REFLECTIVE PRACTICE

Whew! You have made it through your first videotaping experience, and now you can relax. This activity should have given you valuable feedback on your oral presentation skills—and additional insight into the values and beliefs that influence your decisions as well.

Go through each of your artifacts and your documentation and rating sheets again, and highlight your choices that differ from your partner's choices. For each item highlighted, ask yourself the questions that follow this paragraph. On a clean piece of paper, make notes of your responses to the questions. When you have completed the task, share your responses with your partner. Discuss the differences in your responses: Do not attempt to persuade your partner to your point of view. There is more than enough educational theory and research to support almost any point of view, and this activity is not intended to create arguments. The purpose of this reflective task is for you to clarify for yourself what your beliefs are and to recognize how they influence your decisions.

- In what ways do your responses differ from those of your partner?

- Why do you think the responses are different? Of the broad areas for improvement at the school—curriculum, students, community, staff, facilities—why did you select the particular areas to address first in your recommendations to the board? What does this tell you about your beliefs and values?

- You were required to make a presentation without all the information that you would like to have had. How did that make your feel? Did you feel that you were going out on a limb to make recommendations?

- The board of education is committed to site-based decision making and wanted to meet with you to discuss your plan. Does that mean that site-based decision making is just between district administrators and site administrators? Or, in your plan, did you extend the decision-making process to the staff? Students? Parents?

- What elements of your presentation were influenced by what you believe to be the purpose of education?

- What did you observe about your personal manner in the oral presentation? What behavioral aspects will you have to focus on: nervous or repetitive mannerisms, eye contact, body movement, voice, and volume control?

- What has the oral presentation activity revealed to you about your skills in analyzing problems, exercising judgment, organizing and planning, making decisions, managing stress, oral communication, oral presentation, and expressing professional values?

- If you were to make another presentation to the board of education after completing this reflective practice exercise, would you make your presentation differently? How would it differ and why? Or why not?

In the next chapter, you will have an opportunity to practice your oral communication skills and leadership in a group. This should be an enjoyable activity as you will be able to discuss educational issues with one or more colleagues.

6

Providing Leadership in Groups

OVERVIEW

In this chapter, you'll experience another powerful leadership activity that consists of a videotaped group problem-solving discussion. Focused on you and your partner, the activity provides video as well as paper and pencil artifacts for documentation, analysis, and rating. You will need a volunteer to join you to enrich the discussion.

Group leadership involves persuading others to support a plan of action, reigning in disparate views to reach consensus, and getting everyone on the same page without making enemies. Besides the force of your personality, what kinds of skills does it demand? It's hard enough to get others to line up behind a perfect, inspired solution to a problem—a solution that you believe in because you created it yourself. But what do you do when you need the group's support for a plan of action that is not your own? One that might not be perfect? Sound familiar?

By participating in the simulation in this chapter, you'll discover how strong you already are in group leadership skills and what you still need to practice. When you've finished, you'll have paper and pencil, and videotape artifacts that will provide the substance for analysis, reflection, performance documentation, and rating. Scripting the performance is not required. In place of a script are detailed performance checklists. For this simulation, the use of video technology makes it possible for accurate performance documentation that stimulates powerful leadership development.

Having already prepared one plan and analyzed three school improvement plans—the example in Chapter 3, your partner's and your own—you now have an opportunity to see three more plans. In this simulation, you will not develop a plan of your own, but you will have an opportunity to carefully examine and evaluate plans prepared by other people. In a random drawing, you will get one of the plans to present and defend in a small group of three participants: you, your partner, and a volunteer. As you read these three plans—each of which is for a different school in imaginary Normal City—you will find grammatical and other errors. To help make this experience as authentic as possible, we have intentionally left in flaws.

The most prominent skill area in this problem-solving discussion is group leadership. You will be working with only your partner and another person whom you enlist as a volunteer to join your team to enrich the discussion.

STEPS FOR DEVELOPMENT

Unless you have someone else to take care of the physical arrangements, you and your partner will need to assist each other in the setup and operation of the video camera. The camera should be focused on both of you—ideally on your faces and upper torsos. It is important to have a good video recording of your voices and faces. Your image will look better if the background is without distractions and is dark. Light-colored backgrounds reflect light and cause the camera iris to automatically adjust to the brightness, producing images with poorly defined features.

This activity requires an hour to complete. In order to save time and videotape, *you should not begin recording until after the initial preparation and presentations of plans.* When you begin to work on achieving consensus, that's the time to record. When you do begin to record, be sure the camera is running; sometimes, after a few minutes, a video camera switches to standby and needs to be awakened.

The group discussion developmental tasks consist of the following:

1. Read about the group discussion and performance areas.

2. Study the group discussion setup with tables, video camera, and flip chart.

3. Prepare for videotaping your three-member group discussion.

4. Videotape the discussion.

5. Exchange paper and pencil artifacts and documentation forms with your partner.

6. Document the paper and pencil artifacts and view the videotaped discussion with your partner.

7. Document each of your performances on the videotape.

8. When you have finished documenting each other's performance, exchange the completed documentation forms.

9. After completing and discussing documentation results, rate your performance in this activity.

Group Problem-Solving Discussion and Group Report

The emphasis in the group discussion is on your ability to help resolve a typical administrative task: evaluating work completed by others. In this case, you and your partner (and volunteer group member) are called on to present and defend school improvement plans and arrive at a recommendation for the superintendent.

The activity is in three parts:

1. In the first part, you individually evaluate and rank three different school improvement plans.

2. In the second part, (a) you each present and defend the plan you are randomly assigned, and then (b) as a group, you reach consensus on the best plan.

3. The final part of this activity challenges your group to prepare a report detailing the process used to arrive at its recommendation. Both elementary and secondary school improvement plans are included in this activity.

Group Problem-Solving Performance Areas

This activity gives you an opportunity to demonstrate your skills in:

- Analyzing Problems
- Exercising Judgment
- Group Leadership
- Interpersonal Sensitivity
- Managing Stress
- Oral Communication
- Oral Presentation
- Expressing Professional Values

As in all program activities, problem-solving performance areas are related to the ISLLC Standards. Detailed performance aspects are found in the linkages made in this book. As before, you will find performance aspects in the Standards that relate to the performance areas for this activity in the Resources section of this book.

Standards, Performance Areas, and Aspects

Each of the related standards presented below is an abbreviated statement followed by program skill areas and the number of related performance aspects. In some instances the activity calls for skills not identified in the ISLLC Standards. Specific performance aspects are not included here but may be found in the Resources section. This information is presented to show the linkages between the group problem-solving discussion and the performance aspects of the ISLLC Standards.

STANDARD 1

Developing, articulating, implementing, and stewarding a shared vision of learning.

Analyzing Problems
> 7 ISLLC performance aspects related to analyzing problems

Exercising Judgment
> No ISLLC-related performance aspects

Making Decisions
> No ISLLC-related performance aspects

Group Leadership
> 4 ISLLC performance aspects related to group leadership

Interpersonal Sensitivity
> 3 ISLLC performance aspects related to interpersonal sensitivity

Expressing Professional Values
> 8 ISLLC performance aspects related to professional values

Managing Stress
> No ISLLC-related performance aspects

Oral Communication
> 3 ISLLC performance aspects related to oral communication

STANDARD 2

Advocating, nurturing, and sustaining a school culture and effective instructional program conducive to student learning and staff professional growths

Exercising Judgment
> 1 ISLLC performance aspect related to exercising judgment

Organizing and Planning
> 10 ISLLC performance aspects related to organizing and planning

Making Decisions
> No ISLLC-related performance aspects

Interpersonal Sensitivity
> 6 ISLLC performance aspects related to interpersonal sensitivity

Oral Communication
> No ISLLC-related performance aspects

STANDARD 3

Ensuring management of the organization, operations, and resources for a safe, efficient, and effective learning environment

Analyzing Problems
> 10 ISLLC performance aspects related to analyzing problems

Making Decisions
> 3 ISLLC performance aspects related to making decisions

Group Leadership
> 1 ISLLC performance aspect related to group leadership

Interpersonal Sensitivity
> 8 ISLLC performance aspects related to interpersonal sensitivity

Expressing Professional Values
> 2 ISLLC performance aspects related to professional values

Oral Communication
> 1 ISLLC performance aspect related to oral communication

ISLLC STANDARDS (Continued)

STANDARD 4

Collaborating with families and community members, responding to diverse community interests and needs, and mobilizing community resources

Exercising Judgment
    5 ISLLC performance aspects related to exercising judgment
Making Decisions
    No ISLLC-related performance aspects
Expressing Professional Values
    11 ISLLC performance aspects related to professional values
Oral Communication
    4 ISLLC performance aspects related to oral communication

STANDARD 5

Promoting success of all students through integrity, fairness, and an ethical manner

Exercising Judgment
    10 ISLLC performance aspects related to exercising judgment
Making Decisions
    No ISLLC-related performance aspects
Group Leadership
    No ISLLC-related performance aspects
Interpersonal Sensitivity
    9 ISLLC performance aspects related to interpersonal sensitivity
Expressing Professional Values
    19 ISLLC performance aspects related to professional values
Oral Communication
    No ISLLC-related performance aspects

STANDARD 6

Promoting the success of all students by understanding, responding to, and influencing the larger political, social, economic, legal, and cultural context

Analyzing Problems
    7 ISLLC performance aspects related to analyzing problems
Exercising Judgment
    4 ISLLC performance aspects related to exercising judgment
Making Decisions
    No ISLLC-related performance aspects
Group Leadership
    No ISLLC-related performance aspects
Interpersonal Sensitivity
    No ISLLC-related performance aspects
Expressing Professional Values
    6 ISLLC performance aspects related to professional values
Oral Presentation
    2 ISLLC performance aspects related to oral presentation
Oral Communication
    4 ISLLC performance aspects related to oral communication

---

Note: Linkages were identified by the principal author and verified by education experts.
SOURCE: Adapted from Council of Chief State School Officers (1996).

THE SIMULATION

The Situation

This is a group leadership simulation completed with your partner and a colleague. Ask a colleague to participate so you will have a three-person group. The simulation requires approximately 1 hour.

You and your partner are to assume the role of school principals serving on a subgroup of a school improvement committee. A staff member from your school has prepared the plan you are presenting and defending strongly. Of course you want your school's plan to win. Following a 10-minute preparation period, you will have 35 minutes to discuss the plans and reach consensus on your group's recommendation for the best school improvement plan. There is no designated chairperson for this group problem-solving discussion.

Reading the Three Plans

First, read the three improvement plans for three different schools in Normal City (Figures 6.1, 6.2, and 6.3). The Normal City school board has decided to give an award for the best-written school improvement plan. Their goal is to encourage the writing of better school improvement plans. Actual school improvement is not linked to this contest. The goal is to write the best improvement plan and win the improvement plan writing contest. Your job is to choose the winning plan. The plans contain errors of spelling, grammar, syntax, and structure to make them as realistic as possible. The errors will, no doubt, shock you. However, you and your partner will have an opportunity to practice identifying and documenting them. Even minor errors in printed materials get in the way of our being able to judge what might otherwise be a well-written plan. Each of the school improvement plans was prepared by a participant in leadership training to address one of the problems at Normal School. One plan is for an elementary school and two are for secondary schools. Care has been taken to retain the flavor, language, and structure of the plans as originally written.

Figure 6.1 School Improvement Plan 1

Normal Elementary School

PROBLEM IDENTIFICATION STATEMENT:

Overall student performance on both norm-referenced and standardized achievement tests have dropped significantly over the past few years. This may be simptomatic of a number of factors. An analysis of our current situation reveals that:

- The curriculum and instructional delivery system has not been reviewed, revised, or modified in 15 years even though the student population has changed dramatically.
- English is a second language for many students. Some students come from home backgrounds that are not language rich, some lack background experiences that hamper their understanding of content, and many are dealing with emotional and social issues that create barriers to learning.
- Teachers are teaching according to old paradims that are not working with our current student body. This has resulted in frustration, confusion, and "burn out." At this point our students do not have equitable access to a challenging and appropriate instructional program using curricula that reflects their cultures and future needs.

These situations must be corrected before student achievement scores can improve.

GOALS AND OBJECTIVES:

A school has two goals (or purposes) for existing, productivity (attainment of knowledge and skills), and satisfaction (sense of value, esteem and belonging). Currently, our students are not being productive and, in some cases, do not feel satisfied within their school. It is imperative that we change this situation so that we can become a viable institution again.

Goal: Become a productive and satisfying school for students, staff, and parents.

Objectives:

- Improve the instructional delivery system so that students will master the skills and concepts taught and be able to demonstrate competency in all areas of the curriculum.
- Increase staff opportunities to improve their skills and participate in decisions made about the school organization.

Evaluation indicators:

- In June, report card grades for all students will verify that they were legitimately promoted to the next grade.
- Ninety percent of all students tested by the ITBS will score above the 50th percentile on all subtests.
- In January, log entries will show that 100% of the teachers participated in scheduled staff development and 80% integrated the strategies learned into their instructional planning.
- Student performance on all three sections of the State Literacy Test and on all seven strands of the Program of studies mathematics test will show a 50% increase when compared to the most recent scores.
- Base line data on the number of hour's parents volunteer in the classroom will be collected for the fist marking period of the year. Data collected for the second and third marking periods will show a 25% increase each period when compared to the previous marking period. Data collected for the second and third marking periods

Figure 6.1 School Improvement Plan 1 (continued)

will show a 25% increase each period when compared to the previous marking period. Data collected in June will show a 100% increase when compared with November.

- A school climate/attitudinal survey administered to the staff, students and parents in June will show a 75% increase in satisfaction with school when compared to the one previously administered in September.

10-MONTH WORK PLANS:

1. August: Schedule a 2-hour faculty meeting to discuss status, goals, issues, concerns, instructional and climatic factors related to student performance. During this session, collaboratively plan a staff retreat for the first weekend in September. The school system will find this retreat (primary responsibility: principal and counselor.)

2. September: Conduct a 2-day retreat to review fifth grade student data/records. The objective will be to find ways to "level the playing field" for all students and to improve overall student performance. The review should help staff determine what experiences perceived successful students have had that perceived unsuccessful students have not had. Records of 20 fifth grade students will be studied.

Criteria for selection of student samples:

Fifth grade students perceived by staff as, and whose reported cards identify, achievers and underachievers. These definitions include students who are socially, emotionally, and academically well and successful, and students who have experienced difficulty socially, emotionally, and academically. Ten students in each category will be selected.

Data to be reviewed:

The student review will include cumulative records, child study reports, At-Risk Students List, records of special programs and services provided.

What to look for:
- Positive or negative expectations articulated in teacher comments
- Pacing and placement
- Actions taken to assist child when trouble was noted
- Instructional modifications
- Parent/school communication
- Enrichment/assessment of interests
- Applications of test data to instructional decisions
- Progress trends and reactions if achievement declined
- Monitoring processes

Anticipated outcomes:

It is anticipated that old assumptions are challenged or affirmed, expectations will be validated or questioned, and practices and processes when scrutinized will either prove worthy or lay sound pedagogical foundations. Teachers should discover which nonacademic factors are powerful mediators of success and

Figure 6.1 School Improvement Plan 1 (continued)

failure. These insights will lead to recommendations for improving the learning environment and, ultimately, result in greater student achievement.

Staff will record a summary of findings indicating what was learned and suggest next steps to correct for problem areas. (primary responsibility: principal, team leaders, and counselor.)

3. October: Create a Collaborative School Team to assist with the implementation of "next steps" identified at the retreat and to develop and monitor implementation of the school plan. The composition shall include parents, teaches, and support staff. Each grade level will select a representative to serve on the team. Parents' selection will reflect the student population. The group will appoint a chair. Members of the superintendent's office will train the team in the collaborative process. Following the training, the collaborative team will meet monthly. (primary responsibility: principal and appointed chair.)

4. October: Begin the process of developing a school mission statement of shared values. Staff, parents, and students will participate. Hire an outside consultant to facilitate these sessions. Sessions should begin not later than October 15. Sessions will be held on the second and fourth Mondays each month until the mission and shared values are completed. The Collaborative Team will develop a Likert Scale measurement instrument to be administered to the parents and teachers in the spring to determine how well we acted upon our beliefs. (primary responsibility: faculty advisory committee, collaborative team, and PTO board.)

5. November: Create an advisory board consisting of Parents, teachers, sixth grade students, business and industry personnel for the purpose of obtaining support for academic programs, locating enrichment experiences for staff and students, improving communication and creating good public relations for the school. The first meeting will take place the first week in November. (primary responsibility: principal, NAC, and PTO board.)

6. November-April: Schedule staff development in areas identified at the staff retreat. Two staff development days will be set aside per month for teachers to improve their repertoire or strategies for teaching in heterogeneous classrooms. Fifty percent of the staff will participate on the fist day and 50% on the second day of training. All training will be conducted from a multi-cultural perspective. Training is mandatory. (Primary responsibility: collaborative team.)

7. November: Establish a student achievement task force who will:
   - Identify student experiencing learning difficulties and/or who scored in the lower quar on a standardized test. Create a monitoring list of those students.
   - Meet monthly with teachers to monitor student progress and make recommendations f instructional modifications for targeted students.
   - Monitor and collect achievement data on the targeted students, report findings, and recommend staff development initiatives. (Primary responsibility: chair appointed by t collaborative team.)

8. May: Schedule a staff retreat for the purpose of reflecting on the progress made during the school year and implications for school planning. All data collected for the evaluation will reviewed and analyzed by the total staff. Recommendations for additional initiatives will t made. (Primary responsibility: collaborative team.)

Figure 6.2 School Improvement Plan 2

Normal High School

PROBLEM IDENTIFICATION:

Examination of achievement data in the summer showed that test scores at Normal City School have dropped drastically. This information along with input from the Area Office Analysis Report and a growing concern expressed by a parent group led to the development of a plan that focuses on improving the academic performance of all of its students.

The Normal City School Plan is a strong general education program that emphasizes reading, writing, thinking, mathematics, social studies, science, and the arts, supported by and in conjunction with the latest available technology. In addition, this plan reflects an appreciation and understanding of varied learning styles through an integration of auditory, visual, tactile, and kinesthetic experiences for students.

SCHOOL PLAN TASK FORCE COMMITTEE:

The Normal City School Plan reflects the active, collaborative efforts of representatives from across the school community. The Committee, headed by Principal Page Turner, was composed of staff students, and parents. There was a teacher representative from each department, three parents from the PTO to include one Hispanic and one African American parent, a student from each grade level to include one Hispanic and African American student, and a counselor.

GOAL:

To improve student academic performance through the implementation of strategies that can be used by teachers, parents, and other staff of Normal City School.

OBJECTIVE:

IMPLEMENT STRATEGIES THAT IMPROAVE THE ACADEMIC PERFORMANCE OF STUDENS, PARTICULARLY FOR THOSE AFRICAN AMERICANS AND HISPANICS FOR WHOM TEST RESULTS ARE LEAST FAVORABLE.

This plan is designed to address one strategy per month that will enhance the understanding and awareness of teachers, parents, and counselors as to how best the current student population of Normal School may be served. Representatives from the staff development team will be responsible for providing follow-up activities for those strategies which cannot be adequately addressed in one meeting. The school year would be broken up as follows.

August
- Staff development team meets to design individual monthly strategies beginning with September and ending in May
- Team members will consist of administration, department chairs, experienced teachers from schools where similar programs have been successful, interested Normal City staff members who responded to Principal's letter, Staff Development Office member, and parents from PTO Board

Figure 6.2 School Improvement Plan 2 (continued)

September

Implement a teacher inservice that addresses an understanding and response to ethnic, national, and cultural diversity in the school environment

Demonstrate strategies that have proven successful at schools with similar problems (cooperative learning, intro-disciplinary curriculum, cultural projects, and learning style theory)

October

Implement a mentoring/tutoring/after-school study hall program

Invite all interested school staff, business partnership and community members to orientation session

Distribute a mentoring guidelines/activities handbook

Match mentor/mentee

Set up schedules for tutoring and study hall

November

Provide an open-house day and coffee for African American and Hispanic Parents

Distribute a guidance handbook (in Spanish also) for such topics as: role of the counselor, calendar dates for interims and quarter grades, course selection process, choices students need to consider, and steps in planning for college

Encourage participation in PTSA and volunteer for classrooms, library, or career center

Encourage responsibility in signing interims and Students Rights and Responsibilities

Stress the importance of children being in school every day

December

No inservice. Holiday reception for staff

Invite targeted students to reception 7th period (Invite minority college graduates to return to give encouragement to African American and Hispanic students. Invite college minority recruiters to give an informal talk)

January

Implement portfolio work plan in English department

Mentors/tutors assist their mentees with developing materials for portfolio to include the college essay for juniors

Portfolio to include representative pieces from across the curriculum

February

Focus in the guidance department

Counselors advise and investigate with targeted students grants, endowments, and other financial aid available to African American and Hispanic high school graduates for college study

March

Staff development inservice on conflict resolution for students and instructional strategies for disruptive students

Figure 6.2 School Improvement Plan 2 (continued)

April

Technology inservice for teachers

Technology committee facilitates session on how to integrate computers in the classroom (Hands on sessions in various locations throughout the building)

Basic computer programs workshop (Word Perfect, Microsoft Word, spreadsheet, database) as well as use of supplemental subject content software sponsored by business department

May

Hold exhibits of students' cultural and ethnic projects (i.e., model of Aztec capitol city, African mosaics and folk art)

Invite parents, superintendent, area office representative, and key community members to reception in fine arts wing.

EVALUATION:

At the conclusion of the school year there should be a noticeable difference in the Normal City School community as seen in the following areas:

- Increase in school attendance, particularly for Hispanics and African Americans
- Increase in grade point average, particularly for Hispanics and African Americans
- Increase of computers as aides to learning
- Increase in students' writing skills

A comparison of previous year survey results with this year survey results will show that staff, students, parents, and community are more knowledgeable about Normal City School with particular emphasis on Hispanic and African American families within the school community.

In June, there would be an end-of-the-year assessment to evaluate the overall results of this plan.

Evaluation would include:

- Student, staff and PTO input
- Statistical data (grade marks, attendance figures, SAT scores)
- Open discussion on the plan's success and problems.

Figure 6.3 School Improvement Plan 3

Normal Secondary School
Plan for achieving success with site-based management

STAFF DEVELOPMENT PROPOSAL

BACKGROUND:

Important changes will take effect at Normal School next year. Site-based management has been mandated by the acting superintendent. Up to the present time most decisions concerning the operation of the school have been made at the district level under the direction of the school superintendent. The superintendent believes site-based management is the wave of the future and necessary for improving the schools in his district. This is fully supported by the local school board. Since this decision by the superintendent, many concerns have developed.

GOAL SETTING:

A staff development program is needed to assist in changing the paradigm from centralized control to one of school based management that focuses on addressing individual school needs through collaborative decision-making. In studying the demographics of the student population of Normal School it is evident that changes have occurred. Since it is in the best interest of the total community that all young people receive an education, students should be counseled to stay in school. The school leadership must ensure that all students are given the opportunity to learn through instruction that best accommodates their needs. Offering staff development opportunities for teachers, counselors, and administrative staff will improve understanding and acceptance of the required changes in the school climate.

The implementation of a well-defined staff-development program is critical to building a positive school climate, which in turn will lead to improving academic achievement. Since a positive school climate must be built before change can occur, an on-going staff development process should be implemented immediately. This process should be based on a vision that is clearly defined in the school mission statement. A school committee should be formed to develop a plan of objectives that correspond to the mission statement. Each objective should have specific work plans designed for meeting the objective. An evaluation component should be determined for each objective. The committee should focus on what they determine to be the priority concerns of the school in the coming year. This proposal will outline a sample school plan that empowers teachers to take on leadership roles. This will in turn help to build the school climate and ensure the success of site-based management.

NORMAL SCHOOL OPERATING PLAN
AUGUST – JUNE
MISSION STATEMENT

The mission of Normal School is to provide students with the knowledge, skills, and values they will need to succeed in a changing society. We emphasize excellence in the academic achievement of all students; Stress respect for the diversity of each individual; and strive to improve the ethical conduct of our student-body.

Figure 6.3 School Improvement Plan 3 (continued)

OBJECTIVE 1: Improve academic achievement of students.

Evaluation Component

By June, academic achievement will improve as indicated by:
1. Increased enrollment in grades 10-12 when compared to 4th quarter.
2. Increased number of honor roll students in all grade levels.
3. Reduced percentage of final D/F marks for targeted students.

Work Plans
1. Define, implement, and monitor reading and writing activities across the curriculum.
2. Offer a study skills course as a requirement for all D/F targeted students and for all 9th grade students.
3. Identify African American and other minority candidates and develop strategies to encourage enrollment and success in upper level courses. Involve parents and the business community as mentors for students whose first language is not English.
4. Offer staff development opportunities focusing on students with language and cultural differences.
5. Schedule faculty meetings that provide opportunities for interdisciplinary discussion on curricular and instructional issues.
6. Implement ways of recognizing student achievement – i.e., certificates, pizza lunches, awards ceremony.
7. Explore techniques which increase the success of minority and other targeted students, i.e., team teaching, cooperative learning, providing for Teaming styles, computer technology, and alternative assessment. Offer staff development to support these practices.

OBJECTIVE 2: Increase awareness of diversity issues and cultural sensitivity.

Evaluation Component
By June, cultural sensitivity will improve as indicated by:
1. Increased recognition, understanding, and acceptance of the cultural diversity of the student population.
2. Increased enrollment of second language and other minority students in core courses.
3. Increased involvement of minority parents in the school.
4. Increased use of diverse instructional materials that reflect a pluralistic society.

Work Plans
1. Schedule cultural awareness session for total faculty.
2. Offer ongoing staff development opportunities that focus on prejudice reduction, conflict resolution, understanding diversity, instructional decision-making, and collaborative partnerships with parents and community.
3. Incorporate instructional strategies that build on students' experiences.
4. Promote language minority parent involvement in the school by offering back to school night and parent coffees designed with translator services.
5. Encourage minority student participation in all school activities.

Figure 6.3 School Improvement Plan 3 (continued)

OBJECTIVE 3: Improve student conduct

Evaluation Component

1. By June, student conduct will improve as indicated by:
2. Decreased yearly number of discipline referrals when compared to June.
3. Decreased yearly incidents of vandalism when compared to June.
4. Decreased yearly number of students with alcohol and other drug violations when compared to June.
5. Improved language and behavior as reported by teachers in an end-or-year survey.

Work Plans

1. Hold grade-level class meetings to address expectations for student behavior.
2. Promote community service by students through courses and extra curricular activities.
3. Reinforce positive behavior of students by enforcing rules consistently.
4. Encourage student organizations to take an active role in fostering an atmosphere of respect and responsibility.
5. Implement school-wide efforts to reduce alcohol and other drug use.

SUGGESTIONS FOR STAFF DEVELOPMENT   August – June

The following suggestions include the development of a school operating plan and means of accomplishing that task. Other ideas may be put into the school plan as determined by the shared governance council. Although much of the staff development will be ongoing, specific programs should be prioritized considering what is feasible for the time.

Increase opportunities for team and consensus budding by organizing a team budding activity for staff at the beginning of the school year.

Conduct a strengths and needs assessment of the school.

Form committee to identify school wide priorities and develop a mission statement and school plan of measurable objectives, work plans, and an evaluation component.

Elect a shared-governance council to serve with the principal as the instructional decision-making group of the school.

Plan staff development programs to include workshop on: multi cultural sensitivity, cooperative learning, teaming, alternative assessment, and the collaborative decision-making process.

Appoint an Academic Concerns group to oversee and advise targeted at-risk students. Hold faculty retreat on teacher workday to get feedback on school plan.

Analyze data from retreat and reassess school plan.

Establish teams to formulate ideas for interdisciplinary curriculum development. Work with social services and community organizations to serve student needs.

Schedule a school wide assembly on drug awareness.

Establish a mentor program with members of the community.

Figure 6.3 School Improvement Plan 3 (continued)

Form a school-business partnership with a community corporation.

Offer technology training for all staff.

Schedule an activities fair for students.

Sponsor an International Night for students and parents.

Plan a special awards ceremony to recognize students who have improved their grades.

Instructions

Prepare to videotape. You and your partner share one video camera and videotape. Figure 6.4 represents a sample setup with one camera focusing on two partners. You will not need to record the third member of your group. In addition to the camera, you will need access to a flip chart and felt pens. Also, you will need three notepads with pencils or pens for preparing paper and pencil artifacts.

10-Minute Preparation and Individual Ranking

Now put the numbers of the plans on small strips of paper and turn them face down. Shuffle them. You, your partner, and the volunteer should each pick a slip. The school improvement plan named on that slip is the school you are now assigned to defend, and you are the principal of that school, although you did not write the plan.

Figure 6.4 Setup for Group Discussion

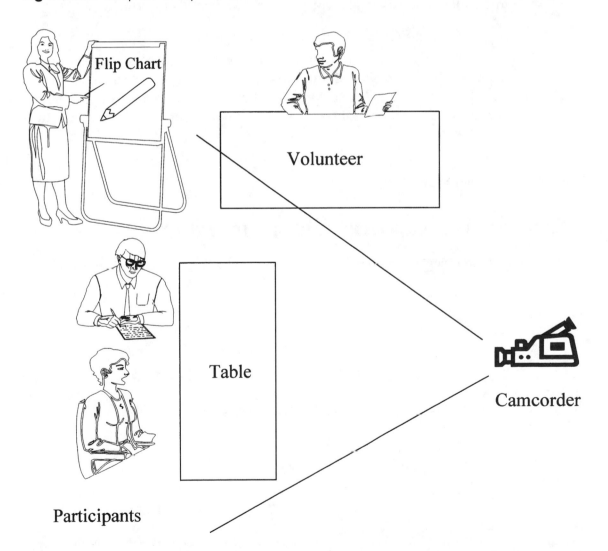

Before the first videotaped discussion period, you have 10 minutes to prepare for the discussion. During this period, each of you should rank all three plans from the weakest to the strongest, in your opinion. This is in the reverse order of most ranking tasks. Make notes about all three school improvement plans and record your rankings in part A of Form 6.1.

You will need to keep track of the timing for this 10-minute preparation period. At the end, one of you will need to turn on the camera and make sure it is focused on your team. Let the camera run continuously through the second and third segments: group problem-solving (consensus-ranking) discussion (35 minutes) and group preparation of written consensus report to the superintendent (10 minutes).

35-Minute Group Problem-Solving Discussion

During the 35-minute, recorded, group problem-solving discussion, your group of three will (a) discuss the merits of the assigned plans, each defending your own; (b) agree on the selection criteria to use in ranking the plans; (c) reach consensus on your subcommittee's recommended winning plan; and (d) record your rankings in part B of Form 6.1.

10-Minute Creation of Consensus Report

Following the selection of the winning plan, you have another discussion period, lasting 10 minutes. Instructions for this discussion are in Box 6.1. The assignment is to create an outline for a consensus report that, in a similar real-world situation, would be written for the superintendent of schools.

Form 6.1   Ranking Sheet

A.   PERSONAL RANKING OF SCHOOL IMPROVEMENT PLANS

Rank the school improvement plans.

_____   Weakest Plan
_____   Middle Plan
_____   Strongest Plan

B.   GROUP RANKING OF SCHOOL IMPROVEMENT PLANS

Complete this section after you have reached consensus through your videotaped group discussion.

_____   Weakest Plan
_____   Middle Plan
_____   Strongest Plan

> **Box 6.1** Instructions for the Creation of a Consensus Report
>
> During the final problem-solving discussion, your group will develop an outline for a report that, in a similar real-world situation, would be written for the superintendent. One of you will need to take notes on a blank piece of paper. The report outline should include the following items:
>
> - Name of the winning plan
> - Summary statement outlining the unique qualifications of the winning plan
> - Selection criteria and processes used to decide on the plan
> - Ways your subgroup solved possible conflicts and disagreements
> - Your group's consensus ranking of all three plans
>
> When this 10-minute taped session is over, discard the outline for the report. It provides a focus for this discussion, but will not be used again.

The Camera

Keep the camera running throughout both discussion periods (35 minutes for ranking the plans and then 10 minutes to create a consensus report) for a total of 45 minutes. You and your partner will need to keep track of time during both discussion periods. At the conclusion of this activity, you should see that the camera is turned off. Rewind the tape. You and your partner will share the task of documenting each other's performance in the group.

GROUP PROBLEM-SOLVING PERFORMANCE DOCUMENTATION AND RATING

You and your partner should review the videotaped consensus discussion and the report preparation. If possible, you should do this together, helping each other identify the performance indicators. The third person need not participate from this point on. To get the most from this activity, you should review again the Steps for Development at the beginning of this chapter. Take particular note of steps 6 through 9.

It's now time to document your partner's paper and pencil and videotape artifacts. You will note that the listing of performance indicators to be documented includes related performance areas: analyzing problems, exercising judgment, group leadership, interpersonal sensitivity, expressing professional values, managing stress, oral presentation, and oral communication.

Watch the videotape and, on the Documentation and Rating Form, Part Ia, document and rate your first review of your partner's performance in the 35-minute, group problem-solving discussion. In Resources, Form R.9 is an example of this form filled in. Watch the tape again and repeat your review, documenting and rating your second review of your partner's taped performance again on the Documentation and Rating Form, Part Ib.

Next, use the Documentation and Rating Form, Part IIa to document and rate your partner's performance. Form R.10 in Resources is an example of this form filled in. Watch the videotaped 10-minutes again and on the Documentation and Rating Form, Part IIb complete the documentation and rating of your partner's performance. Lastly, give an overall group discussion performance summary rating.

Documentation and Rating Form— Group Problem-Solving Discussion

Part 1a: Ranking Discussion (first review of videotaped discussion period)

Instructions

Examine your partner's completed Ranking Sheet (Form 6.1) and complete the following:

Step 1

Place a check (✓) to the left of the two statements that follow, when they are true. Do not check a statement if it is false; instead, place a dot (•) to the left.

ANALYZING PROBLEMS

_____ 1. Listed and ranked all three school improvement plans on the Ranking Sheet (upper half).

_____ 2. Listed the consensus ranking of school improvement plans on the Ranking Sheet (lower half).

Step 2

When you view the videotape of the first discussion period, place a tally mark (/) on the blank line to the right for the most appropriate listed performance indicators. If a given indicator was observed more than one time, tally it each time it occurs. If you are documenting this discussion with your partner, the task may be shared. You may document the performance on one page while your partner documents performance on the other page. You may view the videotape as often as needed: start, stop, and replay.

When you finish documenting the first discussion period, pause and place one check (✓) on the blank line to the left of each statement in this section that has one or more tally marks. Do not check a statement if it is not true; instead, place a dot (•) to the left

GROUP LEADERSHIP	Example or Quote	Tally (/)
_____ 1. Initiated the discussion.		_____
_____ 2. Suggested solutions.		_____
_____ 3. Suggested criteria for selecting the plan.		_____
_____ 4. Clarified or restated the group's tasks.		_____
_____ 5. Initiated a new topic, redirecting the discussion.		_____
_____ 6. Kept group on task.		_____
_____ 7. Summarized and restated the other member's arguments.		_____
_____ 8. Pointed out areas of agreement.		_____
_____ 9. Supported other member who was leading the discussion.		_____
_____ 10. Called attention to time constraints.		_____
_____ 11. Took action to end the discussion phase and to complete the ranking.		_____
_____ 12. Freely participated in the discussion.		_____
(Make an overall judgment here—yes or no—don't tally)		
_____ 13. Stopped irrelevant discussions.		_____
_____ 14. Avoided or stopped arguments.		_____

Documentation and Rating Form—
Group Problem-Solving Discussion (continued)

GROUP LEADERSHIP	**Example or Quote**	**Tally (/)**
_____ 15. Successfully dominated the discussion.		_____
_____ 16. Influenced the group in productive directions.		_____
_____ 17. Attempted to influence the group, but without success.		_____
_____ 18. Stopped active participation following criticism.		_____
_____ 19. The group completed the task within the time allotted.		_____

INTERPERSONAL SENSITIVITY	**Example or Quote**	**Tally (/)**
_____ 1. Suggested compromises.		_____
_____ 2. Used a group member's name.		_____
_____ 3. Acknowledged positive aspects of other plans.		_____
_____ 4. Interrupted another group member.		_____
(When this happens, subtract each tally mark from the total Interpersonal Sensitivity tally before entering the final total below.)		
_____ 5. Modified arguments based on the reactions of others.		_____
_____ 6. Engaged in a side conversation with another group member.		_____
(When this happens, subtract each tally mark from the total Interpersonal Sensitivity tally before entering the final total below.)		
_____ 7. Dealt tactfully with others.		_____
_____ 8. Helped others save face when arguing against a position taken.		_____
_____ 9. Used tension-reducing language.		_____

ANALYZING PROBLEMS	**Example or Quote**	**Tally (/)**
_____ 1. Followed instructions by helping to develop ranking criteria.		_____
_____ 2. Quoted information from the instructions.		_____
_____ 3. Clarified or paraphrased the problem.		_____
_____ 4. Used information or quoted from improvement plans.		_____
_____ 5. Commented on strengths and weaknesses of plans.		_____
_____ 6. Asked clarifying questions.		_____

Now summarize the tally marks and ratings below. The tally marks indicate the frequency of participation; the check marks indicate the related skills shown. Both help to document what the participant did in each designated skill area.

Documentation and Rating Form— Group Problem-Solving Discussion (continued)

GROUP LEADERSHIP

Tally the Group Leadership Performance Indicators:

Total the statements documented with tally marks (/) under GROUP LEADERSHIP.

Record the total number of tally marks. _____

Rating symbols and ranges: 1-3 = ⊖, 4 – 6 = –, 7 - 9 = (–), 10 -12 = (+), 13 -15 = +, 16 or more = ⊕

Rating Symbol _____

Check the Group Leadership Performance Indicators:

Total the number of check marks (✓) under GROUP LEADERSHIP.

Record the total number of check marks. _____

Rating symbols and ranges: 1-3 = ⊖, 4 – 6 = –, 7 - 9 = (–), 10-12 = (+), 13 –15 = +, 16 or more = ⊕

Rating Symbol _____

INTERPERSONAL SENSITIVITY

Tally the Interpersonal Sensitivity Performance Indicators:

Total the statements documented with tally marks (/) under INTERPERSONAL SENSITIVITY.
Remember to subtract tally marks for items 4 and 6 before recording number. _____

Rating symbols and ranges: 1 = ⊖, 2 = – , 3 = (–), 4 = (+), 5 = + , 6 or more = ⊕

Rating Symbol _____

Check the Sensitivity Performance Indicators:

Total the number check marks (✓) under INTERPERSONAL SENSITIVITY. Subtract checks for 4 and 6 before recording number. _____

Rating symbols and ranges: 1= ⊖, 2 = –, 3 = (–), 4 = (+), 5 = + , 6 = ⊕

Rating Symbol _____

ANALYZING PROBLEMS

Tally the Analyzing Problems Performance Indicators:

Total the statements documented with tally marks (/) under ANALYZING PROBLEMS.

Record the total number of tally marks. _____

Rating symbols and ranges: 1 = ⊖, 2 = – , 3 = (–), 4 = (+), 5 = + , 6 = ⊕

Rating Symbol _____

Check the Analyzing Problems Performance Indicators:

Total the check marks (✓) made under ANALYZING PROBLEMS.

Record the total number of check marks. _____

Rating symbols and ranges: 1 = ⊖, 2 = – , 3 = (–), 4 = (+), 5 = + , 6 = ⊕

Rating Symbol _____

Documentation and Rating Form—
Group Problem-Solving Discussion (continued)

EXERCISING JUDGMENT

Tally the Exercising Judgment Performance Indicators:

Total the statements documented with tally marks (/) under EXERCISING JUDGMENT.

Record the total number of tally marks. _____

Rating symbols and ranges: $1 = \ominus$, $2 = -$, $3 = (-)$, $4 = (+)$, $5 = +$, $6 = \oplus$

Rating Symbol _____

Check the Exercising Judgment Performance Indicators:

Total the check marks (✓) made under EXERCISING JUDGMENT.

Record the total number of check marks. _____

Rating symbols and ranges: $1 = \ominus$, $2 = -$, $3 = (-)$, $4 = (+)$, $5 = +$, $6 = \oplus$

Rating Symbol _____

MANAGING STRESS

Tally the Managing Stress Performance Indicators:

Total the statements documented with tally marks (/) under MANAGING STRESS.

Subtract tally marks for 2.

Record the total number of tally marks. _____

Rating symbols and ranges: $1 = \ominus$, $2 = -$, $3 = (-)$, $4 = (+)$, $5 = +$, $6 = \oplus$

Rating Symbol _____

Check the Managing Stress Performance Indicators:

Total the check marks (✓) made under MANAGING STRESS.

Record the total number of check marks. _____

Rating symbols and ranges: $1 = \ominus$, $2 = -$, $3 = (-)$, $4 = (+)$, $5 = +$, $6 = \oplus$

Rating Symbol _____

Part 1b: Ranking Discussion
(Second review of videotaped discussion period)

Instructions

Rewind the tape and view the first discussion period again to complete the following leadership performance indicators. If you are documenting with your partner you will want to share the documentation tasks.

Step 1

Study the listings of performance indicators on this page.

As you view the videotape of the first discussion period a second time, place tally marks (/) to the right for the most appropriate performance indicators listed below. If a given indicator was observed more than one time, tally it each time it occurs. You may review the tape as often as needed; start and stop the video as needed.

When you complete viewing this entire discussion, pause and place one check (✓) to the left of each statement having one or more tally marks. Do not check a statement if it is not true; instead, place a dot (•) to the left.

Documentation and Rating Form—
Group Problem-Solving Discussion (continued)

EXERCISING JUDGEMENT	**Example or Quote**	**Tally (/)**

_____ 1. Contributed to setting the ranking criteria. _____

_____ 2. Made statements about the importance of setting ranking criteria. _____

_____ 3. Gave supportive reasons for solutions suggested. _____

_____ 4. Acknowledged weaknesses in own arguments. _____

_____ 5. Attempted to incorporate own views into the discussion. _____

MANAGING STRESS	**Example or Quote**	**Tally (/)**

_____ 1. Accepted criticism without showing defensiveness.
(If no criticism took place, leave blank.) _____

_____ 2. Showed anger.
(When this happens, subtract each tally mark from the total Managing Stress tally.) _____

_____ 3. Raised voice.
(When this happens, subtract each tally mark from the total Managing Stress tally.) _____

_____ 4. Was patronizing of peer.
(When this happens, subtract each tally mark from the total Managing Stress tally.) _____

_____ 5. Withdrew from the discussion.
(When this happens, subtract each tally mark from the total Managing Stress tally.)

EXPRESSING PROFESSIONAL VALUES	**Example or Quote**	**Tally (/)**

_____ 1. Expressed strongly held professional values. _____

ORAL PRESENTATION—Do not tally Oral Presentation Indicators.

_____ 1. Ideas were clearly expressed in the first group discussion.

_____ 2. Used a flip-chart or other visual aid.

Now, summarize these tally marks and ratings below. The tally marks indicate the frequency of participation; the check marks indicate the related skills shown. Both of you should help each other document each other's performance.

EXERCISING JUDGMENT

Tally the Exercising Judgment Performance Indicators:

Total the statements documented with tally marks (/) under EXERCISING JUDGMENT.

Record the total number of tally marks. _____

Rating symbols and ranges: $1 = \ominus$, $2 = -$, $3 = (-)$, $4 = (+)$, $5 = +$, $6 = \oplus$

Rating Symbol _____

Check the Exercising Judgment Performance Indicators:

Total the number of check marks (✓) under EXERCISING JUDGMENT.

Rating symbols and ranges: $1 = \ominus$, $2 = -$, $3 = (-)$, $4 = (+)$, $5 = +$, $6 = \oplus$

Rating Symbol _____

Documentation and Rating Form—
Group Problem-Solving Discussion (continued)

MANAGING STRESS

Tally the Managing Stress Performance Indicators:

Total the statements documented with tally marks (/) under MANAGING STRESS.

Subtract tally marks for 2 through 5 before recording total. _____

Rating symbols and ranges: 1 = ⊖, 2 = – , 3 = (–), 4 = (+), 5 = + , 6 = ⊕

Rating Symbol _____

Check the Managing Stress Performance Indicators:

Total the number check marks (✓) under MANAGING STRESS.

Subtract checks for 2 through 5 before recording total. _____

Rating symbols and ranges: 1 = ⊖, 2 = – , 3 = (–), 4 = (+), 5 = + , 6 = ⊕

Rating Symbol _____

EXPRESSING PROFESSIONAL VALUES

Tally the Professional Values Performance Indicators:

Total the statements documented with tally marks (/) under EXPRESSING PROFESSIONAL VALUES.

Record the total number of tally marks._____

Rating symbols and ranges: 1 = ⊖, 2 = – , 3 = (–), 4 = (+), 5 = + , 6 = ⊕

Rating Symbol _____

Documentation and Rating Form—
Group Problem-Solving Discussion (continued)

Rating Group Problem-Solving Discussion

On the Group Discussion Performance Summary Ratings form below, rate each performance area on a scale of ⊖ to ⊕ (very little skill shown to very high skill shown). This information is later combined with performance on all items and summarized on a School Board Presentation Performance Summary form and on a final performance summary chart in the last chapter of this book. After viewing the final chart you will reach consensus with your partner on areas of strength and areas for improvement.

Symbols — **Interpretations**

⊕ — Very high skill shown
+ — More than moderate skill
(+) — Moderate skill shown
(−) — Less than moderate skill
− — Little skill shown
⊖ — Very little skill shown

Group Discussion Performance Summary Ratings (pages 183–186)

Performance Areas	Rating Symbols
Analyzing Problems Performance Ratings: ____, ____	____
Exercising Judgment Performance Ratings: ____, ____	____
Group Leadership Performance Ratings: ____, ____	____
Interpersonal Sensitivity Performance Ratings: ____, ____	____
Managing Stress Performance Ratings: ____, ____	____
Expressing Professional Values Performance Ratings: ____, ____	____

Note: *Extreme ratings of ⊕ or ⊖ are seldom appropriate.*

Documentation and Rating Form—
Group Problem-Solving Discussion (continued)

Part 2a: Report Preparation Discussion
(first review of the videotaped discussion period)

Instructions
Study the listings of performance indicators that follow.

Step 1
1. As you view the videotape of the second 10-minute discussion preparing the outline for a report for the superintendent, place a tally mark (/) to the right for the most appropriate performance indicator in the list that follows. If a given indicator was observed more than one time, tally each time it occurs. If you are documenting this discussion with your partner, as before, the task may be shared. You may document the performance on one page while your partner documents on the other. Review the tape as often as needed: start, stop, and replay the videotape.

2. When you complete documenting this 10-minute discussion, pause and place one check (✓) to the left of each statement having one or more tally marks. Do not check a statement if it is not true; place a dot (•) to the left.

GROUP LEADERSHIP	Example or Quote	Tally (/)
_____ 1. Initiated the second, 10-minute, part of the discussion.		_____
_____ 2. Suggested solutions.		_____
_____ 3. Clarified or restated the tasks.		_____
_____ 4. Initiated a new topic, redirecting the discussion.		_____
_____ 5. Summarized and restated the other member's arguments.		_____
_____ 6. Pointed out areas of agreement.		_____
_____ 7. Supported the other member who was leading the discussion.		_____
_____ 8. Called attention to time constraints.		_____
_____ 9. Took action to end the discussion and complete the report.		_____
_____ 10. Freely participated in the discussion. (Make an overall judgment here—yes or no— but don't tally)		
_____ 11. Stopped irrelevant discussions.		_____
_____ 12. Avoided or stopped arguments.		_____
_____ 13. Successfully dominated the discussion.		_____
_____ 14. Influenced the group in productive directions.		_____
_____ 15. Attempted to influence the group but without success.		_____
_____ 16. Stopped active participant following criticism.		_____
_____ 17. The group completed the task within the time allotted.		_____

Documentation and Rating Form—
Group Problem-Solving Discussion (continued)

INTERPERSONAL SENSITIVITY	Example or Quote	Tally (/)

_____ 1. Suggested compromises. _____

_____ 2. Used a group member's name. _____

_____ 3. Acknowledged positive aspects of other plans. _____

_____ 4. Interrupted colleague. _____
(When this happens, subtract each tally mark
from Interpersonal Sensitivity tally.)

_____ 5. Modified arguments based on the reactions of peer. _____

_____ 6. Engaged in a side conversation with other group members. _____
(When this happens, subtract each tally mark
from the Interpersonal Sensitivity tally.)

_____ 7. Dealt tactfully with other group members. _____

_____ 8. Helped a group member save face when arguing against a position taken. _____

_____ 9. Used tension-reducing language. _____

ANALYZING PROBLEMS	Example or Quote	Tally (/)

_____ 1. Followed instructions by helping to develop the report. _____

_____ 2. Quoted information from the instructions. _____

_____ 3. Asked clarifying questions. _____

_____ 4. Summarized the problem-solving process used. _____

_____ 5. Commented on incidences of conflict. _____

Now, summarize the tally marks and ratings on the following form.

GROUP LEADERSHIP

Tally the Group Leadership Performance Indicators:

Total the statements documented with tally marks (/) under GROUP LEADERSHIP.

Record the total number of tally marks. _____

Rating symbols and ranges: $1 - 3 = \ominus$, $4 - 6 = -$, $7 - 9 = (-)$, $10 - 12 = (+)$, $13 - 15 = +$, 16 or more $= \oplus$

Rating Symbol _____

Check the Group Leadership Performance Indicators:

Total the number of check marks (✓) under GROUP LEADERSHIP.

Rating symbols and ranges: $1 - 2 = \ominus$, $3 - 4 = -$, $5 - 6 = (-)$, $7 - 8 = (+)$, $9 - 10 = +$, 11 or more $= \Phi$

Rating Symbol _____

Documentation and Rating Form—
Group Problem-Solving Discussion (continued)

INTERPERSONAL SENSITIVITY

Tally the Interpersonal Sensitivity Performance Indicators:

Total the statements documented with tally marks (/) under INTERPERSONAL SENSITIVITY.
Subtract tally marks for items 4 and 6. _____

Rating symbols and ranges: $1 = \ominus$, $2 = -$, $3 = (-)$, $4 = (+)$, $5 = +$, $6 = \oplus$

Rating Symbol _____

Check the Interpersonal Sensitivity Performance Indicators:

Total the number check marks (✓) under INTERPERSONAL SENSITIVITY.

Subtract checks for 4 and 6 before recording total. _____

Rating symbols and ranges: $1 = \ominus$, $2 = -$, $3 = (-)$, $4 = (+)$, $5 = +$, $6 = \oplus$

Rating Symbol _____

ANALYZING PROBLEMS

Tally the Analyzing Problems Performance Indicators:

Total the statements documented with tally marks (/) under ANALYZING PROBLEMS.

Record the total number of tally marks. _____

Rating symbols and ranges: $1 = \ominus$, $2 = -$, $3 = (-)$, $4 = (+)$, $5 = +$, $6 = \oplus$

Rating Symbol _____

Check the Analyzing Problems Performance Indicators:

Total the check marks (✓) made under ANALYZING PROBLEMS.

Record the total number of tally marks. _____

Rating symbols and ranges: $1 = \ominus$, $2 = -$, $3 = (-)$, $4 = (+)$, $5 = +$, $6 = \oplus$

Rating Symbol _____

Part 2b: Report Preparation Discussion (Second review of the videotaped discussion period)

Instructions

Rewind the tape and view the 10-minute discussion a second time to complete documenting the following leadership performance indicators for preparing an outline for a report. If you are viewing the videotape with your partner, documentation tasks may be shared.

Step 1

Examine and study the listings of performance indicators.

1. As you view the videotape of the second discussion period a second time, place a tally mark (/) to the right for the most appropriate performance indicators listed below. If a given indicator was observed more than one time, tally it whenever it occurs. You may start and stop the video as needed.

2. When you complete viewing this entire discussion, pause and place one check (✓) to the left of each statement having one or more tally marks. Do not check a statement if it is not true; instead, place a dot (•) to the left.

Documentation and Rating Form—
Group Problem-Solving Discussion (continued)

EXERCISING JUDGMENT	Example or Quote	Tally (/)
_____ 1. Gave supportive reasons for solutions suggested.		_____
_____ 2. Acknowledged weaknesses in own arguments.		_____
_____ 3. Attempted to incorporate own views into the group's decisions.		_____

MANAGING STRESS	Example or Quote	Tally (/)
_____ 1. Accepted criticism without showing defensiveness. (If no criticism occurred, leave blank.)		_____
_____ 2. Showed anger. (When this happens, subtract each tally mark from the total Stress Management tally.)		_____
_____ 3. Raised voice. (When this happens, subtract each tally mark from the total Managing Stress tally.)		_____
_____ 4. Was patronizing of peer. (When this happens, subtract each tally mark from the total Managing Stress tally.)		_____
_____ 5. Withdrew from the discussion. (When this happens, subtract each tally mark from the total Managing Stress tally.)		_____

EXPRESSING PROFESSIONAL VALUES		Tally (/)
_____ 1. Expressed strongly held professional values.		_____

ORAL PRESENTATION—Do not tally Oral Presentation indicators.

_____ 1. Ideas were clearly expressed in the first group discussion.

_____ 2. Used a flip-chart or other visual aid.

Now, summarize the tally marks and ratings on the following form.

EXERCISING JUDGMENT

Tally the Exercising Judgment Performance Indicators:

Total the statements documented with tally marks (/) under EXERCISING JUDGMENT.

Record the total number of tally marks. _____

Rating symbols and ranges: 1 = ⊖, 2 = –, 3 = ( ), 4= (+), 5 = + , 6 = ⊕

Rating Symbol _____

Check the Exercising Judgment Performance Indicators:

Total the number of check marks (✓) under EXERCISING JUDGMENT. _____

Rating symbols and ranges: 1 = ⊖, 2 = –, 3 = (–), 4= (+), 5 = + , 6 = ⊕

Rating Symbol _____

Documentation and Rating Form— Group Problem-Solving Discussion (continued)

MANAGING STRESS

Tally the Managing Stress Performance Indicators:

Total the statements documented with tally marks (/) under MANAGING STRESS.

Subtract tally marks for 2 through 5 before recording total. _____

Rating symbols and ranges: $1 = \ominus$, $2 = -$, $3 = (-)$, $4 = (+)$, $5 = +$, $6 = \oplus$

Rating Symbol _____

Check the Managing Stress Performance Indicators:

Total the number check marks (✓) under MANAGING STRESS.

Subtract checks for 2 through 5 before recording total. _____

Rating symbols and ranges: $1 = \ominus$, $2 = -$, $3 = (-)$, $4 = (+)$, $5 = +$, $6 = \oplus$

Rating Symbol _____

EXPRESSING PROFESSIONAL VALUES

Tally the Professional Values Performance Indicators:

Total the statements documented with tally marks (/) under EXPRESSING PROFESSIONAL VALUES.

Record the total number of tally marks. _____

Rating symbols and ranges: $1 = \ominus$, $2 = -$, $3 = (-)$, $4 = (+)$, $5 = +$, $6 = \oplus$

Rating Symbol _____

Check the Expressing Professional Values Performance Indicators:

Total the number check marks (✓) under EXPRESSING PROFESSIONAL VALUES. _____

Rating ranges: $0 = (-)$, $1 = (+)$

Rating Symbol _____

Instructions

Place a check (✓) to the left of the two statements below when they are true. Do not check a statement if it is false; instead, place a dot (•) to the left.

ORAL PRESENTATION

_____ 1. Ideas were clearly expressed throughout the activity.

　　　Examples:

_____ 2. Used a flip-chart or other visual aid.

OVERALL ORAL PRESENTATION

Total the number of checks (✓) above to determine the number of desirable oral presentation performance indicators. Rating ranges: $0 = -$, $1 = (+)$, $2 = +$

Rating Symbol _____

Documentation and Rating Form— Group Problem-Solving Discussion (continued)

Read the components of Oral Communication in the list that follows, and record a rating on the blank to the right. The rating range is presented as guidance to help you make a decision regarding the rating you will use. If you assign a score lower than a (+), you must give examples to help the participant.

ORAL COMMUNICATION

Components	Ratings	Example(s)	Symbols and Rating Ranges	
Voice easy to hear	_____		⊕	Very high*
Voice quality	_____		+	More than moderate
Word articulation	_____		(+)	Moderate
Pronunciation	_____		(−)	Less than moderate
Grammar	_____		−	Little or poor
Confidence	_____		⊖	Very little*

* Ratings rarely used

OVERALL ORAL COMMUNICATION

Examine all component ratings on the preceding list and determine an overall rating: _____

Documentation and Rating Form—
Group Problem-Solving Discussion (continued)

Rating Group Report Discussion Performance

The symbols below are used to represent demonstrated levels of skill. After studying the completed documentation form, above, with particular attention to the skill areas and frequency of checked performance indicators, rate each performance area in the Performance Ratings below. In some instances, a particular performance indicator may be assigned to more than one skill areas.

When you have completed rating this group problem solving activity complete the Overall Performance Summary that follows.

Symbols	Interpretations
⊕	Very high skill shown
+	More than moderate skill
(+)	Moderate skill shown
(−)	Less than moderate skill
−	Little skill shown
⊖	Very little skill shown

Group Discussion Performance Summary Ratings:
(pages 188–193)

Performance Areas	Rating Symbols
Analyzing Problems Performance Ratings: ____ , ____	____
Exercising Judgment Performance Ratings: ____ , ____	____
Group Leadership Performance Ratings: ____ , ____	____
Interpersonal Sensitivity Performance Ratings: ____ , ____	____
Managing Stress Performance Ratings: ____ , ____	____
Oral Communication Performance Ratings: ____ , ____	____
Oral Presentation Performance Ratings: ____ , ____	____
Expressing Professional Values Performance Ratings: ____ , ____	____

Note: *Extreme ratings of ⊕ or ⊖ are seldom appropriate.*

Documentation and Rating Form—
Group Problem-Solving Discussion (continued)

Rating Overall Group Discussion Performance Summary

On the Overall Group Discussion Performance Summary form below, rate each performance area on a scale of
⊖ to ⊕ (very little skill shown to very high skill shown). This information is summarized here and later used on
the final performance summary chart in the last chapter of this book. After viewing the final chart you will reach
consensus with your partner on areas of strength and areas for improvement.

Overall Group Discussion Performance Summary Ratings
(pages 186 and 194)

Performance Areas	Rating Symbols
Analyzing Problems Performance Ratings: ____, ____	____
Exercising Judgment Performance Ratings: ____, ____	____
Group Leadership Performance Ratings: ____, ____	____
Interpersonal Sensitivity Performance Ratings: ____, ____	____
Managing Stress Performance Ratings: ____, ____	____
Oral Communication Performance Ratings: ____	____
Oral Presentation Performance Ratings: ____, ____	____
Expressing Professional Values Performance Ratings: ____, ____	____

Note: *Extreme ratings of ⊕ or ⊖ are seldom appropriate.*

Symbols	Interpretations
⊕	Very high skill shown
+	More than moderate skill
(+)	Moderate skill shown
(−)	Less than moderate skill
−	Little skill shown
⊖	Very little skill shown

REFLECTIVE PRACTICE

The 35-minute problem-solving discussion and 10-minute preparation of a report in this chapter are followed in Chapter 7 by two structured interviews. Reflection on your performance in the group problem-solving discussion and preparation of a report takes place during the first structured interview. There you will have an opportunity to ask questions of your partner concerning performance during the group activity. Your partner will ask also you questions about your performance.

7

Conducting Structured Interviews

OVERVIEW

In this chapter you will practice an important leadership responsibility requiring highly-developed listening skills as you and your partner take turns interviewing each other. The first of two interviews relates to your performance in the group problem-solving discussion from the previous chapter. The second interview focuses on your personal and professional life. Questions for both interviews, along with performance indicators, are included. The interview guides also serve as your documentation forms. Although interviews do not provide reliable information regarding performance, they do verify perceptions of performance. Links to key performance aspects of the ISLLC Standards are provided in Resources (Form R.17).

INTERVIEWING

At this point in your career, you've probably been interviewed a number of times. You've come to know what to expect generally, and you've probably sensed when an interview went well and when it didn't. There may have been times when an interview seemed fair, and perhaps you've had the unfortunate experience of sensing that an interview wasn't quite impartial. You might have had the feeling that you'd rather be the one conducting the interview than the one being interviewed. After all, asking the questions is easier than answering them, isn't it? How hard could interviewing be? Does it require special skills?

Now that you're approaching the responsibilities of leadership from the interviewer's side of the desk, it's time for some specialized practice. We believe that conducting fair and impartial interviews really does require special skills that are important ingredients in effective leadership. As a principal, you will conduct many interviews in your career; by engaging in the interview simulations in this chapter, you will gain particular experience in the skills of listening to and documenting responses. These two skills are particularly important in those situations where you must select one candidate over another—especially when both are highly qualified. The quality of your documentation may make all the difference.

Structured Interviewing

A *structured interview* is one in which the questions asked are exactly the same for each interviewee. This is particularly important when individuals are competing for the same position. In structured interviews, interviewees are all asked the same questions in the same sequence without added comments or explanations. By practicing and conducting these two interviews with your partner, both of you will learn a great deal about each other.

The first interview, about your group problem-solving discussion in Chapter 6 should be conducted in a highly professional, yet comfortable and relaxed manner. However, you will need to listen very carefully to the responses in order to accurately classify them.

Steps for Development

The tasks you are to complete for the interview consist of the following:

1. Read about the interview and the relevant performance areas.

2. Conduct the interview, documenting your partner's answers in his or her book.

3. Exchange your books with the completed interview guides. The guides also serve as documentation forms.

4. Discuss and reach consensus on your partner's responses to your answers.

5. After completing and discussing documentation results, rate your performance in this activity. Use the rating symbols for this program.

This interview is used for both elementary and secondary school partners. See Figure 7.1 for a suggested setup.

Figure 7.1 Structured Interview Setup

Group Problem-Solving Discussion Performance Areas

The interview about the group discussion in Chapter 6 gives you an opportunity to verify your experiences in the group discussion by telling about your performance in the following areas:

- Analyzing Problems
- Exercising Judgment
- Organizing and Planning
- Making Decisions
- Group Leadership
- Interpersonal Sensitivity
- Managing Stress
- Oral Communication
- Expressing Professional Values

As with all the other leadership activities in this book, the same questions arise: What performance aspects in the ISLLC Standards are related to the performance areas in the interviews? What skills are needed in order to be successful in meeting the standards? The interviews you will engage in for this chapter provide a bridge to the performance aspects of the ISLLC Standards.

Standards and Performance Areas and Aspects

Each of the related standards is presented below as an abbreviated statement followed by program skill areas and the number of related per-

formance aspects. In some instances the activity calls for a skill not identified in the ISLLC Standards. The following information is presented to
show the linkages between the structured interviews and the performance
aspects of the ISLLC's standards. For convenience, the linkages for both
interviews have been combined. As in the previous chapters in the book,
specific performance aspects are not included here but may be found in the
Resources (Form R.17).

STANDARD 1
Developing, articulating, implementing, and stewarding a shared vision of learning

Analyzing Problems
  7 ISLLC performance aspects related to analyzing problems
Exercising Judgment
  No ISLLC-related performance aspects
Organizing and Planning
  13 ISLLC performance aspects related to organizing and planning
Making Decisions
  No ISLLC -related performance aspects
Group Leadership
  4 ISLLC performance aspects related to group leadership
Interpersonal Sensitivity
  3 ISLLC performance aspects related to interpersonal sensitivity
Range of Interests
  No ISLLC-related performance aspects
Professional Motivation
  5 ISLLC performance aspects related to professional motivation
Expressing Professional Values
  8 ISLLC performance aspects related to expressing professional values
Managing Stress
  No ISLLC-related performance aspects
Oral Communication
  3 ISLLC performance aspects related to oral communication

STANDARD 2
Advocating, nurturing, and sustaining a school culture and effective instructional program conducive to student learning and staff professional growth

Exercising Judgment
  1 ISLLC performance aspect related to exercising judgment
Making Decisions
  No ISLLC-related performance aspects
Interpersonal Sensitivity
  6 ISLLC performance aspects related to interpersonal sensitivity
Range of Interests
  No ISLLC-related performance aspects
Professional Motivation
  4 ISLLC performance aspects

ISLLC STANDARDS (Continued)

Expressing Professional Values

10 ISLLC performance aspects related to expressing professional values

Managing Stress

No ISLLC-related performance aspects

Oral Communication

No ISLLC-related performance aspects

STANDARD 3

Ensuring management of the organization, operations, and resources for a safe, efficient, and effective learning environment

Exercising Judgment

7 ISLLC performance aspects related to exercising judgment

Making Decisions

3 ISLLC performance aspects related to making decisions

Group Leadership

1 ISLLC performance aspect related to group leadership

Range of Interests

No ISLLC-related performance aspects

Professional Motivation

No ISLLC-related performance aspects

Expressing Professional Values

2 ISLLC performance aspects related to expressing professional values

Managing Stress

No ISLLC-related performance aspects

Oral Communication

1 ISLLC performance aspect related to oral communication

STANDARD 4

Collaborating with families and community members, responding to diverse community interests and needs, and mobilizing community resources

Exercising Judgment

5 ISLLC performance aspects related to Exercising Judgment

Making Decisions

No ISLLC-related performance aspects

Group Leadership

5 ISLLC performance aspects related to group leadership

Interpersonal Sensitivity

11 ISLLC performance aspects related to interpersonal sensitivity

Range of Interests

No ISLLC-related performance aspects

Professional Motivation

8 ISLLC performance aspects related to professional motivation

Expressing Professional Values

11 ISLLC performance aspects related to expressing professional values

Oral Communication

4 ISLLC performance aspects related to oral communication

ISLLC STANDARDS (Continued)

STANDARD 5
Promoting success of all students through integrity, fairness, and an ethical manner

    Exercising Judgment
      10 ISLLC performance aspects related to exercising judgment
    Making Decisions
      No ISLLC-related performance aspects
    Group Leadership
      No ISLLC-related performance aspects
    Interpersonal Sensitivity
      9 ISLLC performance aspects related to interpersonal sensitivity
    Range of Interests
      No ISLLC-related performance aspects
    Professional Motivation
      No ISLLC-related performance aspects
    Expressing Professional Values
      19 ISLLC performance aspects related to expressing professional values
    Managing Stress
      No ISLLC-related performance aspects
    Oral Communication
      No ISLLC-related performance aspects

STANDARD 6
Promoting the success of all students by understanding, responding to, and influencing the larger political, social, economic, legal, and cultural context

    Exercising Judgment
      4 ISLLC performance aspects related to exercising judgment
    Making Decisions
      No ISLLC-related performance aspects
    Group Leadership
      No ISLLC-related performance aspects
    Interpersonal Sensitivity
      No ISLLC-related performance aspects
    Range of Interests
      3 ISLLC performance aspects related to range of interests
    Professional Motivation
      3 ISLLC performance aspects related to professional motivation
    Expressing Professional Values
      6 ISLLC performance aspects related to expressing professional values
    Oral Communication
      4 ILSSC performance aspects related to oral communication

Note: Linkages were made by the principal author and verified by education experts.
SOURCE: Adapted from Council of Chief State School Officers (1996).

YOUR TWO INTERVIEWS

Guidelines

The primary task for you as interviewer is to read the questions just as they are written and to listen to your partner's responses. Do not elaborate on, modify, or change the wording of the questions. After reading the question, listen for the associated criteria listed in the phrases in the interview guide; check (✓) the most appropriate responses below each question. If you do not hear evidence for a particular phrase, do not check it; leave it blank until later. To do the job accurately, you will need to wait until your peer has completely finished answering the question.

Before you go on to the next question, place a dot (•) to the left of all phrases for which you have heard no evidence. Do not worry that this results in poor interview performance; it simply indicates that no information was available for that particular criterion. You should, however, enhance the reliability and completeness of your documentation by writing notes consisting of brief examples and quotes to clarify or explain your partner's answers.

Avoid asking "why" questions. Such questions often result in defensive responses and change the friendly character of interviews. A neutral and preferred way to probe for more information is to ask, "Can you tell me more?" Your partner's response to such a probe may often include additional information to help you decide whether to check a phrase on the list.

Adhere to the questions in the interview script. If your partner wants clarification of a question, read the question again. Avoid guiding or limiting the answers the interviewee gives. The interviewee should feel free to answer any way he or she chooses. If the interviewee does not want to answer a particular question, that's perfectly okay. Just put dots beside each related phrase for that question and go on to the next question.

It is important that you treat the information gained about each other with *strict confidentiality.* Without confidentiality, trust will be lacking; and where trust is lacking, interview responses are less meaningful. Also, no one should feel pressure to answer any question they do not wish to answer. Remember to put your partner at ease. One way to do this is to open with a question like, "How are you doing today?"

After listening to the response, begin by telling your peer what you will be doing. You might, before the first interview, say, "I will be asking you seven questions concerning the group problem-solving discussion. I'll be making some notes and may need your help. I may also need to ask you to clarify some of your answers."

Additionally, before beginning with the scripted questions, you might include something like, "Do you have any questions?" or "Are you ready to begin?"

Combined Interviewing

One of the unusual aspects of this interview process here in this leadership development book is that the interviewer and interviewee exchange roles at designated times during the interviews. This exchange helps to remind you that the purpose of this activity is for you and your partner, as prospective administrators, to learn how to conduct structured interviews. When conducting the first interview with your partner, one of you will ask all the questions first while the other answers; then you will switch roles. When it's your turn to respond to the interview questions, do not look at the questions or performance indicators; this will only tend to inhibit your responses. Set aside the interview script so that you can respond freely.

We can assure you from our experience that the first interviewer does not have an advantage over the second interviewer. In fact, both of you have the advantage of seeing all the questions before beginning. Remember that the purpose of the first interview is to learn how to conduct a fair and impartial structured interview, not to learn how to remember the listen-fors so you can be sure to address them all.

Group Problem-Solving Interview, Documentation, and Rating

The first short interview focuses on the group problem-solving discussion in Chapter 6 and, therefore, should be held soon after that discussion. This interview is a brief, introductory experience that provides practice in accurately documenting answers to seven questions. You and your partner will take turns interviewing one another to verify the accuracy of each other's documentation work in the previous chapter. You will each ask the same questions, which are scripted on the Group Discussion Interview and Rating Guide, and will exchange documentation when you're finished. This form also serves as the documentation form. You can use the times in the time column as guides—they indicate the average cumulative time for the interview in minutes. If you use a stopwatch, begin timing at 00:00. Take time to get thoughtful answers. Do not rush through the interview or you won't get the information you need. Next, switch roles and repeat the scripted interview. After you and your partner have completed interviewing each other, rate your partner's responses and return the completed interview guides. Rating will most likely take another 10 minutes. You may want to examine the sample of a completed version of this form in Resources (Form R.14).

7a: Group Discussion Interview and Rating Guide (for two)

Instructions

This activity serves as reflective practice for the group problem-solving discussion in Chapter 6. Use a total of 20 minutes for both you and your partner to interview each other. Take turns interviewing each other with the seven numbered questions in the script that follows. When you finish, rate your partner's responses and return the completed interview guide. You probably need at least 10 more minutes to analyze, reflect, and rate your partner's documentation of your responses. Listen carefully to all your partner's responses and check (✓) the phrases that accurately represent what your partner revealed. You may add notes and examples in the desig-nated space. This should help explain or clarify your interpretation of your partner's response. If your partner does not answer in ways that align well with the listed phrases, that's okay. In such instances, do not check those particular phrases. Instead, place dots (•) to the left of the phrases. This is to be done only after your partner has completely finished responding to the current question.

Time

0:00

1. Think back to the 35-minute group problem-solving discussion in Chapter 6. How did you approach the task of helping to reach consensus on ranking school improvement plans? [2 minutes]

GROUP LEADERSHIP, MAKING DECISIONS

_____ Suggested ideas to get the activity underway

_____ Suggested a specific plan or approach to solve the problem

_____ Immediately seized the leadership

_____ Reserved active participation until later

YOUR NOTES:

2:00

2. Now think about the second part of the group discussion that dealt with preparing a consensus report for the superintendent. Did you use the same approach as you did in the first part of the discussion? [2 minutes]

ANALYZING PROBLEMS, EXERCISING JUDGMENT,
INTERPERSONAL SENSITIVITY, MANAGING STRESS

_____ More analytical approach the second time

_____ More cautious approach the second time

_____ More collaborative approach the second time

_____ More productive approach overall

_____ More resistant to the leadership attempts of others

_____ More defensive the second time

YOUR NOTES:

Group Discussion Interview and Rating Guide (continued)

Time

4:00

3. What do you think you did particularly well in either one or both parts of the group discussion? [1 minute]

INTERPERSONAL SENSITIVITY, GROUP LEADERSHIP,
ORAL COMMUNICATION, MANAGING STRESS

_____ Acknowledged other group members' ideas

_____ Resolved conflicts among other group members

_____ Supported other individuals who showed signs of stress

_____ Kept the group on task

_____ Expressed ideas well

_____ Handled criticism well

_____ Did well despite personal frustrations with the process

YOUR NOTES:

5:00

4. How do you feel about the group's conclusions? [2 minutes]

MANAGING STRESS, EXERCISING JUDGMENT, GROUP LEADERSHIP

_____ Feel good overall

_____ Feel the group reached the right conclusion

_____ Feel frustrated overall

_____ Disagree with the conclusions of the group

YOUR NOTES:

7:00

5. If you could participate in another group problem-solving situation right away, what, if anything, would you try to do differently? [1 minute]

ANALYZING PROBLEMS, ORGANIZING AND PLANNING, INTERPERSONAL
SENSITIVITY, GROUP LEADERSHIP, MANAGING STRESS

_____ Develop better procedures for accomplishing group tasks

_____ Provide more frequent leadership and direction to the group

_____ Support each other more often

Group Discussion Interview and Rating Guide (continued)

Time

_____ Increase personal level of participation
_____ Show more interpersonal sensitivity to others
_____ Remain more calm
YOUR NOTES:

8:00

6. What was the most difficult part of the group activity? [1 minute]

ANALYZING PROBLEMS, EXERCISING JUDGMENT, MANAGING STRESS,
INTERPERSONAL SENSITIVITY

_____ Ranking the plans
_____ Defending the assigned school improvement plan
_____ Reaching consensus on the ranking of plans
_____ Reaching consensus on the report to the superintendent
_____ Remaining calm
_____ Dealing with other group members.
YOUR NOTES:

9:00

7. What, if anything, prevented you from doing your best? [1 minute]

ORGANIZING AND PLANNING, MANAGING STRESS,
INTERPERSONAL SENSITIVITY

_____ Lack of sufficient time
_____ Defensiveness of other group members
_____ Own defensiveness
_____ Limited expertise in planning
YOUR NOTES:

10:00

THIS CONCLUDES THE GROUP DISCUSSION INTERVIEW—Rate Oral Communication and the Group Discussion Performance Summary Ratings on the next two pages. See the way it was done on page 226 in the second interview.

Group Discussion Interview and Rating Guide (continuted)

Oral Communication Ratings

Place a check (✓) to the left of each true statement below. Do not check a false statement; instead, place a dot (•) to the left of the statement. The information recorded below will determine the final score for the participant's oral communication skill noted in this interview.

Voice Audibility

____	Exceptionally easy to hear	=	+
____	Moderately easy to hear	=	(+)
____	Less than moderately easy to hear	=	(−)
____	Difficult to hear	=	−
____	Very difficult to hear	=	⊖

Voice Quality

____	Very high quality	=	⊕
____	More than moderate quality	=	+
____	Moderate quality	=	(+)
____	Less than moderate quality	=	(−)
____	Poor quality	=	−
____	Very poor quality	=	⊖

Word Articulation

____	Very high clarity	=	⊕
____	More than moderate clarity	=	+
____	Moderate clarity	=	(+)
____	Less than moderate clarity	=	(−)
____	Little clarity	=	−
____	Very little clarity	=	⊖

Pronunciation

____	0 errors and very high skill	=	⊕
____	0 errors and more than moderate skill	=	+
____	0 errors and moderate skill	=	(+)
____	2 errors and less than moderate skill	=	(−)
____	4 errors and poor skill	=	−
____	5+ errors and very little skill	=	⊖

Grammar

____	0 errors and very high skill	=	⊕
____	0 errors and more than moderate skill	=	+
____	0 errors and moderate skill in grammar	=	(+)
____	2 errors and less than moderate skill	=	(−)
____	4 errors and poor skill in grammar	=	−
____	5+ errors and very poor skill in grammar	=	⊖

Eye Contact

____	Very high frequency	=	⊕
____	More than moderate frequency	=	+
____	Moderate frequency	=	(+)
____	Less than moderate frequency	=	(−)
____	Seldom	=	−
____	Never	=	⊖

Confidence

____	Very high confidence	=	⊕
____	More than moderate confidence	=	+
____	Moderate confidence	=	(+)
____	Less than moderate confidence	=	(−)
____	Little confidence	=	−
____	No confidence	=	⊖

Comments:

Overall Ratings: ____

Group Discussion Interview and Rating Guide (continuted)

Overall Group Discussion Performance Summary
Rate your partner on each performance area on a scale of ⊖ to ⊕ (very little overall to very high overall). Remember that these two extreme ratings are rarely appropriate.

Use the following guidelines for determining overall performance summary ratings for all areas documented in the 10-minute interview. Due to the complexity of the interview documentation task, you will need to survey your checks and dots and then use your best judgment regarding the performance levels.

Symbols	Interpretations
⊕	Very high skill shown
+	More than moderate skill
(+)	Moderate skill shown
(−)	Less than moderate skill
−	Little skill shown
⊖	Very little skill shown

Overall Group Discussion Interview Summary Ratings

Performance Areas	Rating Symbols
Analyzing Problems	_____
Exercising Judgment	_____
Organizing and Planning	_____
Making Decisions	_____
Group Leadership	_____
Interpersonal Sensitivity	_____
Managing Stress	_____
Oral Communication	_____

Note: *Extreme ratings ⊕ or ⊖ are seldom appropriate.*

Personal Interview and Documentation

Now decide who will be the first interviewee on the next and longer personal interview, which is scripted in the Personal Interview and Rating Guide. You may want to examine the sample of this completed form in Resources (Form R.15). Periodically during this interview, you will be asked to switch roles: The interviewer will become the interviewee and vice versa.

Repeat the process using a fresh copy of the Personal Interview and Rating Guide. Each partner should answer the sets of questions not answered before, so that by the end of the time period, you have both answered all the questions. When you and your partner have both answered all the questions on both interviews, rate each other's performances on the personal interview, using the Oral Communication Ratings section of the form. An example of the filled-in Personal Interview Form and Rating Guide is in the Resources (Form R. 15}.

7b: Personal Interview and Rating Guide (for two)

Instructions

Use a total of two and a half hours for you and your partner to take turns interviewing each other with the 35 numbered questions that follow. Listen carefully to all your partner's responses and check (✓) the phrases that accurately represent what your partner revealed. You may add notes and examples in the designated space. This should help explain or clarify your interpretation of your partner's response. If your partner does not answer in ways that align well with the listed phrases, that's okay. In such instances, do not check those particular phrases. Instead, place dots (●) to the left of the phrases. This is to be done only after your partner has completely finished responding to the current question.

Time

0:00

1. We either will learn, or we have already learned, some things about each other from our work together, but we don't know much about our personal lives. Tell me about your family, your early background, and your experiences growing up. [2 minutes]

INTERPERSONAL SENSITIVITY, MANAGING STRESS

_____ Talked about early years with little or no difficulty

_____ Talked about early years with some difficulty

YOUR NOTES:

2:00

2. Now let's talk about any early work experiences you may have had. How old were you when you got your first part-time job? And what did you do? [2 minutes]

RANGE OF INTERESTS, PROFESSIONAL MOTIVATION

_____ Jobs varied

_____ Jobs were relatively similar

_____ Jobs represented increasing responsibilities

_____ No part-time jobs before high school

YOUR NOTES:

4:00

3. What other kinds of work experiences did you have while you were in high school or college? [2 minutes]

Personal Interview and Rating Guide (continued)

Time

RANGE OF INTERESTS, PROFESSIONAL MOTIVATION

_____   Jobs varied

_____   Jobs were relatively similar

_____   Jobs represented increasing responsibilities

_____   No part-time jobs in high school or college

YOUR NOTES:

6:00

4.   What was your first full-time job? [2 minutes]

PROFESSIONAL MOTIVATION

Job:

YOUR NOTES:

8:00

5.   Let's discuss you college experiences. What subjects or courses did you like best? In which courses did you do your best work? [2 minutes]

ANALYZING PROBLEMS, RANGE OF INTERESTS

Liked best:

Did best in:

10:00

6.   What subjects, if any, did you choose as electives outside your major field of study? [1 minute]

Personal Interview and Rating Guide (continuted)

Time

PROFESSIONAL MOTIVATION, RANGE OF INTERESTS

_____ 1 or 2 electives

_____ 3 or 4 electives

_____ 5 or more electives

YOUR NOTES:

11:00

7. In what extracurricular activities were you involved? [1 minute]

PROFESSIONAL MOTIVATION, RANGE OF INTERESTS

Extracurricular Activities:

_____ 1 or 2 extracurricular activities

_____ 3 or 4 extracurricular activities

_____ 5 or more extracurricular activities

YOUR NOTES:

12:00

8. Did you have any significant achievements that you were particularly proud of when you were in school? [1 minute]

PROFESSIONAL MOTIVATION

Achievements:

_____ 1 or 2 significant achievements

_____ 3 or 4 significant achievements

_____ 5 or more significant achievements

YOUR NOTES:

Personal Interview and Rating Guide (continuted)

Exchange Roles

Time
13:00

9.   Let's shift to the present. What do you enjoy doing when you aren't working?
     [3 minutes]

RANGE OF INTERESTS, PROFESSIONAL MOTIVATION
Activities Include:
_____   Activities primarily career-related
_____   Activities both solitary and group based
_____   Activities both career and family related
_____   Some outside activities
_____   Many outside activities
          YOUR NOTES:

16:00

10.   What clubs or organizations do you currently belong to? Are you active in any of
      them? Do you hold leadership positions in any of them? [2 minutes]

GROUP LEADERSHIP, PROFESSIONAL MOTIVATION
Clubs and Organizations:
_____   Sometimes holds leadership positions
_____   Often holds leadership positions
_____   Holds no leadership positions
          YOUR NOTES:

18:00

11.   Other than this program, have you participated in any other professional
      development activities recently? If so, tell me about them. [2 minutes]

Personal Interview and Rating Guide (continuted)

Time

PROFESSIONAL MOTIVATION , RANGE OF INTERESTS

Professional Development Activities:

_____ 1 or 2 professional development activities

_____ 3 or 4 professional development activities

_____ 5 or more professional development activities

_____ No recent professional development activities

YOUR NOTES:

20:00

12. Now let's talk about how you approach your life and work. All of us encounter problems and obstacles in both our personal and professional lives. Can you recall such a situation in your life? [3 minutes]

MANAGING STRESS, INTERPERSONAL SENSITIVITY

How did you handle the situation?

How was the problem resolved?

ANALYZING PROBLEMS, EXERCISING JUDGMENT,
PROFESSIONAL MOTIVATION

_____ Could not recall encountering problems or obstacles

_____ Occasionally encountered problems or obstacles

_____ Almost always faced up to problems or obstacles

YOUR NOTES:

23:00

13. Have you ever encountered any problems in working with a particular individual or group? Tell me about the experience. How did you deal with the situation? How was the problem resolved? [2 minutes]

Personal Interview and Rating Guide (continued)

Time

ANALYZING PROBLEMS, INTERPERSONAL SENSITIVITY,
PROFESSIONAL MOTIVATION, EXERCISING JUDGMENT

_____ Could not recall encountering problems with others

_____ Occasionally encountered problems with others

_____ Almost always faced up to problems with others

YOUR NOTES:

25:00

14. All of us encounter work situations that require us to make adjustments. What adjustments did you have to make? How was the situation resolved? [2 minutes]

ANALYZING PROBLEMS, INTERPERSONAL SENSITIVITY,
PROFESSIONAL MOTIVATION, EXERCISING JUDGMENT

_____ Could not recall needing to make adjustments

_____ Occasionally required to make adjustments

_____ Successful adjustments were made

_____ Adjustments made were not accepted by others

YOUR NOTES:

27:00

15. Have you ever encountered a situation in which you demonstrated initiative by calling a group of people together to solve a problem? What was the situation? How did you approach the situation? How was the problem resolved? [3 minutes]

ANALYZING PROBLEMS, PROFESSIONAL MOTIVATION, INTERPERSONAL
SENSITIVITY, EXERCISING JUDGMENT, GROUP LEADERSHIP

_____ Could not recall needing to call a group together

_____ Occasionally needed to call a group together

_____ Initiative taken resulted in a successful outcome

_____ Initiative taken was not accepted by others

YOUR NOTES:

Personal Interview and Rating Guide (for two) (continued)

16. Can you recall a work situation in which you had to learn new skills or techniques because you didn't have sufficient background in the particular area? How did you go about acquiring the necessary skills? To what degree were you successful in measuring up to the situation? [2 minutes]

ANALYZING PROBLEMS, PROFESSIONAL MOTIVATION, MAKING DECISIONS, EXERCISING JUDGMENT

_____ Could not recall needing to learn new skills

_____ Took immediate action to learn new skills

_____ Attempted to learn new skills

_____ Did not attempt to learn new skills

YOUR NOTES:

32:00

17. Can you think of any work situation in which others came to you for assistance in solving a problem? What was the situation? What did you do to solve the problem? How was the situation resolved? [2 minutes]

ANALYZING PROBLEMS, PROFESSIONAL MOTIVATION, MAKING DECISIONS, EXERCISING JUDGMENT, INTERPERSONAL SENSITIVITY

_____ Could not recall being called upon by others for assistance

_____ Took action to assist solving a problem presented by others

_____ Attempted different solutions

_____ Did not attempt different solutions

_____ Called on frequently by others

_____ Called on occasionally by others

YOUR NOTES:

34:00

18. Sometimes we work very hard to solve a problem but ultimately are unable to resolve it to our satisfaction. Can you recall such a situation in your career? What did you do to resolve the situation? How was the situation resolved? [2 minutes]

Personal Interview and Rating Guide (continuted)

Time

ANALYZING PROBLEMS, MAKING DECISIONS, PROFESSIONAL MOTIVATION, EXERCISING JUDGMENT

_____ Could not recall needing to resolve problems

_____ Took action to resolve a problem

_____ Attempted different solutions

_____ Did not attempt different solutions

YOUR NOTES:

36:00

19. What do you think your colleagues think of your performance on the job? How do you know? [2 minutes]

ANALYZING PROBLEMS, PROFESSIONAL MOTIVATION,
EXERCISING JUDGMENT, EXPRESSING PROFESSIONAL VALUES

_____ Gets feedback from colleagues and peers

_____ Gets feedback from formal organization channels and processes

_____ Gets feedback from those served

_____ Gets little or no feedback from anyone

YOUR NOTES

Personal Interview and Rating Guide (continuted)

Exchange Roles

Time
38:00

20. Tell me more about your current position. What do you do and what do you consider your most important responsibilities? [2 minutes]

PERSONAL MOTIVATION, EXPRESSING PROFESSIONAL VALUES,
INTERPERSONAL SENSITIVITY, GROUP LEADERSHIP

Current position:

_____ A variety of routine tasks

_____ Requires new learning

_____ Professionally challenging

_____ Serve as a role model for others

_____ Positive view of self as a result of current job

YOUR NOTES:

40:00

21. What do you think you have done especially well in your current position? [2 minutes]

PERSONAL MOTIVATION, EXPRESSING PROFESSIONAL VALUES

Things done well:

_____ Made no direct references to personal work standards

_____ Made some references to personal work standards

_____ Made many references to personal work standards

YOUR NOTES:

42:00

22. Has there ever been a time when you were not especially pleased with your performance in a job situation? What was the situation? How did you deal with it? How was the situation resolved? [2 minutes]

Personal Interview and Rating Guide (continuted)

Time

PROFESSIONAL MOTIVATION, EXPRESSING PROFESSIONAL VALUES

Not pleased with:

_____ Made no direct references to personal work standards

_____ Made some references to personal work standards

_____ Made many references to personal work standard.

YOUR NOTES:

44:00

23. What are your career goals? [2 minutes]

Career goals:

_____ Cited no career goals

_____ Cited general career goals

_____ Cited specific career goals

_____ Spoke of a special commitment to the field of education

YOUR NOTES:

Personal Interview and Rating Guide (continuted)

Exchange Roles

Time
46:00

24. What do you consider some of the most important characteristics and abilities of leaders in your field? [2 minutes]

EXPRESSING PROFESSIONAL VALUES

Instructions: Interviewer: Note reported leadership characteristics and abilities in the following section.

List:

On a scale of 1 to 10, how would you rank yourself on the preceding list of characteristics and abilities?

EXPRESSING PROFESSIONAL VALUES, ANALYZING PROBLEMS

Instructions: Interviewer: Number the ranking of leadership characteristics and abilities noted in the preceding section.

YOUR NOTES:

48:00

25. What would you identify as the most significant current trends in the delivery of instruction at your level? [2 minutes]

YOUR NOTES:

Personal Interview and Rating Guide (continuted)

Time
50:00

26. What would you identify as the most significant current trends in the management and administration of schools at your level? [1 minute]
    YOUR NOTES:

51:00

27. What would you identify as the standards or values you have set for your own performance on the job? [1 minute]

PERSONAL MOTIVATION, EXPRESSING PROFESSIONAL VALUES

_____ Personal standards and values set

_____ Did not identify personal standards or values

YOUR NOTES:

52:00

28. Have you ever encountered a situation in which you stood up for your beliefs by stating publicly what is important to you about education? What was the situation? What beliefs did you stand up for? What was the result of your action? [2 minutes]

EXPRESSING PROFESSIONAL VALUES, ANALYZING PROBLEMS, PROFESSIONAL MOTIVATION

_____ Gave an example

_____ Gave several examples

_____ Taking a personal stand on beliefs is too risky because . . .

_____ Taking a personal stand on beliefs is worth the risk because . . .

54:00

29. Can you identify a situation in which you needed to employ your most strongly held educational beliefs? [2 minutes]

Personal Interview and Rating Guide (continued)

Time

EXPRESSING PROFESSIONAL VALUES, GROUP LEADERSHIP

_____ Gave an example

_____ Gave several examples

_____ Applied personal beliefs, convictions, and standards

_____ Built support for ideas and opinions

YOUR NOTES:

56:00

30. What do you consider to be your strongest characteristic or ability? Can you describe a situation in which you capitalized on that characteristic or ability? What did you do? What was the result of your action? [3 minutes]

EXPRESSING PROFESSIONAL VALUES, INTERPERSONAL SENSITIVITY

Strongest characteristic or ability:

_____ Freely talked about abilities

_____ Talked about abilities with some difficulty

_____ Described no situations

_____ Described no results of actions taken

YOUR NOTES:

59:00

31. Now, let's talk about the opposite. What would you identify as your greatest short-coming? Can you think of anything you have done to make up for that shortcoming? What did you do? What was the result of your action? [2 minutes]

ANALYZING PROBLEMS, INTERPERSONAL SENSITIVITY

Shortcomings:

_____ Freely talked about shortcomings

_____ Talked about shortcomings with some difficulty

_____ Described no shortcomings

YOUR NOTES:

Personal Interview and Rating Guide (continued)

32. Can you identify a situation in which you came up with an idea to solve a problem that occurred at work? What was the idea for addressing the situation? What was the result of your suggestion? [2 minutes]

ANALYZING PROBLEMS, EXPRESSING PROFESSIONAL VALUES, EXERCISING JUDGMENT, PROFESSIONAL MOTIVATION, INTERPERSONAL SENSITIVITY

The situation:

_____ Came up with ideas so solve the problem

_____ Ideas were accepted by others

_____ Ideas were in line with conventional practice

_____ Ideas were not accepted by others

YOUR NOTES:

33. Have you ever stated publicly an opinion that you knew was not popular? What was the opinion? What happened with you expressed your opinion? [2 minutes]

EXPRESSING PROFESSIONAL VALUES, PROFESSIONAL MOTIVATION, MANAGING STRESS, INTERPERSONAL SENSITIVITY

_____ Expressed an unpopular opinion

_____ Opinions were accepted by others

_____ Opinions were in line with conventional practice

_____ Opinions were not accepted by others

YOUR NOTES:

34. Have you ever been called upon to defend an instructional strategy or teaching technique about which you felt strongly? What was the situation? What was the result of your defense of the strategy? [2 minutes]

Personal Interview and Rating Guide (continuted)

Time

ANALYZING PROBLEMS, EXPRESSING PROFESSIONAL VALUES,
EXERCISING JUDGMENT, PROFESSIONAL MOTIVATION

The situation:

_____ Built support for the instructional strategy

_____ The instructional strategy was accepted by others:

_____ The instructional strategy was not accepted by others:

_____ When others resisted the strategy, remained silent:

YOUR NOTES:

67:00

35. What would you identify as your most outstanding achievement on the job?
[3 minutes]

PROFESSIONAL MOTIVATION

Outstanding achievement on the job: 70:00

The interview stops here.

You and your partner should each thank the other by saying this: "I have truly enjoyed getting to know more about you and some of your educational beliefs and values. Thanks very much for sharing your ideas and experiences with me."

Additional Information
Additional information about the interview is provided below.
The statements are addressed after the interview ends. [5 minutes]

INTERPERSONAL SENSITIVITY, ANALYZING PROBLEMS, MANAGING STRESS

My interviewee:

_____ Helped to maintain an easy two-way discussion

_____ Asked for clarification or interpretation

_____ Answered questions freely

_____ Made references to frustration and stress

_____ Freely admitted to having no answers for some questions

_____ Gave brief, direct answers to questions

_____ Couldn't remember some events or incidents

_____ Asked for time to think about an answer

_____ Asked to stop the interview early

_____ Criticized some interview questions

75:00

Personal Interview and Rating Guide (for two) (continuted)

Oral Communication Ratings

Place a check (✓) to the left of each true statement below. Do not check a false statement; instead, place a dot (•) to the left of the statement. The information recorded below will determine the final score for the participant's oral communication skills noted in this interview.

Voice Audibility

____ Exceptionally easy to hear	=	+
____ Moderately easy to hear	=	(+)
____ Less than moderately easy to hear	=	(−)
____ Difficult to hear	=	−
____ Very difficult to hear	=	⊖

Voice Quality

____ Very high quality	=	⊕
____ More than moderate quality	=	+
____ Moderate quality	=	(+)
____ Less than moderate quality	=	(−)
____ Poor quality	=	−
____ Very poor quality	=	⊖

Word Articulation

____ Very high clarity	=	⊕
____ More than moderate clarity	=	+
____ Moderate clarity	=	(+)
____ Less than moderate clarity	=	(−)
____ Little clarity	=	−
____ Very little clarity	=	⊖

Pronunciation

____ 0 errors and very high skill	=	⊕
____ 0 errors and more than moderate skill	=	+
____ 0 errors and moderate skill	=	(+)
____ 2 errors and less than moderate skill	=	(−)
____ 4 errors and poor skill	=	−
____ 5+ errors and very little skill	=	⊖

Grammar

____ 0 errors and very high skill	=	⊕
____ 0 errors and more than moderate skill	=	+
____ 0 errors and moderate skill in grammar	=	(+)
____ 2 errors and less than moderate skill	=	(−)
____ 4 errors and poor skill in grammar	=	−
____ 5+ errors and very poor skill in grammar	=	⊖

Eye Contact

____ Very high frequency	=	⊕
____ More than moderate frequency	=	+
____ Moderate frequency	=	(+)
____ Less than moderate frequency	=	(−)
____ Seldom	=	−
____ Never	=	⊖

Confidence

____ Very high confidence	=	⊕
____ More than moderate confidence	=	+
____ Moderate confidence	=	(+)
____ Less than moderate confidence	=	(−)
____ Little confidence	=	−
____ No confidence	=	⊖

Comments:

Overall Ratings: ____

Personal Interview and Rating Guide (continuted)

Overall Personal Interview Performance Summary Ratings

Rate your partner on each performance area on a scale of ⊖ to ⊕ (very little overall to very high overall). Remember that these two extreme ratings are rarely appropriate.

After you complete the personal interview, you will complete this overall performance summary form. As with other activities, you will summarize your overall ratings here and later use them to complete the final overall performance ratings form in Chapter 8. Use the following guidelines for determining overall ratings for all areas documented in this interview. Due to the complexity of the interview documentation task, you will need to survey the checks and dots and then use your best judgment regarding the performance levels.

Symbols	Interpretations
⊕	Very high skill shown
+	More than moderate skill
(+)	Moderate skill shown
(–)	Less than moderate skill
–	Little skill shown
⊖	Very little skill shown

Overall Personal Interview Performance Summary Ratings

Performance Areas	Rating Symbols
Analyzing Problems	_____
Exercising Judgment	_____
Organizing and Planning	_____
Making Decisions	_____
Group Leadership	_____
Interpersonal Sensitivity	_____
Managing Stress	_____
Oral Communication	_____
Expressing Professional Values	_____
Range of Interests	_____
Professional Motivation	_____

Note: *Extreme ratings ⊕ or ⊖ are seldom appropriate.*

8

Planning for Personal Development

OVERVIEW

This chapter is the shortest but not the least important. Here is where your performance data for the seven activities are summarized and culminate in your making a decision about what skill areas you should improve. After completing all the previous activities, you are ready to develop your own personalized developmental action plan. This is where you get to apply all you've learned about leadership and your own behavior as demonstrated throughout the various activities. By rating your performance in each activity and then summarizing your overall performance across all activities, you will have a very strong awareness of your personal strengths and development needs. The next step is to prepare your professional development action plan, carry it out, and evaluate its effects on improving the effectiveness of your leadership. Then revise your plan and repeat with a new action plan. And don't forget the importance of practice, practice, practice!

THE PROOF IS IN THE PUDDING

This old truism takes on new meaning when it comes to taking charge of our learning and development. We often do a lot of seemingly pointless preparation for planning our personal development, but seldom do we actually write down steps that can be observed and measured: an action plan. We sometimes take a shotgun approach—signing up for a course or workshop, or reading a book or two—without knowing whether the contents of the experience mesh with our real performance improvement needs. When beginning to make plans, we usually say something like, "I want to improve my skills of delegation" or "I want to make better oral presentations." This is a good start, but it hardly specifies what action steps we should take to achieve our goals.

Now that you have nearly finished this book, you should have a much better idea of what you should be doing to demonstrate your improved performance as a leader. First, let's have a look at the Overall Performance Ratings (Figure 8.1) as well as a sample of completed Overall Performance Ratings in Resources (Figure R.1).

We hope you find these forms interesting and useful. If you haven't looked at the examples of filled-in forms in Resources, now is the time to do so: Forms R.2, R.4, R.6, R.8, R.12, and R.16. Then transfer your own performance summary ratings to the appropriate blank lines on Figure 8.1. This profile of your performances will help you decide what you want to stress in your action plan.

EXAMPLE OF AN ACTION PLAN

R.1 in Resources is an example of a completed action plan. Though there were three areas with below-average skills, the person whose plan it is selected only one of them, oral presentation, as the target improvement area. Later, when you work on your own plan, you may also choose one of your strengths as well as a weakness for further improvement, and that's okay; one strength and one weakness are usually quite enough to work on.

Effective Communication Skills

The action plan in Form 8.1 reflects the fact that communication pervades all aspects of effective leadership. Goal setting, decision making, problem solving, and delegating responsibilities, among others, are administrative tasks closely tied to communication. Communication with parents and citizens affects community support of schools. One of the most obvious roles of an outstanding leader is that of being an effective oral presenter. This role requires the ability to make clear and effective presentations of information and ideas. It also requires the ability to present to various audiences and cultural groups, small and large, in both formal and informal settings.

Improving oral presentation skills before different audiences includes using appropriate visual aides to strengthen communication and using verbal and nonverbal skills effectively. Other skills include the use of appropriate volume, tone, rate of speech, use of pauses, modulation, pronunciation, and enunciation. Nonverbal skills include the use of appropriate body language, stance, eye contact, gestures for emphasis, movement, and so forth. All these aspects are suggested by the action plan in Form 8.1.

Figure 8.1 Overall Performance Ratings

Activity Performance—
Rating Descriptors and Symbols:

Very high skill shown	= ⊕
More than moderate skill shown	= +
Moderate skill shown	= (+)
Less than moderate skill shown	= (−)
Little skill shown	= −
Very little skill shown	= ⊖

Overall Performance—
Rating Descriptors and Symbols:

Outstanding skills shown	= ⊕
Above average skills shown	= +
Average skills shown	= (+)
Below average skills shown	= (−)
Poor skills shown	= −
Very poor skills shown	= ⊖

Instructions: Record the overall performance area summary ratings for each activity in the columns below. Then summarize, in the last column, overall performance levels across all activities.

Compare the *activity-rating* descriptors in the box to the left with the *overall-rating* descriptors in the box to the right. After determining the overall ratings, check the skill areas you want to improve.

Note: Extreme ratings, identified by shading in the boxes, are seldom used.

ACTIVITIES

Chapters:

Performance	2 Case Study	3 Improvement Plan	4 Office Deskwork	5 Oral Presentation	6 Group Discussion	7a Discussion Interview	7b Personal Interview	OVERALL (Check √) Areas for Improvement
PROBLEM-SOLVING CLUSTER								
1. Analyzing Problems								
2. Exercising Judgment								
3. Organizing and Planning								
4. Making Decisions								
INTERPERSONAL CLUSTER								
5. Group Leadership								
6. Delegating Effectively								
7. Interpersonal Sensitivity								
8. Managing Stress								
COMMUNICATION CLUSTER								
9. Oral Communication								
10. Written Communication								
11. Oral Presentation								
PERSONAL CHARACTERISTICS CLUSTER								
12. Expressing Professional Values								
13. Range of Interests								
14. Professional Motivation								

231

Form 8.1   Sample of a Completed Action Plan Worksheet

ACTION PLAN WORKSHEET

1. What is my objective? What do I want the result to be?

   Example: *I want to improve my oral presentation skills so that I can be effective before an audience that, most likely, will question and challenge my responses. I will make two presentations of 10 minutes each and put into practice all of the steps of my action plan. An evaluation session will be held with a coach of my choosing immediately after each presentation.*

2. How big a risk am I taking to pursue this objective? Is it worth it?

   Example: *The personal risk is small and, if successful, will be worth the time and effort. I will need this skill throughout the rest of my career whether in the classroom or in the front office.*

3. If I do this, what will result? How will things be better?

   Example: *If I improve my oral presentation skills, I will be recognized as a leader and be able to face the challenges ahead with more confidence than I currently have.*

4. What may I gain and risk if I try to reach the objective? Is it a Go or a No go?

   Example (Go): *What I learn by getting feedback on targeted attempts to improve my presentation skills outweighs the risk of appearing to be drawing attention to myself. Ultimately, improving my communication skills with groups of people will have an important influence on my effectiveness as a leader.*

   Example (No go): *I am not comfortable making a commitment to improve my oral presentation skills at this time. I would like to read more about public speaking before I pledge to change significantly my communication skills in this area.*

5. What are some things I should do to reach my objective?

   Example: *Develop an action plan to incorporate the oral presentation performance indicators into my plan. I should also review the ISLLC Standards and the NPBEA Dimensions outlined in the first chapter of Powerful Leadership Development, and consider their importance to my career. I could observe others at a variety of public speaking events and find a mentor to help me improve.*

Form 8.1   Sample of a Completed Action Plan Worksheet (continued)

6. What is my action plan? What specific steps will I take?

    Example: *I will select specific performance indicators to practice demonstrating, whenever I am scheduled to speak before a group. I will develop measurable objectives for each indicator and evaluate each at the conclusion of my presentation.*

Oral Presentation Performance Indicators are as follows:

- Standing for formal presentations
- Using appropriate volume, tone, rate of speech
- Using pauses when speaking
- Varying pitch when speaking
- Making no errors in grammar
- Making enthusiastic presentations
- Demonstrating a confident manner with eye contact, gestures, word emphasis, and so on
- Clearly presenting facts and ideas
- Presenting supportive reasons for recommendations
- Expressing well-organized thoughts
- Maintaining eye contact with the audience
- Making opening statements to the audience
- Making closing statements to the audience
- Using visual aids effectively

The performance indicators I have selected include the following:

1. *Standing for formal presentations*
2. *Making an opening statement to the audience*
3. *Using visual aids effectively*
4. *Maintaining eye contact with the audience*
5. *Demonstrating a confident manner with gestures and emphasizing important words and ideas*
6. *Making a closing statement to the audience*

I will arrange to make at least two oral presentations during the next 3 months and receive performance feedback from a coach. The coach will be someone I know that is skilled in public speaking and is aware of my development plans for improving my oral presentation skills.

Form 8.1   Sample of a Completed Action Plan Worksheet (continued)

I will make note cards and list the oral presentation performance indicators selected. I will review the indicators two days before each scheduled presentation. After reviewing the performance indicators on each card, I will plan how to meet my own expectations.

Listing each performance indicator, I will prepare these observable and measurable objectives:

1. **Standing for formal presentations**

   After my introduction, I will rise, face the audience, and thank the moderator or chairperson. I will remain standing throughout the presentation and move to a chalkboard or some other kind of writing surface.

2. **Making an opening statement to the audience**

   I will make an opening statement for the presentation that is judged by my coach to be engaging and interesting; something like, "Ladies and gentlemen, I am pleased to be here to share with you information about . . ."

3. **Maintaining eye contact with the audience**

   I will identify three individuals positioned in different locations in the audience and will alternate eye contact among them. The individuals I identify will be reported to my coach prior to the presentation.

4. **Organizing for and using visual aides**

   I will plan to prepare in advance, writing on a flip chart or some other suitable material, key points (or other important information) that I will cover in my presentation. I will ensure that the writing is legible from a distance. My coach will assist me in evaluating the clarity of the visual aids I use.

5. **Demonstrating a confident manner**

   I will practice, before a mirror or video camera, how to effectively emphasize important aspects of my presentation. This may be done by hand movements for emphasis, moving in on the audience, briefly acknowledging one or two known individuals in the audience, smiling, appearing relaxed and confident, and so on.

Form 8.1   Sample of a Completed Action Plan Worksheet (continued)

6. Making a closing statement to the audience

I will make a closing statement for the presentation: something like, "Ladies and gentlemen, I am pleased to have been able to address you today. In summary, we have discussed the following points . . . any questions? Thank you."

7. How am I going to evaluate the outcomes; how will I know how I'm doing?

I will have my coach videotape the two presentations and I will review the tape and document the number of identified performance indicators I have successfully used. Additionally, I will get feedback from my coach.

Form 8.1 implies that its creator remembered that volume, tone, rate of speech, use of enough pauses in sentences, varying the pitch when you speak, and using correct pronunciation and grammar are important. Also, presenting supportive reasons for any recommendations is important. And finally, it is important to enhance the clarity of your ideas as presented, with opening and closing statements, sufficient eye contact, the use of visual aids, organization of thoughts presented, confident mannerisms, and enthusiasm. These are all important aspects of effective oral presentations. These skills are seldom acquired except through practice and experience.

Similarly, your own action plan will have many details on which to focus in the area you target for improvement.

Performance Indicators

Most people ask, "So what do I do next?" For those of you who have completed all the activities in this book, that's easy. Before you begin your own action plan, review the relationships, summarized in the Resources, with the ISLLC Standards and the National Policy Board for Educational Administration's (NPBEA) Domains and Dimensions (see Form R.18) with regard to whatever area you choose for improvement. The creator of Form 8.1, for example, would examine the performance indicators in the clusters that are shown in Table 8.1; these are the specific indicators on which the action plan in Form 8.1 is structured.

Table 8.1 Performance Indicators for Form 8.1

9. ORAL COMMUNICATION	*Capsule Definition:* Orally expressing ideas clearly, effectively; using appropriate eye contact; using correct grammar, diction, pronunciation.
ISLLC Relationships	Standard 1 (Vision), Standard 3 (Management), Standard 4 (Community), Standard 6 (Context)
NPBEA Relationships	Domain 3 (Interpersonal), Domain 4 (Contextual)
Performance Indicators	• Speaking with appropriate volume
	• Articulating words clearly
	• Pronouncing words correctly
	• Making no errors in grammar
	• Making eye contact when listening or speaking
	• Expressing ideas clearly

Table 8.2 Force Field Analysis for Form 8.1

OBJECTIVE: Register for Saturday course in Eloquent Elocution

Forces in Favor	Forces Against
1. Nationally known presenters	1. $3,000 registration fee
2. Would build my confidence in making oral presentations	2. I don't have the time
3. Better communications skills will improve my chances for career advancement	3. I don't think I can round up the fee

Force Field Analysis

You can enhance, in a number of ways, the likelihood that your own plan of action will be successful. Take time to analyze the forces that may work for or against fulfilling your plan. A force field analysis is one way of identifying the elements that can help or block self-improvement efforts. Listing those forces makes clear the difficulties that must be faced and the factors that can help you fulfill the planned changes. Begin by stating the objective you are going to work on. Then list in two separate columns forces that you believe will help or inhibit your accomplishing the objective. Sometimes it is helpful to identify the source of the forces. Are they within you? Are they within or outside the work environment? Table 8.2 provides an example of a force field plan tied to the action plan in Form 8.1.

Any improvement plan you decide to implement will require a commitment of time—the scarcest resource in education. You will want to use blank paper to write out the questions and your responses. More space will be needed than what is provided for you on Form 8.2. There will never be enough time to finish all that you have to do, and it will always appear on the forces-against side of your force field analysis. But rethink your position. For example, if you had written the force field in Table 8.2, you might ask yourself, if someone were to pay you $20,000 to take the Saturday course, would you be able to find the time to do it? Of course you probably would— it's usually not a matter of time; it's a matter of priorities.

YOUR OWN ACTION PLAN

The Nine Steps

Remember the important nine steps recommended in the first chapter of this book? Here they are again:

1. Become familiar with the entire book before starting the activities.

2. Complete the leadership simulations and related activities.

3. Reflect on the completed activity, your choices, and the beliefs and reasons underlying your choices.

4. Share with your partner your reflections on your choices.

5. With your partner, review any differences between your choices and underlying belief systems.

6. In each chapter, complete your performance summary forms and the overall form for all activities.

7. Review the final outcomes and compare with your self-inventory, which you completed earlier.

8. Based on the summary performance form, as well as the entire experience, write your targeted, professional leadership development plan—your action plan.

9. Share your action plan with others; implement it and evaluate your growth in leadership skills.

Getting Started

With the nine steps in mind, you can take several preliminary steps toward implementing your action plan.

1. Analyze your support system. A support system is composed of those individuals at work or in your personal life on whom you can depend for help or comfort when you need it. If you find that your support system isn't as strong as you'd like, you may want to develop and strengthen it. Are there colleagues who may be cynical about your efforts?

ACTION PLAN WORKSHEET

1. What is my objective? What do I want the result to be?

2. How big a risk am I taking to pursue this objective? Is it worth it?

3. If I do this, what will result? How will things be better?

4. What may I gain and risk if I try to reach the objective? Is it a go or a no go?

5. What are some things I should do to reach my objective?

6. What is my action plan? What specific steps will I take?

If so, don't confide in them. Avoid their presence except for required business interactions. You don't need toxic people poisoning your resolve. Seek out those you can count on to support and help you.

2. Make a contract with a peer, a superior, or a subordinate covering one or more elements of your action plan. By making a contract with someone from whom you will receive help, you are more apt to stick to your promises. It's even more effective if you work out a mutual arrangement in which you serve as a monitor of your partner's progress.

3. Go public with your plan. This is particularly a good idea if you are embarking on a long and demanding path, such as an advanced degree in your selected area of improvement. Sharing your objectives with others will strengthen your resolve. When you've declared your intentions publicly, you are more likely to follow through on your plan. In addition, others can be of help and support to you during the process. Select only one or two areas at a time for improvement. If you try to take on too many self-improvement projects, time will truly become an issue. You will give less than the required attention to each project and will only create frustration and disappointment with your results.

4. After you have selected the first area for improvement, brainstorm about all the possibilities for a personal-development plan: Register for a course; attend a conference; research the literature and build a professional reading list; find a colleague who is skilled in the area and form a mentor relationship; job shadow; join a discussion group on a professional organization's Web site; and so on.

5. Once you know the possibilities, select those activities that seem best suited to help you reach your objective.

6. Create a detailed action plan. This may be the most critical step for your success. If there is not enough specificity in your actions, you may not know whether or not you have completed the activities, and you may not be able to tell when you have finished. Break the actions down into small, measurable steps, and set the timeline for each activity. Identify the resources you will need for each step of the action plan (time, finances, materials, people) and be sure they are in place prior to starting. If you have a lengthy plan (such as earning an advanced degree), be sure to establish benchmarks at regular intervals to measure progress toward the goal.

7. Implement your action plan.

8. Celebrate your success! If you have a lengthy action plan, plan minicelebrations as you meet benchmarks along the way.

Action Plan Worksheet

Examine and complete the sample action plan worksheet (Form 8.2). When you have completed your action plan, spend some quality time reflecting on your experience. What parts were the most successful? Which activities provided you with the greatest learning experiences? What does that tell you about your preferred learning style? Be sure to plan similar learning experiences when you develop your next action plan. Which activities did you keep putting off—or avoid altogether? What does that tell you about your preferred learning style? In your next action plan, think twice before committing to activities that you know you are unlikely to complete. Careful selection of activities in your action plan is an important component of building success into your plan.

Now revisit your leadership self-inventory that you completed in the first chapter (Form 1.1). Would you answer the questions differently now? Are you able to recognize your personal growth? Now is the time to build on your success and select another area for building your leadership skills. Continuous improvement is the key to powerful leadership development.

And this concludes our book about a powerful leadership development program illustrating a unique approach to professional development that bridges theory and practice.

How tasty will your pudding be?

Resources

These Resources contain

- An example of the three lists you were asked to make in Chapter 2 listing Normal School's strengths, weaknesses, and urgent problems

- Examples of some pages from completed documentation forms from Chapters 2, 3, 4, 5, 6, 7

- ISLLC standards and the number of performance aspects in the program skill areas covered in this book

- Summary analysis of National Policy Board for Educational Administration's domains and knowledge and the Interstate Leadership Licensure Consortium performance aspects related to the program skill areas covered in this book

THE GOAL

Figure R.1 shows you the information you will have when you have completed all the activities in this book.

Figure R.1 Example of Completed Overall Performance Ratings

OVERALL PERFORMANCE RATINGS

Activity Performance—
Rating Descriptors and Symbols:

Very high skill shown	= ⊕
More than moderate skill shown	= +
Moderate skill shown	= (+)
Less than moderate skill shown	= (−)
Little skill shown	= │
Very little skill shown	= ⊖

Instructions: Record the overall performance area summary ratings for each activity in the columns below. Then summarize, in the last column, overall performance levels across all activities.

Compare the *activity-rating* descriptors in the box to the left with the *overall-rating* descriptors in the box to the right. After determining the overall ratings, check the skill areas you want to improve. *Note:* Extreme ratings, identified by shading in the boxes, are seldom used.

Overall Performance—
Rating Descriptors and Symbols:

Outstanding skills shown	= ⊕
Above average skills shown	= +
Average skills shown	= (+)
Below average skills shown	= (−)
Poor skills shown	= │
Very poor skills shown	= ⊖

ACTIVITIES

Chapters: Performance	2 Case Study	3 Improvement Plan	4 Office Deskwork	5 Oral Presentation	6 Group Discussion	7a Discussion Interview	7b Personal Interview	OVERALL (Check (√) Areas for Improvement)
PROBLEM-SOLVING CLUSTER								
1. Analyzing Problems	+ / (+)	(+) / (+)	(+) / (+)	(+) / (+)	(+) / (+)	(+) / (+)	(+) / (+)	+ / (+) / (+)
2. Exercising Judgment	(+)	(+) / (+)	(+) / (+)	(+) / (+)		(+) / (+)	+ / (+)	(+) / (+)
3. Organizing and Planning	(+)	(+) / (+)	(+) / (+)	(+) / (+)		(+) / (+)	(+) / (+)	(+) / (+)
INTERPERSONAL CLUSTER								
5. Group Leadership					(+)	(+)	(+)	(+)
6. Delegating Effectively		(−)	(−)		+ / (+)	(+) / (+)	+ / (+)	(−) / (+)
7. Interpersonal Sensitivity			(−)	(+)				(+) / (+)
8. Managing Stress								
COMMUNICATION CLUSTER								
9. Oral Communication	(+)	(−)	(+)	(+)	+ / (−)	(−)	(+)	(−) / (+) / (+)
10. Written Communication				(+)				
11. Oral Presentation								
PERSONAL CHARACTERISTICS CLUSTER								
12. Expressing Professional Values	(+)	(+)	(−)	(+)	(−)		(+) / (+) / (+)	(+) / (+) / (+)
13. Range of Interests								
14. Professional Motivation								

CASE STUDY
(CHAPTER 2)

The First Three Lists

Here (Box R.1) are samples of the lists you made in chapter two on three blank sheets of paper.

Box R.1   Examples Lists of Normal School's Strengths, Weaknesses, and Urgent Problems (Prepared in Chapter 1 With Headings on Blank Paper)

List 1: Normal School's Strengths

1. Reputation for the basics
2. Teachers provide for activity-centered learning
3. Serves students well from middle- to upper-income families
4. Ethnic diversity
5. Many teachers have master's degrees
6. Outstanding after-school programs
7. Good physical education program—many awards
8. Strong music program with both a band & strings classes
9. Media center is well staffed, stocked, and used
10. Building is well maintained

List 2: Normal School's Weaknesses

1. Upper grades' dropout steadily increasing
2. Steadily declining average daily attendance
3. Diminishing tax revenues
4. Lower-income students feel left out
5. Significant drop in basic skills test scores—noted by PTO
6. Teachers not interested in curriculum review/ revision
7. Staff animosity—seasoned vs. new
8. Few students attend after-school activities

Box R.1 Continued

9. ELS program

10. Spelling bee situation

11. PTO has weak support from parents and faculty

12. Instructional technology

13. Inconsistent follow-through of dress policy

14. Mixed feelings concerning education procedures and teachers observing colleagues

List 3: Normal School's Most Urgent Problems

1. Significant drop in test scores (basic skills)

2. Steadily declining average daily attendance

3. Dropout rate steadily increasing

4. Staff feelings—evaluation procedures

5. Weak PTO—need strong community support (neighborhood drug issue, etc.)

6. Technology

7. Teacher attitude toward curriculum—review/revise

8. Staff animosity and inconsistent follow-through

9. Diminishing tax revenue—affects site-based management

10. Principal not believed to be competent to evaluate instruction

Form R.1 and Form R.2 are examples of filled-in forms from Chapter 2.

From R.1   Example of Completed Case Study Documentation Form—Urgent Problems
See the Documentation Forms in Chapter 2 for the instructions.

ANALYZING PROBLEMS—EXERCISING JUDGMENT—
EXPRESSING PROFESSIONAL VALUES—MAKING DECISIONS

  __3__ **1. The dropout rate is steadily increasing.**

  __2__ **2. There is a steadily declining average daily attendance.**

  __•__ **3. The school board has decided to implement districtwide, site-based management without inservice.**

  __•__ **4. The current principal feels threatened by the decision to start site-based management.**

  __•__ 5. Many seasoned teachers are burned out.

  __•__ **6. Resentment expressed by younger faculty over class assignments.**

  __•__ 7. PTO programs are poorly attended by parents and teachers.

  __•__ 8. There is a disturbing rumor that the school board is planning total renovation.

  __5__ **9. There are drug wars in the neighborhood of the school.**

  __•__ 10. There is increasing vandalism in the school.

  __6__ 11. Teachers are not getting support for needed instructional technology.

  __6__ 12. Children are not taught the technology needed for success in secondary school.

  __•__ 13. There are too many public address system interruptions during the school day.

  __•__ 14. There is too much instructional time lost to assemblies and other special events.

  __•__ 15. Children upset because dress policy is unfairly administered.

  __•__ **16. Parents demand to know what will be done to improve test scores.**

  __1__ **17. Basic skills test scores have dropped significantly.**

  __4__ 18. Tenured teachers do not like the new evaluation procedures.

  __10__ **19. Teachers are convinced the principal is not competent to evaluate their teaching.**

ANALYZING PROBLEMS—EXERCISING JUDGMENT—EXPRESSING PROFESSIONAL VALUES

  __✓__ 20. Your partner listed 10 urgent problems as directed.

  __✓__ 21. Your partner's listing of urgent problems differs from the order listed above.

  __✓__ 22. Your partner identified some of the most urgent problems
(those identified in bold type).

  __8__ Total the number of most urgent problems identified in bold on the preceeding list.

Form R.2 Example of Completed Overall Performance Summary: Case Study,
See blank documentation forms in Chapter 2 for the instructions.

Symbols	Interpretations
⊕	Very high skill shown
+	More than moderate skill
(+)	Moderate skill shown
(−)	Less than moderate skill
−	Little skill shown
⊖	Very little skill shown

Overall Performance Summary
Case Study
(use ratings on pages 33, 36 and 38)

Performance Areas	Overall Rating Symbols
Overall Rating for Analyzing Problems	(+)
Performance Ratings: (+) , (+) , (+)	
Overall Rating for Exercising Judgment	(+)
Performance Ratings: (+) , (+) , +	
Overall Rating for Making Decisions	+
Performance Rating: +	
Overall Rating for Written Communication	(+)
Performance Ratings: (+) , (+) , (+)	
Overall Rating for Expressing Professional Values	(+)
Performance Ratings: + , (+) , (+)	

Note: *Extreme ratings of ⊕ or ⊖ are seldom appropriate.*

SCHOOL IMPROVEMENT PLAN
(CHAPTER 3)

Forms R.3 and R.4 are examples of filled-in forms from Chapter 3.

Form R.3   Example of Completed School Improvement Plan Rating Form
See blank documentation forms in Chapter 3 for the instructions.

ANALYZING PROBLEMS

The goals and objectives of the plan relate directly to:

- __•__ 1. Afterschool programs
- __•__ 2. Attendance and absenteeism rates
- __•__ 3. Community involvement
- __•__ 4. Curriculum development
- __•__ 5. First language of students
- __•__ 6. Guidance and counseling program
- __✓__ 7. Improving instruction
- __✓__ 8. Inservice and staff development
- __•__ 9. Leadership
- __•__ 10. Mentoring and tutoring
- __✓__ 11. Parent involvement
- __•__ 12. Research and evaluation
- __•__ 13. Scheduling
- __✓__ 14. School climate
- __•__ 15. Student demographics
- __✓__ 16. Student morale
- __•__ 17. Teacher burnout
- __✓__ 18. Teacher involvement
- __✓__ 19. Teacher morale
- __✓__ 20. Test results and student achievement
- __•__ 21. Test-taking preparation

Total matches (checks) in this column: __8__

EXERCISING JUDGMENT

The plans include measurable outcomes that relate to:

- __•__ 1. Absenteeism
- __•__ 2. Curriculum
- __•__ 3. Emphasis placed on test results
- __•__ 4. GPA
- __•__ 5. Information given to parents concerning the testing program
- __•__ 6. Language of students taking tests
- __•__ 7. Preparing students for taking tests
- __✓__ 8. Promotion rates
- __•__ 9. Scheduling tests
- __•__ 10. Student demographics
- __•__ 11. Teacher morale
- __✓__ 12. Test results
- __•__ 13. The plan for improving scores does not include outcomes stated in *measurable terms*

Total matches (checks) in this column: __2__

Form R.4 Example of Completed Overall Performance Summary School Improvement Plan. See blank documentation forms in Chapter 3 for the instructions.

Symbols	Interpretations
⊕	Very high skill shown
+	More than moderate skill
(+)	Moderate skill shown
(−)	Less than moderate skill
−	Little skill shown
⊖	Very little skill shown

Overall Performance Summary
School Improvement Plan
(Use Ratings on Pages 52, 53, and 54)

Performance Areas	Rating Symbols
Overall Rating for Analyzing Problems Performance Ratings: (+) , (−)	(+)
Overall Rating for Exercising Judgment Performance Ratings: (+) , (−)	(+)
Overall Rating for Organizing and Planning Performance Ratings: (+)	(+)
Overall Rating for Making Decisions Performance Ratings: (+)	(+)
Overall Rating for Interpersonal Sensitivity Performance Ratings: (+)	(−)
Overall Rating for Written Communication Performance Ratings: (−)	(−)
Overall Rating for Expressing Professional Values Performance Ratings: (+)	(+)

Note: *Extreme ratings ⊕ or ⊖ are seldom appropriate.*

OFFICE DESKWORK
(CHAPTER 4)

Froms R.5 and R.6 are examples of filled-in forms from Chapter 4.

Form R.5   Example of Completed Form DW#1—Handling of Deskwork Item #1 (Figure 4.1)

GUIDANCE
Review the paragraphs beneath the Deskwork Instructions and Preparing Your Responses headings earlier in this chapter before documenting your partner's work on this form. Mark an item with a check (✓) if the applicable performance indicator is in evidence, with a dot (●) if it is not. Give examples where you can.

Task Completion

ORGANIZING AND PLANNING, and MAKING DECISIONS

  ✓   1. Handled the guidance memo   (Read performance definitions)
           re: memorial service as a high-priority item.
           If not, enter a dot and go on to the next deskwork item.

  ✓   2. Took some action.   (Read performance definition)
           If not, mark with a dot and go on to the next
           deskwork item.

ANALYZING PROBLEMS

  ✓   3. Sought more information   (Read performance definition)
           on the memorial service issue.
  ●   4. Sought more information on the family.
  ●   5. Sought information on the neighborhood drug situation.
  ●   6. Sought information on scheduling the memorial service.
  ✓   7. Sought policy information on holding memorial services at school.

ORGANIZING AND PLANNING

  ✓   8. Prepared a plan for the school   (Read performance definition)
           memorial service issue.

INTERPERSONAL SENSITIVITY and DELEGATING EFFECTIVELY

  ✓   9. Contacted Guidance about the memorial service.
  ✓   10. Directly acknowledged the viewpoint held by Guidance.
  ✓   11. Shared some memorial service information with Guidance.
  ✓   12. Used tact when contacting Guidance.   (Read performance definition)
  ●   13. Had someone else contact Guidance about the memorial service issue.

EXERCISING JUDGMENT

  ✓   14. Showed that the memorial service is a priority issue.   (Read performance definition)
  ●   15. Committed to having a memorial service at school.   (Read performance definition)

EXPRESSING PROFESSIONAL VALUES

  ✓   16. Stated strong personal value about the memorial service.   (Read performance definition)
  ●   17. Stated a strong value about the memorial being held at school.
  ●   18. Stated a strong value about excusing students to attend a school memorial service.
  ●   19. Stated another strong value. Describe here:

Form R.6   Example of Completed Overall Performance Summary—
Office Deskwork Ratings From Forms DW#1–DW#13
See blank documentation forms in Chapter 4 for the instructions.

Symbols	Interpretations
⊕	Very high skill shown
+	More than moderate skill
(+)	Moderate skill shown
(−)	Less than moderate skill
−	Little skill shown
⊖	Very little skill shown

Overall Performance Summary—
Office Deskwork Summary Ratings From
Forms DW#1–DW#13

Performance Areas   **Rating Symbols**

Analyzing Problems   (−)
Performance Ratings: (−), (−), (−), + , ___ ,
 + , (+), − , − , (+), (−), ___ , (+)

Exercising Judgment   (+)
Performance Ratings: (+), (+), (+), (+), ___ ,
 + , (+), (−), (+), (+), (+), (+), +

Organizing and Planning   (+)
Performance Ratings: (+), (+), (−), (−), (+),
(+), (+), (+), (+), (+), (+), (−), (−)

Making Decisions   (+)
Performance Ratings: (+), (+), (+), (+), (−),
(+), (+), (+), (+), (+), (+), (+), (−)

Delegating Effectively   (−)
Performance Ratings: (−), NA, (−), (−), ___ ,
(−), NA, NA, NA, − , (−), (+), (−)

Interpersonal Sensitivity   (−)
Performance Ratings: + , (−), (−), ___ , ___ ,
 + , (+), (−), (+), + , (−), + , (+)

Written Communication   (+)
Performance Ratings: (+), (+), (−), (+), ___ ,
(+), (+), (−), (−), (+), (+), (+), (+)
(Overall written response throughout deskwork activity)

Expressing Professional Values   (−)
Performance Ratings: (−), (−), NA, (+), ___ ,
(−), NA, NA, (−), − , − , (+), (+)

Note: *Extreme ratings of ⊕ or ⊖ are seldom appropriate.*

MAKING ORAL PRESENTATIONS
(CHAPTER 5)

Forms R.7 and R.8 are examples of filled-in forms from Chapter 5.

Form R.7 Example of Completed Rating for School Board Presentation

ANALYZING PROBLEMS

Noted Information Areas	Tally (/)
• 1. Board expectations—flagship school, mainstreaming, new and enhanced programs, etc.	
• 2. Budget—amounts for construction, renovation, program development and inservice, etc.	
✓ 3. Buildings and grounds—age, condition, parking, and space available	//
• 4. Classrooms—media center/library, numbers by grade levels, current and projected additional number needed each year, etc.	
• 5. Climate control—air conditioning and heating, etc.	
• 6. Community—expectations, involvement, resources, etc.	
✓ 7. Enrollment—current and projected	//
• 8. Equipment and technology—materials, supplies, current and projected, etc.	
• 9. Floor plan—current, classroom and office location, etc.	
✓ 10. In-service and staff development—current and projected needs, etc.	
• 11. Instruction—teaching, quality, needs, etc.	/
✓ 12. Programs—extracurricular, curriculum, special, current and projected needs, etc.	/
• 13. Staff—current and projected needs, etc.	
✓ 14. Teacher morale—current, contributing causes, etc.	/
• 15. Testing—test results, trends, etc.	
✓ 16. Time frame—approval processes, completion, duration, etc.	/
✓ 17. Other areas	///

ANALYZING PROBLEMS

Tally the analyzing problems performance indicators:

Total the tally marks (/) to determine the **number of facts** noted during the information-seeking period: __10__

Rating symbols and ranges: 1-2 = ⊖, 3-4 = –, 5 -6 = (–), 7-8 = (+), 9-10 = +, 11 or more = ⊕

Rating Symbol: __+__

ANALYZING PROBLEMS

Check the analyzing problems performance indicators:

Total the check marks (✓) to determine the **number of areas** covered (1-17): __7__

Rating symbols and ranges: 1 = ⊖, 2 = –, 3 = (–), 4 = (+), 5 = +, 6 or more = ⊕

Rating Symbol: __+__

Form R.8   Example of Completed Overall Rating for School board Presentation Performance Summary Ratings
See blank documentation forms in Chapter 5 for the instructions.

Symbols	Interpretations
⊕	Very high skill shown
+	More than moderate skill
(+)	Moderate skill shown
(–)	Less than moderate skill
–	Little skill shown
⊖	Very little skill shown

Overall Rating for School Board Presentation Performance Summary Ratings
(Use ratings on pages 148–157)

Performance Areas	Rating Symbols
Analyzing Problems Performance Rating: _(+)_	_(+)_
Exercising Judgment Performance Rating: _(+)_	_(+)_
Organizing and Planning Performance Rating: _(+)_	_(+)_
Making Decisions Performance Rating: _(+)_	_(+)_
Managing Stress Performance Rating: _(+)_	_(+)_
Oral Communication Performance Rating: _(+)_ , _(+)_	_(+)_
Oral Presentation Performance Rating: _(+)_	_(+)_
Expressing Professional Values Performance Rating: _(+)_	_(+)_

Note: *Extreme ratings of ⊕ or ⊖ are seldom appropriate.*

PROVIDING LEADERSHIP GROUPS
(CHAPTER 6)

Forms R.9, R.10, and R.11 are examples of filled-in forms from Chapter 6.

Form R.9 Example of Completed Part 1a: Ranking discussion
(first review of discussion period)

Instructions
Examine your partner's completed Ranking Sheet (Form 6.1) and complete the following:

Step 1
Place a check (✓) to the left of the two statements that follow, when they are true. Do not check a statement if it is false; instead, place a dot (•) to the left.

ANALYZING PROBLEMS

____3____ 1. Listed and ranked all three school improvement plans on the Ranking Sheet (upper half).

____•____ 2. Listed the consensus ranking of school improvement plans on the Ranking Sheet (lower half).

Step 2
When you view the videotape of the first discussion period, place a tally mark (/) on the blank line to the right for the most appropriate listed performance indicators. If a given indicator was observed more than one time, tally it each time it occurs. If you are documenting this discussion with your partner, the task may be shared. You may document the performance on one page while your partner documents performance on the other page. You may view the videotape as often as needed: start, stop, and replay.

When you finish documenting the first discussion period, pause and place one check (✓) on the blank line to the left of each statement in this section that has one or more tally marks. Do not check a statement if it is not true; instead, place a dot (•) to the left

GROUP LEADERSHIP	Example or Quote	Tally (/)
____•____ 1. Initiated the discussion.		_____
____3____ 2. Suggested solutions.	Said, "I think we need to listen to each report first, then decide what our ranking criteria should be." Later suggested a rating system.	____///____
____•____ 3. Suggested criteria for selecting the plan.		_____
____•____ 4. Clarified or restated the group's tasks.		_____
____•____ 5. Initiated a new topic, redirecting the discussion.		_____
____•____ 6. Kept group on task.		_____
____•____ 7. Summarized and restated the other member's arguments.		_____
____•____ 8. Pointed out areas of agreement.		_____
____3____ 9. Supported other member who was leading the discussion.	On a least three occasions, nodded head in support. One occasion said, "I think you have a good idea . . . let's go with it."	____///____
____3____ 10. Called attention to time constraints.	On two occasions, looked at watch and announced, "I think we're running out of time . . . we need to move it."	____///____
____•____ 11. Took action to end the discussion phase and to complete the ranking.		_____
____•____ 12. Freely participated in the discussion. (Make an overall judgment here—yes or no—don't tally)		_____
____•____ 13. Stopped irrelevant discussions.		_____
____•____ 14. Avoided or stopped arguments.		_____

Form R.10   Example of Completed Performance Indicators, Part 1a

GROUP LEADERSHIP

Tally the Group Leadership Performance Indicators:

Total the statements documented with tally marks (/) under GROUP LEADERSHIP.

Record the total number of tally marks. __10__

Rating symbols and ranges: 1-3 = ⊖, 4 – 6 = –, 7 - 9 = (–), 10 -12 = (+), 13 -15 = +, 16 or more = ⊕

Rating Symbol __(+)__

Check the Group Leadership Performance Indicators:

Total the number of check marks (✓) under GROUP LEADERSHIP.

Record the total number of check marks. __4__

Rating symbols and ranges: 1-3 = ⊖, 4 – 6 = –, 7 - 9 = (–), 10-12 = (+), 13 –15 = +, 16 or more = ⊕

Rating Symbol ___–___

INTERPERSONAL SENSITIVITY

Tally the Interpersonal Sensitivity Performance Indicators:

Total the statements documented with tally marks (/) under INTERPERSONAL SENSITIVITY. Remember to subtract tally marks for items 4 and 6 before recording number. __5__

Rating symbols and ranges: 1 = ⊖, 2 = – , 3 = (–), 4 = (+), 5 = + , 6 or more = ⊕

Rating Symbol ___+___

Check the Sensitivity Performance Indicators:

Total the number check marks (✓) under INTERPERSONAL SENSITIVITY. Subtract checks for 4 and 6 before recording number. __4__

Rating symbols and ranges: 1= ⊖, 2 = –, 3 = (–), 4 = (+), 5 = + , 6 = ⊕

Rating Symbol __(+)__

ANALYZING PROBLEMS

Tally the Analyzing Problems Performance Indicators:

Total the statements documented with tally marks (/) under ANALYZING PROBLEMS.

Record the total number of tally marks. __7__

Rating symbols and ranges: 1 = ⊖, 2 = – , 3 = (–), 4 = (+), 5 = + , 6 = ⊕

Rating Symbol __(+)__

Check the Analyzing Problems Performance Indicators:

Total the check marks (✓) made under ANALYZING PROBLEMS.

Record the total number of check marks. __6__

Rating symbols and ranges: 1 = ⊖, 2 = – , 3 = (–), 4 = (+), 5 = + , 6 = ⊕

Rating Symbol __(+)__

Form R.11 Example of Completed Overall Group Discussion Performance Summary Ratings

On the Overall Group Discussion Performance Summary form below, rate each performance area on a scale of ⊖ to ⊕ (very little skill shown to very high skill shown). This information is summarized here and later used on the final performance summary chart in the last chapter of this book. After viewing the final chart you will reach consensus with your partner on areas of strength and areas for improvement.

Symbols	Interpretations
⊕	Very high skill shown
+	More than moderate skill
(+)	Moderate skill shown
(−)	Less than moderate skill
−	Little skill shown
⊖	Very little skill shown

Overall Group Discussion Performance Summary Ratings
(pages 186 and 194)

Performance Areas	Rating Symbols
Analyzing Problems Performance Ratings: (+) , (+)	(+)
Exercising Judgment Performance Ratings: (+) , (+)	(+)
Group Leadership Performance Ratings: (+) , (−)	(+)
Interpersonal Sensitivity Performance Ratings: (+) , (+)	(+)
Managing Stress Performance Ratings: (+) , +	(+)
Oral Communication Performance Ratings: +	+
Oral Presentation Performance Ratings: (−) , (−)	(−)
Expressing Professional Values Performance Ratings: (+) , (−)	(−)

Note: *Extreme ratings of ⊕ or ⊖ are seldom appropriate.*

CONDUCTING STRUCTURED INTERVIEWS
(CHAPTER 7)

Forms R.12, R.13, R.14, and R.15 are an examples of filled-in forms from Chapter 7.

Form R.12   Example of Completed 7a: Group Discussion Interview and Rating Guide (for two) Only the first two questions are answered, but they provide a model for the remaining questions.

Instructions

This activity serves as reflective practice for the group problem-solving discussion in Chapter 6. Use a total of 20 minutes for both you and your partner to interview each other. Take turns interviewing each other with the seven numbered questions in the script that follows. When you finish, rate your partner's responses and return the completed interview guide. You probably need at least 10 more minutes to analyze, reflect, and rate your partner's documentation of your responses. Listen carefully to all your partner's responses and check (✓) the phrases that accurately represent what your partner revealed. You may add notes and examples in the designated space. This should help explain or clarify your interpretation of your partner's response. If your partner does not answer in ways that align well with the listed phrases, that's okay. In such instances, do not check those particular phrases. Instead, place dots (•) to the left of the phrases. This is to be done only after your partner has completely finished responding to the current question.

Time

0:00

1. Think back to the 35-minute group problem-solving discussion in Chapter 6. How did you approach the task of helping to reach consensus on ranking school improvement plans? [2 minutes]

GROUP LEADERSHIP, MAKING DECISIONS

__•__   Suggested ideas to get the activity underway
__✓__   Suggested a specific plan or approach to solve the problem
__•__   Immediately seized the leadership
__✓__   Reserved active participation until later
   YOUR NOTES:

   "Said, after 5 minutes into the discussion, "First, I think we should agree on the evaluation standards we are going to apply to all the plans."

2:00

2. Now think about the second part of the group discussion that dealt with preparing a consensus report for the superintendent. Did you use the same approach as you did in the first part of the discussion? [2 minutes]

ANALYZING PROBLEMS, EXERCISING JUDGMENT, INTERPERSONAL SENSITIVITY, MANAGING STRESS

__•__   More analytical approach the second time
__•__   More cautious approach the second time
__✓__   More collaborative approach the second time
__✓__   More productive approach overall
__•__   More resistant to the leadership attempts of others
__•__   More defensive the second time
   YOUR NOTES:

   "I think we should take the time to weigh the merits of each plan before we start pushing for our own plan to win."

Form R. 13 Example of Completed Overall Group Discussion Performance Summary

Rate your partner on each performance area on a scale of ⊖ to ⊕ (very little overall to very high overall). Remember that these two extreme ratings are rarely appropriate.

Use the following guidelines for determining overall performance summary ratings for all areas documented in the 10-minute interview. Due to the complexity of the interview documentation task, you will need to survey your checks and dots and then use your best judgment regarding the performance levels.

Symbols	Interpretations
⊕	Very high skill shown
+	More than moderate skill
(+)	Moderate skill shown
(−)	Less than moderate skill
−	Little skill shown
⊖	Very little skill shown

Overall Group Discussion Interview Summary Ratings

Performance Areas	Rating Symbols
Analyzing Problems	(+)
Exercising Judgment	(+)
Organizing and Planning	(+)
Making Decisions	(+)
Group Leadership	(+)
Interpersonal Sensitivity	+
Managing Stress	(+)
Oral Communication	(−)

Note: *Extreme ratings ⊕ or ⊖ are seldom appropriate.*

Form R. 14 Example of Completed 7b: Personal Interview and Rating Guide (for two).
Only the first two questions are answered, but they provide a model for the remaining
questions.

Instructions

Use a total of two and a half hours for you and your partner to take turns interviewing each other with the 35 numbered questions that follow. Listen carefully to all your partner's responses and check (✓) the phrases that accurately represent what your partner revealed. You may add notes and examples in the designated space. This should help explain or clarify your interpretation of your partner's response. If your partner does not answer in ways that align well with the listed phrases, that's okay. In such instances, do not check those particular phrases. Instead, place dots (•) to the left of the phrases. This is to be done only after your partner has completely finished responding to the current question.

Time
0:00

1. We either will learn, or we have already learned, some things about each other from our work together, but we don't know much about our personal lives. Tell me about your family, your early background, and your experiences growing up. [2 minutes]

INTERPERSONAL SENSITIVITY, MANAGING STRESS

___✓___ Talked about early years with little or no difficulty

___•___ Talked about early years with some difficulty

YOUR NOTES:

"Begin by a detailed description of early childhood experience . . .
beginning with surgery as a 3-year-old. Much detail provided about
early years."

2:00

2. Now let's talk about any early work experiences you may have had. How old were you when you got your first part-time job? And what did you do? [2 minutes]

RANGE OF INTERESTS, PROFESSIONAL MOTIVATION

___✓___ Jobs varied

___•___ Jobs were relatively similar

___✓___ Jobs represented increasing responsibilities

___•___ No part-time jobs before high school

YOUR NOTES:

"At age 11, I had a paper route, My brother was born at 12 and we moved across the state.
Developed an interest in electronics at an early age and experimented with magnets, motors,
Testa coils. . . . Was a shoeshine boy, soda jerk, railroad repair track worker, and a shoe
salesman by age of 18. My parents had communication problems."

Form R. 15 Example of Completed Overall Personal Interview Performance Summary Ratings

Rate your partner on each performance area on a scale of ⊖ to ⊕ (very little overall to very high overall). Remember that these two extreme ratings are rarely appropriate.

After you complete the personal interview, you will complete this overall performance summary form. As with other activities, you will summarize your overall ratings here and later use them to complete the final overall performance ratings form in Chapter 8. Use the following guidelines for determining overall ratings for all areas documented in this interview. Due to the complexity of the interview documentation task, you will need to survey the checks and dots and then use your best judgment regarding the performance levels.

Symbols	Interpretations
⊕	Very high skill shown
+	More than moderate skill
(+)	Moderate skill shown
(−)	Less than moderate skill
−	Little skill shown
⊖	Very little skill shown

Overall Personal Interview Performance Summary Ratings

Performance Areas	Rating Symbols
Analyzing Problems	(+)
Exercising Judgment	+
Organizing and Planning	(+)
Making Decisions	(+)
Group Leadership	(+)
Interpersonal Sensitivity	(+)
Managing Stress	(+)
Oral Communication	(−)
Expressing Professional Values	(+)
Range of Interests	(+)
Professional Motivation	+

Note: *Extreme ratings ⊕ or ⊖ are seldom appropriate.*

Standards and Domains

Forms R.16 and R.17 give you additional information about standards and domains.

Table R.16 ISLLC Standards and Number of Performance Aspects in Program Performance Areas Covered in This Book

PROGRAM PERFORMANCE AREAS AND LEADERSHIP ASPECTS														
ISLLC Standards and Aspects	1. AP	2. EJ	3. PL	4. MD	5. GL	6. DE	7. IS	8. MS	9. OC	10. WC	11. OP	12. PV	13. RI	14. PM
Standard 1 (vision related)	7	-	13	-	4	-	3	-	3	4	2	8	-	5
Standard 2 (instruction related)	6	1	10	-	-	-	6	-	-	-	-	10	-	4
Standard 3 (Management related)	10	7	15	3	1	2	8	-	1	1	1	-	-	-
Standard 4 (Community related)	6	5	11	-	5	-	11	-	4	4	2	11	-	8
Standard (Ethics related)	-	1	-	-	5	-	11	-	-	-	-	19	-	-
Standard 6 (Contest related)	7	4	2	-	-	-	-	-	4	-	2	6	3	3
269 ISLLC Performance Aspects	36	18	51	3	15	2	39	-	12	9	7	54	3	20

Program Key:
1. AP = Analyzing Problems
2. EJ = Exercising Judgment
3. PL = Organizing and Planning
4. MD = Making Decisions
5. GL = Group Leadership
6. DE = Delegating Effectively
7. IS = Interpersonal Sensitivity
8. MS = Managing Stress
9. OC = Oral Communication
10. WC = Written Communication
11. OP = Oral Presentation
12. PV = Expressing Professional Values
13. RI = Range of Interests
14. PM = Professional Motivation

Note: Linkages were identified by the principal author and verified by education experts.

Table R.17 Summary Analysis of National Policy Board for Educational Administration's (NPBEA) Domains, Knowledge and Interstate Leadership Licensure Consortium (ISLLC) Performance Aspects Related to the Performance Areas Covered in This Book

ISLLC Standard1: Developing, articulating, implementing, and stewarding a shared vision of learning

| 1.1 ANALYZING PROBLEMS | Related to the NPBEA Functional Domain: Information collection and problem analysis (S. D. Thomson, S. Hill, & B. M. Conny, 1993, pp. 3.1-3.27) |

Seven performance aspects of the ISLLC knowledge and dispositions are within the program skill area of analyzing problems.

Using information sources; collecting data; using data analysis strategies; using assessment data related to student learning to develop the school vision and goals; using relevant demographic data pertaining to students and their families in developing the school mission and goals; identifying barriers to achieving the vision to clarify and address; regularly monitoring, evaluating and revisiting the vision, mission, and implementation plans.

| 1.2 EXERCISING JUDGMENT | Related to the Functional Domain: Judgment (S. D. Thomson, S. Hill, & B. M. Conny, 1993, pp. 4.1-4.28) |

No performance aspects of the ISLLC Knowledge and Dispositions are within the program skill area of exercising judgment.

| 1.3 ORGANIZING AND PLANNING | Related to the Functional Domain: Organizational oversight (S. D. Thomson, S. Hill, & B. M. Conny, 1993, pp. 5.1-5.30) |

Thirteen performance aspects of the ISLLC Knowledge and Dispositions are within the program skill area of organizing and planning.

Developing and implementing strategic plans; using systems theory; communicating the vision and mission through ceremonies and similar activities; developing a vision with and among stakeholders; communicating progress toward the vision and mission to all stakeholders; involving the school community in school improvement efforts; assuring the vision shapes the educational programs, plans, and actions; developing an implementation plan in which objectives and strategies to achieve the vision and goals are clearly articulated; developing an implementation plan in which objectives and strategies to achieve the vision and goals are clearly articulated; using relevant demographic data pertaining to students and their families in developing the school mission and goals; seeking and obtaining needed resources to support the implementation of the school mission and goals; using existing resources in support of the school vision and goals; regularly monitoring, evaluating, and revising the vision, mission, and implementation plans.

Table R.17 Continued

1. 4 DELEGATING EFFECTIVELY

Related to the Functional Domain: Delegation (S. D. Thomson, S. Hill, & B. M. Conny, 1993, pp. 7.1-7.24)

No performance aspects of the ISLLC Knowledge and Dispositions are within the program skill area of delegating effectively.

1.5 MAKING DECISIONS

Related to the Functional Domain: Implementation (S. D. Thomson, S. Hill, & B. M. Conny, 1993)

No performance aspects of the ISLLC Knowledge and Dispositions are within the program skill area of making decisions.

1.6 GROUP LEADERSHIP

Related to the Functional Domain: Leadership (S. D. Thomson, S. Hill, & B. M. Conny, 1993, pp. 1.1-1.21)

Four performance aspects of the ISLLC Knowledge and Dispositions are within the program skill area of group leadership.
Using effective consensus building and negotiation skills; developing a vision with and among stakeholders; involving the school community in school improvement efforts; assuring the vision shapes the educational programs, plans, and actions.

1.7 INTERPERSONAL SENSITIVITY

Related to the Interpersonal Domain: Interpersonal sensitivity (S. D. Thomson, S. Hill, & B. M. Conny, 1993, pp. 15.1-15.23)

Three performance aspects of the ISLLC Knowledge and Dispositions are within the program skill area of interpersonal sensitivity.
Including all members of the school community; recognizing and celebrating the contributions of school community members to the realization of the vision; involving the school community in school improvement efforts.

1.8 RANGE OF INTERESTS

Related to the Interpersonal Domain: Motivating others (S. D. Thomson, S. Hill, & B. M. Conny, 1993, pp. 14.1-14.21)

No performance aspects of the ISLLC Knowledge and Dispositions are within the program skill area s of range of interests.

Table R.17 Continued

1.9 PROFESSIONAL MOTIVATION

Related to the Interpersonal Domain: Motivating others (S. D. Thomson, S. Hill, & B. M. Conny, 1993, pp.14.1-14.21)

Five performance aspects of the ISLLC Knowledge and Dispositions are within the program skill area of professional motivation.

Conducting continuous school improvement activities; ensuring that students have the knowledge, skills, and values needed to become successful adults; continuously examining one's own assumptions, beliefs, and practices; doing the work required for high levels of personal and organization performance; regularly monitoring, evaluating, and revising the vision, mission—and implementation plans.

1.10 PROFESSIONAL VALUES

Related to the Contextual Domain: Philosophical and cultural values (S. D. Thomson, S. Hill, & B. M. Conny, 1993, pp. 18.1-18.37)

Eight performance aspects of the ISLLC Knowledge and Dispositions are within the program skill area of professional values.

Communicating clear learning goals for all; communicating the belief in the educability of all; communicating a school vision of high standards of learning; including all members of the school community; ensuring that students have the knowledge, skills, and values needed to become successful adults; continuously examining one's own assumptions, beliefs, and practices; modeling the core beliefs of the school vision for all stakeholders; ensuring that the vision shapes the educational programs, plans, and actions.

1.11 MANAGING STRESS

Related to the Interpersonal Domain: Interpersonal sensitivity (S. D. Thomson, S. Hill, & B. M. Conny, 1993, pp. 15.1-15.23)

No performance aspects of the ISLLC Knowledge and Dispositions are within the program skill area of managing stress.

1.12 ORAL PRESENTATION

Related to the Interpersonal Domain: Oral and nonverbal expression (S. D. Thomson, S. Hill, & B. M. Conny, 1993, pp. 16.1-16.27)

Three performance aspects of the ISLLC Knowledge and Dispositions are within the program skill area of oral presentation.

Communicating effectively; communicating the vision and mission through the use of symbols, ceremonies, stories, and similar activities; communicating progress toward the vision and mission to all stakeholders.

Table R.17 Continued

1.13 ORAL COMMUNICATION

Related to the Interpersonal Domain: Oral and nonverbal expression (S. D. Thomson, S. Hill, & B. M. Conny, 1993, pp. 16.1-16.27).

Three performance aspects of the ISLLC Knowledge and Dispositions are within the program skill area of oral communication.

Communicating effectively; communicating the vision and mission through the use of symbols, ceremonies, stories, and similar activities; communicating progress toward the vision and mission to all stakeholders.

1.14 WRITTEN COMMUNICATION

Related to the Interpersonal Domain: Written expression (S. D. Thomson, S. Hill, & B. M. Conny, 1993, pp. 17.1-17.23)

Four performance aspects of the ISLLC Knowledge and Dispositions are within the program skill area of written communication.

Communicating effectively; vision and mission communicated through the use of symbols, ceremonies, stores, and similar activities; communicating progress toward the vision and mission to all stakeholders; developing an implementation plan in which objectives and strategies to achieve the vision and goals are clearly articulated.

ISLLC Standard 2: Advocating, nurturing, and sustaining a school culture and effective instructional program conducive to student learning and staff professional growth

2.1 ANALYZING PROBLEMS

Related to the Functional Domain: Information collection and problem analysis (S. D. Thomson, S. Hill, & B. M. Conny, 1993, pp. 2.1-2.26)

Six performance aspects of the ISLLC knowledge and Dispositions are within the program skill area of analyzing problems.

Identifying, clarifying, and addressing barriers to student learning and addressing them; implementing, evaluating, and refining curriculum decisions on research, and expertise of teachers; assessing school culture and climate on a regular basis; using a variety of sources of information for making decisions; assessing student learning using a variety of techniques; ensures staff and students use multiple sources of information regarding performance.

Table R.17   Continued

2.2 EXERCISING JUDGMENT

Related to the Functional Domain: Judgment (S. D. Thomson, S. Hill, & B. M. Conny, 1993, pp. 4.41-4.28)

One performance aspect of the ISLLC Knowledge and Dispositions is within the program skill area of exercising judgment.

Technologies are used in teaching and learning.

2.3 ORGANIZING AND PLANNING

Related to the Functional Domain: Organizational oversight (S. D. Thomson, S. Hill, & B. M. Conny, 1993, pp. pp. 5.1-5.30)

Ten performance aspects of the ISLLC Knowledge and Dispositions are within the program skill area of organizing and planning.

Using curriculum design, implementation, evaluation, and refinement strategies; using measurement, evaluation, and assessment strategies; using change process for systems, organizations, and individuals; using a variety of ways in which students can learn; using professional development as an integral part of school improvement; ensuring a safe and supportive learning environment; using professional development to promote a focus on student learning consistent with the school vision and goals; considering diversity when developing learning experiences; organizing and aligning the school for success; designing, implementing, evaluating, and refining curricular and extracurricular programs using a variety of supervisory and evaluation models.

2.4 DELEGATING EFFECTIVELY

Related to the Functional Domain: Delegation (S. D. Thomson, S. Hill, & B. M. Conny, 1993, pp. 7.1-7.28)

No performance aspects of the ISLLC Knowledge and Dispositions are within the program skill area of delegating effectively.

2.5 MAKING DECISIONS

Related to the Functional Domain: Implementation (S. D. Thomson, S. Hill, & B. M. Conny, 1993, pp. 6.1-6.15)

No performance aspects of the ISLLC Knowledge and Dispositions are within the program skill area of making decisions.

Table R.17 Continued

2.6 GROUP LEADERSHIP

Related to the Functional Domain: Leadership (S. D. Thomson, S. Hill, & B. M. Conny, 1993, pp.1.1-1.21)

No performance aspects of the ISLLC Knowledge and Dispositions are within the program skill area of group leadership.

2.7 INTERPERSONAL SENSITIVITY

Related to the Interpersonal Domain: Interpersonal sensitivity (S. D. Thomson, S. Hill, & B. M. Conny, 1993, pp. 15.1-14.23)

Six performance aspects of the ISLLC Knowledge and Dispositions are within the program skill area of interpersonal sensitivity.

Bringing diversity and its meaning to educational programs; recognizing school cultures; recognizing the benefits that diversity brings to the school community; treating all individuals with fairness, dignity, and respect; assuring that students and staff feel valued and important; acknowledging the responsibilities and contributions of each individual.

2.8 RANGE OF INTERESTS

Related to the Interpersonal Domain: Motivating others, (S. D. Thomson, S. Hill, & B. M. Conny, 1993, pp. 14.1-14.21)

No performance aspects of the ISLLC Knowledge and Dispositions are within the program skill area of range of interests.

2.9 PROFESSIONAL MOTIVATION

Related to the Interpersonal Domain: Motivating others (S. D. Thomson, S. Hill, & B. M. Conny, 1993, pp. 14.1-14.21)

Four performance aspects of the ISLLC Knowledge and Dispositions are within the professional development program skill area of professional motivation.

Applying motivational theories; preparing students to be contributing members of society; creating a culture of high expectations for self, students, and staff performance; accomplishing and celebrating student and staff accomplishments.

2.10 PROFESSIONAL VALUES

Related to the Contextual Domain: Philosophical and cultural values (S. D. Thomson, S. Hill, & B. M. Conny, 1993, pp. 181.18.37)

Eleven performance aspects of the ILLSC Knowledge and Dispositions are within the program skill area of professional values.

Table R.17 Continued

Communicating student growth and development information; communicating applied learning theories; communicating principles of effective instruction; adult learning and professional development models; communicating the role of technology in promoting student learning and professional growth; communicating student learning as the fundamental purpose of schooling; communicating the proposition that all students can learn; communicating lifelong learning for self and others; encouraging and modeling lifelong leaning; making multiple opportunities to learn available to all students; developing pupil personnel programs to meet the needs of students and their families.

2.11 MANAGING STRESS	Related to the Interpersonal Domain: Interpersonal sensitivity (S. D. Thomson, S. Hill, & B. M. Conny, 1993, pp.15.1-15.23)

No performance aspects of the ISLLC Knowledge and Dispositions are within the program skill area of managing stress.

2.12 ORAL PRESENTATION	Related to the Interpersonal Domain: Oral and nonverbal expression (S. D. Thomson, S. Hill, & B. M. Conny, 1993, pp. 16.1-16.27)

No performance aspects of the ISLLC Knowledge and Dispositions are within the program skill area of oral presentation.

2.13 ORAL COMMUNICATION	Related to the Interpersonal Domain: Oral and nonverbal expression (S. D. Thomson, S. Hill, & B. M. Conny, 1993, pp. 16.1-16.27)

No performance aspects of the ISLLC Knowledge and Dispositions are within the program skill area of oral communication.

2.14 WRITTEN COMMUNICATION	Related to the Interpersonal Domain: Written expression (S. D. Thomson, S. Hill, & B. M. Conny, 1993, pp. 17.1-17.23)

No performance aspects of the ISLLC Knowledge and Dispositions are within the program skill area of written communications.

Table R.17 Continued

ISLLC Standard 3: Ensuring management of the organization, operations, and resources for a safe, efficient, and effective learning environment

3.1 ANALYZING PROBLEMS

Related to the Functional Domain: Information collection and problem analysis (S. D. Thomson, S. Hill, & B. M. Conny, 1993, pp. 2.1-2.26)

Ten performance aspects of the ISLLC Knowledge and Dispositions are within the program skill area of analyzing problems.

Using principles relating to school safety and security; using principles relating to fiscal operations of school management; using principles relating to school facilities and use of space; using legal issues impacting school operations; using current technologies that support management functions; creating and maintaining a safe environment; recognizing, studying, and applying emerging trends as appropriate; identifying potential problems and opportunities; using effective problem-framing and problem-solving skills; using effective conflict resolution skills.

3.2 EXERCISING JUDGMENT

Related to the Functional Domain: Judgment (S. D. Thomson, S. Hill, & B. M. Conny, 1993, pp. 4.1-4.28)

Seven performance aspects of the ISLLC Knowledge and Dispositions are within the program skill area of exercising judgment.

Taking risks to improve schools; using high-quality standards, expectations, and performance; acting entrepreneurially to support continuous improvement; shares responsibility to maximize ownership and accountability; demonstrates effective use of technology to manage school operations; responsibly, efficiently, and effectively managing the fiscal resources of the school; maintaining the confidentiality and privacy of school records.

3.3 ORGANIZING AND PLANNING

Related to the Functional Domain: Organizational oversight (S. D. Thomson, S. Hill, & B. M. Conny, 1993, pp. 5.1-5.30)

Fifteen performance aspects of the ISLLC Knowledge and Dispositions are within the program skill area of organizing and planning.

Using theories and models of organizations and the principals of organizational development; using operational procedures at the school and district level; designing and managing operational procedures to maximize opportunities for successful learning; recognizing, studying, and applying emerging trends as appropriate; using operational plans and procedures to achieve the vision and goals for the school; effectively managing collective bargaining and other contractual agreements related to the school; operating safely, efficiently, and effectively the school plant, equipment, and support systems; managing time to maximize attainment of organizational goals;

Table R.17   Continued

aligning the goals of the school to financial, human, and materials resources; regularly monitoring and modifying organizational systems as needed; effectively using technology to manage school operations; managing responsibly, efficiently, and effectively the fiscal resources of the school; creating and maintaining a safe, clean, and aesthetically pleasing school environment; supporting the attainment of school goals by managing the human resource functions; maintaining confidentiality and privacy of school records.

3.4 EFFECTIVE DELEGATION

Related to the Functional Domain: Delegation (S. D. Thomson, S. Hill, & B. M. Conny, 1993, pp. 7.1-7.24)

Two performance aspects of the ISLLC Knowledge and Dispositions are within the program skill area of effective delegation.

Demonstrating trust of people and their judgments; sharing responsibilities to maximize ownership and accountability.

3.5 MAKING DECISIONS

Related to the Functional Domain: Implementation (S. D. Thomson, S. Hill, & B. M. Conny, 1993, pp. 6.1-6.15)

Three performance aspects of the ISLLC Knowledge and Dispositions are within the program skill area of making decisions.

Making management decisions to enhance learning and teaching; accepting responsibility; confronting and resolving problems in a timely manner.

3.6 GROUP LEADERSHIP

Related to the Functional Domain: Leadership (Thomson, Hill, & Conny, 1993, pp. 1.1-1.21)

One performance aspect of the ISLLC Knowledge and Dispositions is within the program skill area of group leadership.

Using effective group-processes and consensus-building skills.

3.7 INTERPERSONAL SENSITIVITY

Related to the Interpersonal Domain: Interpersonal Sensitivity (S. D. Thomson, S. Hill, & B. M. Conny, 1993, pp. 15.1-15.23)

Eight performance aspects of the ISLLC Knowledge and Dispositions are within the program skill area of interpersonal sensitivity.

Using effective human resources management and development skills; involving stakeholders in the management processes; effectively managing collective bargaining and other contractual agreements related to the school; involving stakeholders in deci-

Table R.17 Continued

sions affecting schools; sharing responsibility to maximize ownership and account-ability; using effective conflict resolution skills; using effective group-process and con-sensus-building skills; maintain confidentiality and privacy of school records.

3.8 RANGE OF INTERESTS	Related to the Interpersonal Domain: Motivating others, (S. D. Thomson, S. Hill, & B. M. Conny, 1993, pp. 14.1-14.21)

No performance aspects of the ISLLC Knowledge and Dispositions are within the pro-gram skill area of range of interests.

3. 9 PROFESSIONAL MOTIVATION	Related to the Interpersonal Domain: Motivating others (S. D. Thomson, S. Hill, & B. M. Conny, 1993, pp. 14.1-14.21)

No performance aspects of the ISLLC Knowledge and Dispositions are within the pro-gram skill area of professional motivation.

3.10 PROFESSIONAL VALUES	Related to the Contextual Domain: Philosophical and cultural values (S. D. Thomson, S. Hill, & B. M. Conny, 1993, pp. 18.1-18.37)

Two performance aspects of the ISLLC Knowledge and Dispositions are within the pro-gram skill area of professional values.

Communicating knowledge of learning, teaching, and student development to inform management decisions; maintaining confidentiality and privacy of school records.

3.11 MANAGING STRESS	Related to the Interpersonal Domain: Interpersonal sensitivity (S. D. Thomson, S. Hill, & B. M. Conny, 1993, pp. 15.1-15.23)

No performance aspects of the ISLLC Knowledge and Dispositions are within the pro-gram skill area of managing stress.

3.12 ORAL PRESENTATION	Related to the Interpersonal Domain: Oral and nonverbal expression (S. D. Thomson, S. Hill, & B. M. Conny, 1993, pp. 16.1-16.27)

One performance aspect of the ISLLC Knowledge and Dispositions is within the pro-gram skill area of oral presentation.

Using effective communication skills.

Table R.17 Continued

3.13 ORAL COMMUNICATION

Related to the Interpersonal Domain: Oral and nonverbal expression (S. D. Thomson, S. Hill, & B. M. Conny, 1993, pp. 16.1-16.27)

One performance aspect of the ISLLC Knowledge and Dispositions is within the program skill area of oral communication.

Using effective communication skills.

3.14 WRITTEN COMMUNICATION

Related to the Interpersonal Domain: Written expression (S. D. Thomson, S. Hill, & B. M. Conny, 1993, pp. 17.1-17.23)

One performance aspect of the ISLLC Knowledge and Dispositions is within the program skill area of written communication.

Using effective communication skills.

ISLLC Standard 4: Collaborating with families and community members, responding to diverse community interests and needs, and mobilizing community resources

4.1 ANALYZING PROBLEMS

Related to the Functional Domain: Information collection and problem analysis (S. D. Thomson, S. Hill, & B. M. Conny, 1993, pp. 2.1-3.27)

Six performance aspects of the ISLLC Knowledge and Dispositions are within the program skill area of analyzing problems.

Using emerging issues and trends that potentially impact the school community; identifying the conditions and dynamics of the diverse school community; identifying community resources; using successful models of school, family, business, community, government, and higher education partnerships; using resources of the family and community needing to be brought to bear on the education of students; regularly using information about family and community concerns, expectations, and needs.

4.2 EXERCISING JUDGMENT

Related to the Functional Domain: Judgment (S. D. Thomson, S. Hill, & B. M. Conny, 1993, pp. 4.1-4.28)

Five performance aspects of the ISLLC Knowledge and Dispositions are within the program skill area of exercising judgment.

Demonstrated understanding of the operation of schools as an integral part of the larger community; demonstrated understanding of families as partners in the education of their children; involving families and other stakeholders in school decision-

Table R.17 Continued

making processes; identifying and nurturing relationships with community leaders; using public resources and funds appropriately and wisely.

4.3 ORGANIZING AND PLANNING

Related to the Functional Domain: Organizational oversight (S. D. Thomson, S. Hill, & B. M. Conny, 1993, pp. 5.1-5.30)

Eleven performance aspects of the ISLLC Knowledge and Dispositions are within the program skill area of organizing and planning.

Using the dynamics of the diverse school community; using community relations and marketing strategies and processes; using the larger community as an integral part of operating the school; bringing to bear on the education of students the resources of the family and community; reaching out to different business, religious, political, and service agencies and organizations; securing available community resources to help the school solve problems and achieve goals; establishing partnerships with area businesses, strengthening programs and support of school goals with institutions of higher education and community groups; integrating community youth family services with school programs; developing and maintaining effective media relations; establishing a comprehensive program of community relations; providing collaborative skills development for staff.

4.4 EFFECTIVE DELEGATION

Related to the Functional Domain: Delegation (S. D. Thomson, S. Hill, & B. M. Conny, 1993, pp. 7.1-7.24)

No performance aspects of the ISLLC Knowledge and Dispositions are within the program skill area of effective delegation.

4.5 MAKING DECISIONS

Related to the Functional Domain: Implementation (S. D. Thomson, S. Hill, & B. M. Conny, 1993, pp. 6.1-6.15)

No performance aspects of the ISLLC Knowledge and Dispositions are within the program skill area of making decisions.

4.6 GROUP LEADERSHIP

Related to the Functional Domain: Leadership (S. D. Thomson, S. Hill, & B. M. Conny, 1993, pp. 1.1-1.21)

Five performance aspects of the ISLLC Knowledge and Dispositions are within the program skill area of group leadership.

Collaborating and communicating with families; involving families and other stakeholders in school decision-making processes; involving families as partners in the education of their children; maintaining high visibility, active involvement, and communication with the larger community; modeling community collaboration for staff.

Table R.17 Continued

4.7 INTERPERSONAL SENSITIVITY

Related to the Interpersonal Domain:
Interpersonal sensitivity (S. D. Thomson,
S. Hill, & B. M. Conny, 1993,
pp. 15.1-15.23)

Eleven performance aspects of the ISLLC Knowledge and Dispositions are within the program skill area of interpersonal sensitivity.

Using the conditions and dynamics of the diverse school community; collaborating and communicating with families; involving families and other stakeholders in school decision-making processes; involving families as partners in the education of their children; identifying and nurturing relationships with community leaders; using community relations, marketing strategies, and processes; giving credence to individuals and groups whose values and opinions may conflict; treating community stakeholders equitably; developing and maintaining effective media relations; establishing a comprehensive program of community relations; modeling community collaboration for staff.

4.8 RANGE OF INTERESTS

Related to the Interpersonal Domain:
Motivating others, (S. D. Thomson, S.
Hill, & B. M. Conny, 1993, pp. 14.1-14.21)

No performance aspects of the ISLLC Knowledge and Dispositions are within the program skill area of range of interests.

4.9 PROFESSIONAL MOTIVATION

Related to the Interpersonal Domain:
Motivating others (S. D. Thomson, S.
Hill, & B. M. Conny, 1993, pp. 14.1-14.21)

Eight performance aspects of the ISLLC Knowledge and Dispositions are within the program skill area of professional motivation.

Using families as partners in the education of their children; adhering to the proposition that families have the best interests in their children in mind; informing the public; bringing to bear the family and community on the education of students; maintaining high visibility; maintaining active involvement and communication with the larger community; maintaining outreach to different business, religious, political, and service agencies and organizations; modeling community collaboration for staff.

4.10 PROFESSIONAL VALUES

Related to the Contextual Domain:
Philosophical and cultural values (S. D.
Thomson, S. Hill, & B. M. Conny, 1993,
pp. 18.1-18.37)

Eleven performance aspects of the ISLLC Knowledge and Dispositions are within the program skill area of professional values.

Table R.17 Continued

Using successful models of school, family, business, community, maintaining government and higher education partnerships; operating the school as an integral part of the larger community; involving families and other stakeholders in school decision-making processes; using diversity to enrich the school; using families as partners in the education of their children; showing that families have the best interests in their children in mind; informing the public; maintaining high visibility, being actively involved, and communicating with the larger community; reaching out to different business, religious, political, and service agencies and organizations; helping the school and community serve one another as resources; integrating community youth family services with school programs; recognizing and valuing diversity.

4.11 MANAGING STRESS	Related to the Interpersonal Domain: Interpersonal Sensitivity (S. D. Thomson, S. Hill, & B. M. Conny, 1993, pp. 15.1-15.23)

No performance aspects of the ISLLC Knowledge and Dispositions are within the program skill area of managing stress.

4.12 ORAL PRESENTATION	Related to the Interpersonal Domain: Oral and nonverbal expression (S. D. Thomson, S. Hill, & B. M. Conny, 1993, pp. 16.1-16.27)

Two performance aspects of the ISLLC Knowledge and Dispositions are within the program skill area of oral presentation.

Communicating with families; informing the public.

4.13 ORAL COMMUNICATION	Related to the Interpersonal Domain: Oral and nonverbal expression (S. D. Thomson, S. Hill, & B. M. Conny, 1993, pp. 16.1-16.27)

Five performance aspects of the ISLLC Knowledge and Dispositions are within the program skill area of oral communication.

Collaborating and communicating with families; informing the public; maintaining high visibility; maintaining active involvement and communication with the larger community; developing and maintaining effective media relations.

Table R.17   Continued

4.14 WRITTEN COMMUNICATION

Related to the Interpersonal Domain: Written expression (S. D. Thomson, S. Hill, & B. M. Conny, 1993, pp. 17.1-17.23)

Four performance aspects of the ISLLC Knowledge and Dispositions are within the program skill area of range of interests.

Collaborating and communicating with families; informing the public; maintaining high visibility; maintaining active involvement and communication with the larger community.

ISLLC Standard 5: Promoting success of all students through integrity, fairness and an ethical manner

5.1 ANALYZING PROBLEMS

Related to the Functional Domain: Information collection and problem analysis (S. D. Thomson, S. Hill, & B. M. Conny, 1993, pp. 2.1-3.27)

No performance aspects of the ISLLC Knowledge and Dispositions are within the program skill area of analyzing problems.

5.2 EXERCISING JUDGMENT

Related to the Functional Domain: Judgment (S. D. Thomson, S. Hill, & B. M. Conny, 1993, pp. 4.1-4.28)

Ten performance aspects of the ISLLC Knowledge and Dispositions are within the program skill area of exercising judgment.

Upholding one's principles and actions despite the consequences; using one's office to constructively and productively influence the service of all students and their families; accepting the responsibility for school operations; using the influence of the office to enhance the educational program rather than for personal gain; protecting the rights and confidentiality of students and staff; recognizing and respecting the legitimate authority of others; expecting that others in the school community will demonstrate integrity and exercise ethical behavior; opening the school to public scrutiny; fulfilling legal and contractual obligations; applying laws and procedures fairly, wisely, and considerately.

5.3 ORGANIZING AND PLANNING

Related to the Functional Domain: Organizational oversight (S. D. Thomson, S. Hill, & B. M. Conny, 1993, pp. 5.1-5.30)

No performance aspects of the ISLLC Knowledge and Dispositions are within the program skill area of organizing and planning.

Table R.17   Continued

5.4 EFFECTIVE DELEGATION

Related to the Functional Domain: Delegation (S. D. Thomson, S. Hill, & B. M. Conny, 1993, pp. 7.1-7.24)

No performance aspects of the ISLLC Knowledge and Dispositions are within the program skill area of effective delegation.

5.5 MAKING DECISIONS

Related to the Functional Domain: Implementation (S. D.   Thomson, S. Hill, & B. M. Conny, 1993, pp.6.1-6.15)

No performance aspects of the ISLLC Knowledge and Dispositions are within the program skill area of making decisions.

5.6 GROUP LEADERSHIP

Related to the Functional Domain: Leadership (S. D. Thomson, S. Hill, & B. M. Conny, 1993, pp. 1.1-1.21)

No performance aspects of the ISLLC Knowledge and Dispositions are within the program skill area of group leadership.

5.7 INTERPERSONAL SENSITIVITY

Related to the Interpersonal Domain: Interpersonal sensitivity (S. D. Thomson, S. Hill, & B. M. Conny, 1993, pp. 15.1-15.23)

Nine performance aspects of the ISLLC Knowledge and Dispositions are within the program skill area of interpersonal sensitivity.

Using the influence of one's office constructively and productively in the service of all students and their families; developing a caring school community; demonstrating values, beliefs, and attitudes that inspire others to higher levels of performance; considering the impact of one's administrative practices on others; treating people fairly, equitably, and with dignity and respect; protecting the rights and confidentiality of students and staff; demonstrating appreciation for and sensitivity to the diversity of the school community; examining and considering the prevailing values of the diverse school community; applying laws and procedures fairly, wisely, and considerately.

5.8 RANGE OF INTERESTS

Related to the Interpersonal Domain: Motivating others (S. D. Thomson, S. Hill, & B. M. Conny, 1993, pp. 14.1-14.21)

No performance aspects of the ISLLC Knowledge and Dispositions are within the program skill area of range of interests.

Table R.17   Continued

5.9 PROFESSIONAL MOTIVATION	Related to the Interpersonal Domain: Motivating others (S. D. Thomson, S. Hill, & B. M. Conny, 1993, pp. 14.1-14.21)

No performance aspects of the ISLLC Knowledge and Dispositions are within the program skill area of professional motivation.

5.10 PROFESSIONAL VALUES	Related to the Contextual Domain: Philosophical and cultural values (S. D. Thomson, S. Hill, & B. M. Conny, 1993, pp. 18.1-18.37)

Nineteen performance aspects of the ISLLC Knowledge and Dispositions are within the program skill area of professional values.

Communicating the purpose of education and the role of leadership in modern society; using various ethical frameworks and perspectives on ethics; communicating the values of the diverse school community; using professional codes of ethics; communicating the philosophy and history of education; communicating the ideal of the common good; communicating the principles in the Bill of Rights; supporting the right of every student to a free, quality education; bringing ethical principles to the decision-making process; subordinating one's own interests to the good of the school community; accepting the consequences for upholding one's principles and actions; examining personal and professional values; demonstrating a personal and professional code of ethics; demonstrating values, beliefs, and attitudes that inspire others to higher levels of performance; serving as a role model; recognizing and respects the legitimate authority of others; demonstrating appreciation for and sensitivity to the diversity of the school community; communicating that others in the school community will demonstrate integrity and exercise ethical behavior; opening the school to public scrutiny.

5.11 MANAGING STRESS	Related to the Interpersonal Domain: Interpersonal sensitivity (S. D. Thomson, S. Hill, & B. M. Conny, 1993, pp. 15.1-15.23)

No performance aspects of the ISLLC Knowledge and Dispositions are within the program skill area of managing stress.

Table R.17 Continued

5.12 ORAL PRESENTATION

Related to the Interpersonal Domain: Oral and nonverbal expression (S. D. Thomson, S. Hill, & B. M. Conny, 1993, pp. 16.1-16.27)

No performance aspects of the ISLLC Knowledge and Dispositions are within the program skill area of oral presentation.

5.13 ORAL COMMUNICATION

Related to the Interpersonal Domain: Oral and nonverbal expression (S. D. Thomson, S. Hill, & B. M. Conny, 1993, pp. 16.1-16.27)

No performance aspects of the ISLLC Knowledge and Dispositions are within the program skill area of oral communication.

5.14 WRITTEN COMMUNICATION

Related to the Interpersonal Domain: Written expression (S. D. Thomson, S. Hill, & B. M. Conny, 1993, pp. 17.1-17.23)

No performance aspects of the ISLLC Knowledge and Dispositions are within the program skill area of written communication.

ISLLC Standard 6: Promoting the success of all students by understanding, responding to, and influencing the larger political, social, economic, legal and cultural context

6.1 ANALYZING PROBLEMS

Related to the Functional Domain: Information collection and problem analysis (S. D. Thomson, S. Hill, & B. M. Conny, 1993, pp. 2.1-3.27)

Seven performance aspects of the ISLLC Knowledge and Dispositions are within the program skill area of analyzing problems.

Communicating the law as related to education and schooling; communicating the political, social, cultural, and economic systems and processes that impact schools; communicating global issues and forces affecting teaching and learning; communicating the dynamics of policy development and advocacy under our democratic political system; acknowledging a variety of ideas, values, and cultures; communicating that the school community works within the framework of policies, laws, and regulations enacted by local, state, and federal authorities; communicating that public policy be shaped to provide quality education for students.

Table R.17   Continued

6.2 EXERCISING JUDGMENT   Related to the Functional Domain:
                                            Judgment (S. D. Thomson, S. Hill, & B.
                                            M. Conny, 1993, pp. 4.1-4.28)

Four performance aspects of the ISLLC Knowledge and Dispositions are within the program skill area of exercising judgment.

Applying the law as related to education and schooling; using legal systems to protect student rights and improve student opportunities; influencing the environment in which schools operate on behalf of students and their families; working for the school community within the framework of policies, laws, and regulations enacted by local, state, and federal authorities.

6.3 ORGANIZING AND PLANNING   Related to the Functional Domain:
                                            Organizational oversight (S. D. Thomson,
                                            S. Hill, & B. M. Conny, 1993, pp. 5.1-5.30)

Two performance aspects of the ISLLC Knowledge and Dispositions are within the program skill area of organizing and planning.

Applying models and strategies of changes and conflict resolution as applied to the larger political, social, cultural, and economic contexts of schooling; shaping public policy to provide quality education for all students.

6. 4 EFFECTIVE DELEGATION   Related to the Functional Domain:
                                            Delegation (S. D. Thomson, S. Hill, & B.
                                            M. Conny, 1993, pp. 7.1-7.24)

No performance aspects of the ISLLC Knowledge and Dispositions are within the program skill area of effective delegation.

6.5 MAKING DECISIONS   Related to the Functional Domain:
                                            Implementation (S. D. Thomson, S. Hill,
                                            & B. M. Conny, 1993, pp. 6.1-6.15)

No performance aspects of the ISLLC Knowledge and Dispositions are within the program skill area of making decisions.

6.6 GROUP LEADERSHIP   Related to the Functional Domain:
                                            Leadership (Thomson, Hill, & Conny,
                                            1993, pp. 1.1-1.21)

No performance aspects of the ISLLC Knowledge and Dispositions are within the program skill area of group leadership.

Table R.17 Continued

6. 7 INTERPERSONAL SENSITIVITY	Related to the Interpersonal Domain: Interpersonal sensitivity (S. D. Thomson, S. Hill, & B. M. Conny, 1993, pp.15.1-15.23)

No performance aspects of the ISLLC Knowledge and Dispositions are within the program skill area of interpersonal sensitivity.

6. 8 RANGE OF INTERESTS	Related to the Interpersonal Domain: Motivating others, (S. D. Thomson, S. Hill, & B. M. Conny, 1993, pp. 14.1-14.21)

Three performance aspects of the ISLLC Knowledge and Dispositions are within the program skill area of range of interests.

Participating in the political and policy-making context in the service of education; influencing the school environment on behalf of students and their families; communicating among the school community concerning trends, issues, and potential changes in the environment in which schools operate.

6.9 PROFESSIONAL MOTIVATION	Related to the Interpersonal Domain: Motivating others (S. D. Thomson, S. Hill, & B. M. Conny, 1993, pp. 14.1-14.21)

Three performance aspects of the ISLLC Knowledge and Dispositions are within the program skill area of professional motivation.

Participating in the political and policy-making context in the service of education; communicating among the school community concerning trends, issues, and potential changes in the environment in which schools operate; maintaining an ongoing dialogue with representatives of diverse community groups.

6.10 PROFESSIONAL VALUES	Related to the Contextual Domain: Philosophical and cultural values (S. D. Thomson, S. Hill, & B. M. Conny, 1993, pp. 18.1-18.37)

Nine performance aspects of the ISLLC Knowledge and Dispositions are within the program skill area of professional values.

Communicating the principles of representative governance that undergird the system of American schools; communicating the role of public education in developing and renewing a democratic society and an economically productive nation; communicating the importance of diversity and equity in a democratic society; communicating education as a key to opportunity and social mobility; communicating a variety of ideas, values, and cultures; communicating the importance of a continuing dialogue with other decision makers affecting education; participating in the political and

Table R.17 Continued

policy-making context in the service of education; influencing the environment in which schools operate on behalf of students and their families; sharing public policy to provide quality education for all students.

6.11 MANAGING STRESS	Related to the Interpersonal Domain: Interpersonal sensitivity (S. D. Thomson, S. Hill, & B. M. Conny, 1993, pp. 15.1-15.23)

No performance aspects of the ISLLC Knowledge and Dispositions are within the program skill area of managing stress.

6.12 ORAL PRESENTATION	Related to the Interpersonal Domain: Oral and nonverbal expression (S. D. Thomson, S. Hill, & B. M. Conny, 1993, pp. 16.1-16.27)

One performance aspect of the ISLLC Knowledge and Dispositions is within the program skill area of oral presentation.

Communicating public policy shaped to provide quality education for all students.

6.13 ORAL COMMUNICATION	Related to the Interpersonal Domain: Oral and Nonverbal expression (S. D. Thomson, S. Hill, & B. M. Conny, 1993, pp. 16.1-16.27)

Four performance aspects of the ISLLC Knowledge and Dispositions are within the program skill area of oral communication.

Maintaining a continuing dialogue with other decision makers affecting education; communicating among the school community concerning trends, issues, and potential changes in the environment in which schools operate; maintaining an ongoing dialogue with representatives of diverse community groups.

6.14 WRITTEN COMMUNICATION	Related to the Interpersonal Domain: Written expression (S. D. Thomson, S. Hill, & B. M. Conny, 1993, pp. 17.1-17.23)

No performance aspects of the ISLLC Knowledge and Dispositions are within the program skill area of written communication.

SOURCES: Principals for Our Changing Schools: Knowledge and Skill Base (1993); S. D. Thomas, S. Hill, & B. m. Conny; Interstate School Leaders Licensure Consortium: Standards for School Leaders (1996); Council

References

Associates for Better Classrooms International, Ltd. (2000). *Coach and director training manual.* Vienna, VA: Author.

Byham, W. C. (1980). Starting an assessment center the correct way. *Personnel Administrator, 25*(2), 27-32.

Caughlin, J. F. (1997, Fall). *Peer-assessment and learning in a technology-assisted leadership development center.* Unpublished doctoral dissertation, George Mason University, Fairfax, VA.

Council of Chief State School Officers. (1996). *Interstate School Leadership Licensure Consortium: Standards for school leaders.* Washington, DC: Author. Retrieved September 12, 2002, from www.ccsso.org/pdfs/isllcstd.pdf

Goleman, D. (1998). *Working with emotional intelligence.* New York: Bantam.

Thomson, S. D., Hill, S., & Conny, B. M. (Eds.). (1993). *Principals for our changing schools: The knowledge and skill base.* Fairfax, VA: National Policy Board for Educational Administration.

National Association of Secondary School Principals. (1988). *Assessment handbook: National assessment center project.* Reston, VA: Author.

Index

PEP*: A LEADERSHIP DEVELOPMENT PROGRAM

Using Peers and Technology

The book *Powerful Leadership Development* by David Lepard and Alice Foster is based on a staff development program used in university leadership academies, state regional service centers, and large and small school districts across the county. The copyrighted leadership development program is called, PEP* (Professional Enhancement Program).

PEP* is a 24-hour, leadership enhancement program using seven, flexibly scheduled, school-based simulations. To strengthen leadership skills, it uses colleagues, coaches, video, and assessment and report-generating software. Developmental coaches reinforce learning for participants and play a key role in assisting them to prepare follow-up action plans. Using PEP* at just one site, both large and small educational organizations may strengthen the skills of from six to 250 participants annually.

Like the book *Powerful Leadership Development*, PEP* is well suited for educational professionals seeking powerful ways to strengthen their leadership performance. It is comprehensive, activity based, and it works well for both prospective and practicing school leaders, K-12. For individuals who desire more guidance and interaction along the way, consider calling ABCI to learn more about PEP*.

District leadership development programs, students in professional preparation programs, workshop leaders—and those searching for new, cost-effective ways to diagnose and prescribe action steps for professional development—find PEP* easy to administer, practical, and useful.

Major PEP* activities include writing, handling deskwork, school improvement planning, oral presentations, group problem-solving situations, interviewing, a self-inventory of leadership skills, and preparing an action plan for continuing improvement. These activities are accomplished by learning how to observe and document performance, by learning how to assume group leadership roles, by learning performance data entry skills to produce personal diagnostic and prescriptive computer-generated reports, and, finally, how to plan for personal staff development—all achieved in a cooperative-learning environment that provides immediate performance feedback.

PEP* has built-in performance linkages between the Interstate Leadership Licensure Consortium's (ISLLC) Leadership Standards and the PEP* performance-based activities; the links provide a bridge between theory and practice.

If you are seeking a safe way for your staff to test the waters of school leadership or are looking for a powerful way for current school leaders to further improve their skills, PEP* is for you—whether you represent a school district, a regional leadership center, or a university educational leadership program.

To learn more about the ABCI's unique computer software that accompanies the Professional Enhancement Program and about how you can get director and coach training, contact ABCI@igc.org or at (703) 242-3939.

Note: Asterisk does not indicate a footnote.

Publisher's Note: The statements made here about the leadership development program are not made on behalf of Corwin Press and do not constitute an endorsement by Corwin Press of the program or its associated materials.

**CORWIN
PRESS**

The Corwin Press logo—a raven striding across an open book—represents the happy union of courage and learning. We are a professional-level publisher of books and journals for K-12 educators, and we are committed to creating and providing resources that embody these qualities. Corwin's motto is "Success for All Learners."